ATOMIC ENERGY
FOR MILITARY PURPOSES

This book is a republication, with the modifications detailed in the author's preface, of the official report issued by the "Manhattan District," U.S. Corps of Engineers (the name given by the War Department to the Atomic Bomb Project). No royalty or other compensation is being paid to the author. Publication has been undertaken by Princeton University Press as a public service in accordance with its purpose as a non-profit organization seeking to disseminate the results of scholarly and scientific research.

Atomic Energy
for Military Purposes

The Official Report
on the Development of the Atomic Bomb
under the Auspices
of the United States Government,
1940–1945

By HENRY DeWOLF SMYTH

CHAIRMAN, DEPARTMENT OF PHYSICS
PRINCETON UNIVERSITY
CONSULTANT, MANHATTAN DISTRICT, U.S. ENGINEERS

Written at the request of
MAJ. GEN. L. R. GROVES, U.S.A.

PRINCETON

PRINCETON UNIVERSITY PRESS

1946

Printed in the United States of America
by Carey Press Corporation, New York

FOREWORD

THE story of the development of the atomic bomb by the combined efforts of many groups in the United States is a fascinating but highly technical account of an enormous enterprise. Obviously military security prevents this story from being told in full at this time. However, there is no reason why the administrative history of the Atomic Bomb Project and the basic scientific knowledge on which the several developments were based should not be available now to the general public. To this end this account by Professor H. D. Smyth is presented.

All pertinent scientific information which can be released to the public at this time without violating the needs of national security is contained in this volume. No requests for additional information should be made to private persons or organizations associated directly or indirectly with the project. Persons disclosing or securing additional information by any means whatsoever without authorization are subject to severe penalties under the Espionage Act.

The success of the development is due to the many thousands of scientists, engineers, workmen and administrators—both civilian and military—whose prolonged labor, silent perseverance, and whole-hearted cooperation have made possible the unprecedented technical accomplishments here described.

L. R. GROVES
Major General, USA

War Department
Washington, D. C.
August 1945

PREFACE

THE ultimate responsibility for our nation's policy rests on its citizens and they can discharge such responsibilities wisely only if they are informed. The average citizen cannot be expected to understand clearly how an atomic bomb is constructed or how it works but there is in this country a substantial group of engineers and scientific men who can understand such things and who can explain the potentialities of atomic bombs to their fellow citizens. The present report is written for this professional group and is a matter-of-fact, general account of work in the United States since 1939 aimed at the production of such bombs. It is neither a documented official history nor a technical treatise for experts. Secrecy requirements have affected both the detailed content and general emphasis so that many interesting developments have been omitted.

References to British and Canadian work are not intended to be complete since this is written from the point of view of the activities in this country.

The writer hopes that this account is substantially accurate, thanks to cooperation from all groups in the project; he takes full responsibility for such errors as may occur.

H. D. SMYTH

July 1, 1945

Minor changes have been made for this edition. These changes consist of the following variations from the report as issued August 12, 1945: (1) Minor clarifications and corrections in wording; (2) Inclusion of a paragraph on radioactive effects issued by the War Department to accompany the original release of this report; (3) Addition of a few sentences on the success of the health precautions; (4) Addition of a few names; (5) Addition of Appendix 6, giving the War Department release on the New Mexico test of July 16, 1945; (6) Inclusion of the photographic section; (7) Inclusion of an index.

H. D. S.

September 1, 1945

For this fifth printing of the Princeton edition two new Appendices have been added—Appendix 7 giving the text of a statement by the British Information Service, and Appendix 8 giving the text of a release by the Canadian Information Service.

H. D. S.

November 1, 1945

CONTENTS

ILLUSTRATION SECTION IS IN CHAPTER VIII

CHAPTER I. INTRODUCTION

1.1. The purpose of this report is to describe the scientific and technical developments in this country since 1940 directed toward the military use of energy from atomic nuclei. Although not written as a "popular" account of the subject, this report is intended to be intelligible to scientists and engineers generally and to other college graduates with a good grounding in physics and chemistry. The equivalence of mass and energy is chosen as the guiding principle in the presentation of the background material of the "Introduction."

THE CONSERVATION OF MASS AND OF ENERGY

1.2. There are two principles that have been cornerstones of the structure of modern science. The first—that matter can be neither created nor destroyed but only altered in form—was enunciated in the eighteenth century and is familiar to every student of chemistry; it has led to the principle known as the law of conservation of mass. The second—that energy can be neither created nor destroyed but only altered in form—emerged in the nineteenth century and has ever since been the plague of inventors of perpetual-motion machines; it is known as the law of conservation of energy.

1.3. These two principles have constantly guided and disciplined the development and application of science. For all practical purposes they were unaltered and separate until some five years ago. For most practical purposes they still are so, but it is now known that they are, in fact, two phases of a single principle for we have discovered that energy may sometimes be converted into matter and matter into energy. Specifically, such a conversion is observed in the phenomenon of nuclear fission of

1

uranium, a process in which atomic nuclei split into fragments with the release of an enormous amount of energy. The military use of this energy has been the object of the research and production projects described in this report.

THE EQUIVALENCE
OF MASS AND ENERGY

1.4. One conclusion that appeared rather early in the development of the theory of relativity was that the inertial mass of a moving body increased as its speed increased. This implied an equivalence between an increase in energy of motion of a body, that is, its kinetic energy, and an increase in its mass. To most practical physicists and engineers this appeared a mathematical fiction of no practical importance. Even Einstein could hardly have foreseen the present applications, but as early as 1905 he did clearly state that mass and energy were equivalent and suggested that proof of this equivalence might be found by the study of radioactive substances. He concluded that the amount of energy, E, equivalent to a mass, m, was given by the equation

$$E = mc^2$$

where c is the velocity of light. If this is stated in actual numbers, its startling character is apparent. It shows that one kilogram (2.2 pounds) of matter, if converted entirely into energy, would give 25 billion kilowatt hours of energy. This is equal to the energy that would be generated by the total electric power industry in the United States (as of 1939) running for approximately two months. Compare this fantastic figure with the 8.5 kilowatt hours of heat energy which may be produced by burning an equal amount of coal.

1.5. The extreme size of this conversion figure was interesting in several respects. In the first place, it explained why the equivalence of mass and energy was never observed in ordinary chemical combustion. We now believe that the heat given off in such a combustion has mass associated with it, but this mass is so small that it cannot be detected by the most sensitive balances available. (It is of the order of a few billionths of a gram per mole.) In the second place, it was made clear that no appreciable quantities of matter were being converted into energy in any familiar terrestrial processes, since no such large sources of energy were known. Further, the possibility of initiating or controlling such a conversion in any practical way seemed very remote. Finally, the very size of the conversion factor opened a magnificent field of speculation to philosophers, physicists, engineers, and comic-strip artists. For twenty-five years such speculation was unsupported by direct experimental evidence, but beginning about 1930 such evidence began to appear in rapidly increasing quantity. Before discussing such evidence and the practical partial conversion of matter into energy that is our main theme, we shall review the foundations of atomic and nuclear physics. General familiarity with the atomic nature of matter and with the existence of electrons is assumed. Our treatment will be little more than an outline which may be elaborated by reference to books such as Pollard and Davidson's *Applied Nuclear Physics* and Stranathan's *The "Particles" of Modern Physics*.

RADIOACTIVITY AND ATOMIC STRUCTURE

1.6. First discovered by H. Becquerel in 1896 and subsequently studied by Pierre and Marie Curie, E. Rutherford, and many others, the phenomena of radioactivity have played leading roles in the discovery of the general laws of atomic structure and in the verification of the equivalence of mass and energy.

IONIZATION BY RADIOACTIVE SUBSTANCES

1.7. The first phenomenon of radioactivity observed was the blackening of photographic plates by uranium minerals. Although this effect is still used to some extent in research on radioactivity, the property of radioactive substances that is of greatest scientific value is their ability to ionize gases. Under normal conditions air and other gases do not conduct electricity—otherwise power lines and electrical machines would not operate in the open as they do. But under some circumstances the molecules of air are broken apart into positively and negatively charged fragments, called ions. Air thus ionized does conduct electricity. Within a few months after the first discovery of radioactivity Becquerel found that uranium had the power to ionize air. Specifically he found that the charge on an electroscope would leak away rapidly through the air if some uranium salts were placed near it. (The same thing would happen to a storage battery if sufficient radioactive material were placed near by.) Ever since that time the rate of discharge of an electroscope has served as a measure of intensity of radioactivity. Furthermore, nearly all present-day instruments for studying radioactive phenomena depend on this ionization effect directly or indirectly. An elementary account of such instruments, notably electroscopes, Geiger-Müller counters, ionization chambers, and Wilson cloud chambers is given in Appendix 1.

The Different Radiations or Particles

1.8. Evidence that different radioactive substances differ in their ionizing power both in kind and in intensity indicates that there are differences in the "radiations" emitted. Some of the radiations are much more penetrating than others; consequently, two radioactive samples having the same effect on an "unshielded" electroscope may have very different effects if the electroscope is "shielded," i.e., if screens are interposed between the sample and the electroscope. These screens are said to absorb the radiation.

1.9. Studies of absorption and other phenomena have shown that in fact there are three types of "radiation" given off by radioactive substances. There are alpha particles, which are high-speed ionized helium atoms (actually the nuclei of helium atoms), beta particles, which are high-speed electrons, and gamma rays, which are electromagnetic radiations similar to X-rays. Of these only the gamma rays are properly called radiations, and even these act very much like particles because of their short wave-length. Such a "particle" or quantum of gamma radiation is called a photon. In general, the gamma rays are very penetrating, the alpha and beta rays less so. Even though the alpha and beta rays are not very penetrating, they have enormous kinetic energies for particles of atomic size, energies thousands of times greater than the kinetic energies which the molecules of a gas have by reason of their thermal motion, and thousands of times greater than the energy changes per atom in chemical reactions. It was for this reason that Einstein suggested that studies of radioactivity might show the equivalence of mass and energy.

THE ATOM

1.10. Before considering what types of atoms emit alpha, beta and gamma rays, and before discussing the laws that govern such emission, we shall describe the current ideas on how atoms are constructed, ideas based partly on the study of radioactivity.

1.11. According to our present view every atom consists of a small heavy nucleus approximately 10^{-12} cm in diameter surrounded by a largely empty region 10^{-8} cm in diameter in which electrons move somewhat like planets about the sun. The nucleus carries an integral number of positive charges, each 1.6×10^{-19} coulombs in size. (See Appendix 2 for a discussion of units.) Each electron carries one negative charge of this same size, and the number of electrons circulating around the nucleus is equal to the number of positive charges on the nucleus so that the atom as a whole has a net charge of zero.

1.12. *Atomic Number and Electronic Structure.* The number of positive charges in the nucleus is called the atomic number, Z. It determines the number of electrons in the extranuclear structure, and this in turn determines the chemical properties of the atom. Thus all the atoms of a given chemical element have the same atomic number, and conversely all atoms having the same atomic number are atoms of the same element regardless of possible differences in their nuclear structure. The extranuclear electrons in an atom arrange themselves in successive shells according to well-established laws. Optical spectra arise from disturbances in the outer parts of this electron structure; X-rays arise from disturbances of the electrons close to the nucleus. The chemical properties of an atom depend on the outermost electrons, and the formation of chemical compounds is accompanied by minor rearrangements of these electronic structures. Consequently, when energy is obtained by oxidation, combustion, explosion, or other chemical processes, it is obtained at the expense of these structures so that the arrangement of the electrons in the products of the process must be one of lowered energy content. (Presumably the total mass of these products is correspondingly lower but not detectably so.) The atomic nuclei are not affected by any chemical process.

1.13. *Mass Number.* Not only is the positive charge on a nucleus always an integral number of electronic charges, but the mass of the nucleus is always *approximately* a whole number times a fundamental unit of mass which is almost the mass of a proton, the nucleus of a hydrogen atom. (See Appendix 2.) This whole number is called the mass number, A, and is always at least twice as great as the atomic number except in the cases of hydrogen and a rare isotope of helium. Since the mass of a proton is about 1,800 times that of an electron, the mass of the nucleus is very nearly the whole mass of the atom.

1.14. *Isotopes and Isobars.* Two species of atoms having the same atomic number but different mass numbers are called isotopes. They are chemically identical, being merely two species of the same chemical element. If two species of atoms have the same mass number but different atomic numbers, they are called isobars and represent two different chemical elements.

RADIOACTIVITY AND NUCLEAR CHANGE

1.15. If an atom emits an alpha particle (which has an atomic number of two and a mass of four), it becomes an atom of a different element with an atomic number lower by two and a mass number lower by four. The emission by a nucleus of a beta particle increases the atomic number by one and leaves the mass number unaltered. In some cases, these changes are accompanied by the emission of gamma rays. Elements which spontaneously change or "disintegrate" in these ways are unstable and are described as being "radioactive." The only natural elements which exhibit this property of emitting alpha or beta particles are (with a few minor exceptions) those of very high atomic numbers and mass numbers, such as uranium, thorium, radium, and actinium, i.e., those known to have the most complicated nuclear structures.

HALF-LIVES; THE RADIOACTIVE SERIES

1.16. All the atoms of a particular radioactive species have the same probability of disintegrating in a given time, so that an appreciable sample of radioactive material, containing many millions of atoms, always changes or "disintegrates" at the same rate. This rate at which the material changes is expressed in terms of the "half-life," the time required for one half the atoms initially present to disintegrate, which evidently is constant for any particular atomic species. Half-lives of radioactive materials range from fractions of a second for the most unstable to billions of years for those which are only slightly unstable. Often, the "daughter" nucleus like its radioactive "parent" is itself radioactive and so on down the line for several successive generations of nuclei until a stable one is finally reached. There are three such families or series comprising all together about forty different radioactive species. The radium series starts from one isotope of uranium, the actinium series from another isotope of uranium, and the thorium series from thorium. The final product of each series, after ten or twelve successive emissions of alpha and beta particles, is a stable isotope of lead.

FIRST DEMONSTRATION OF ARTIFICIAL NUCLEAR DISINTEGRATION

1.17. Before 1919 no one had succeeded in disturbing the stability of ordinary nuclei or affecting the disintegration rates of those that were naturally radioactive. In 1919 Rutherford showed that high-energy alpha particles could cause an alteration

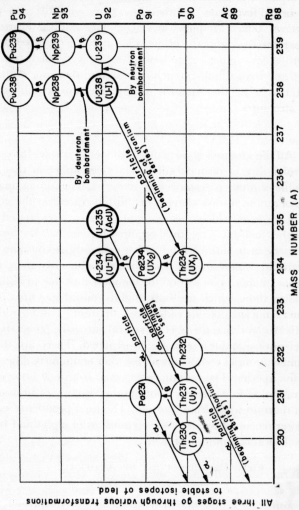

The beginnings of the three natural radioactive series and the new transuranic elements, neptunium and plutonium.

in the nucleus of an ordinary element. Specifically he succeeded in changing a few atoms of nitrogen into atoms of oxygen by bombarding them with alpha particles. The process involved may be written as

$$He^4 + N^{14} \rightarrow O^{17} + H^1$$

meaning that a helium nucleus of mass number 4 (an alpha particle) striking a nitrogen nucleus of mass number 14 produces an oxygen nucleus of mass number 17 and a hydrogen nucleus of mass number 1. The hydrogen nucleus, known as the "proton," is of special importance since it has the smallest mass of any nucleus. Although protons do not appear in natural radioactive processes, there is much direct evidence that they can be knocked out of nuclei.

THE NEUTRON

1.18. In the decade following Rutherford's work many similar experiments were performed with similar results. One series of experiments of this type led to the discovery of the neutron, which will be discussed in some detail since the neutron is practically the theme song of this whole project.

1.19. In 1930 W. Bothe and H. Becker in Germany found that if the very energetic natural alpha particles from polonium fell on certain of the light elements, specifically beryllium, boron or lithium, an unusually penetrating radiation was produced. At first this radiation was thought to be gamma radiation although it was more penetrating than any gamma rays known, and the details of experimental results were very difficult to interpret on this basis. The next important contribution was reported in 1932 by Irene Curie and F. Joliot in Paris. They showed that if this unknown radiation fell on paraffin or any other hydrogen-containing compound it ejected protons of very high energy. This was not in itself inconsistent with the assumed gamma-ray nature of the new radiation, but detailed quantitative analysis of the data became increasingly difficult to reconcile with such an hypothesis. Finally (later in 1932) J. Chadwick in England performed a series of experiments showing that the gamma-ray hypothesis was untenable. He suggested that in fact the new radiation consisted of uncharged particles of approximately the mass of the proton, and he performed a series of experiments verifying his suggestion. Such uncharged particles are now called neutrons.

1.20. The one characteristic of neutrons which differentiates them from other subatomic particles is the fact that they are uncharged. This property of neutrons delayed their discovery, makes them very penetrating, makes it impossible to observe them directly, and makes them very important as agents in nuclear change. To be sure, an atom in its normal state is also uncharged, but it is ten thousand times larger than a neutron and consists of a complex system of negatively charged electrons widely spaced around a positively charged nucleus. Charged particles (such as protons, electrons, or alpha particles) and electromagnetic radiations (such as gamma rays) lose energy in passing through matter. They exert electric forces which ionize atoms of the material through which they pass. (It is such ionization processes that make the air electrically conducting in the path of electric sparks and lightning flashes.) The energy taken up in ionization equals the energy lost by the charged particle, which slows down, or by the gamma ray, which is absorbed. The neutron, however, is unaffected by such forces; it is affected only by a very short-range force, i.e., a force that comes into play when the neutron comes very close indeed to an atomic nucleus. This is the kind of force that holds a nucleus together in spite of the mutual repulsion of the positive charges in it. Consequently a free neutron goes on its way unchecked until it makes a "head-on" collision with an atomic nucleus. Since nuclei are very small, such collisions occur but rarely and the neutron travels a long way before colliding. In the case of a collision of the "elastic" type, the ordinary laws of momentum apply as they do in the elastic collision of billiard balls. If the nucleus that is struck is heavy, it acquires relatively little speed, but if it is a proton, which is approximately equal in mass to the neutron, it is projected forward with a large fraction of the original speed of the neutron, which is itself correspondingly slowed. Secondary projectiles resulting from these collisions may be detected, for they are charged and produce ionization. The uncharged nature of the neutron makes it not only difficult to detect but difficult to control. Charged particles can be accelerated, decelerated, or deflected by electric or magnetic fields which have no effect on neutrons. Furthermore, free neutrons can be obtained only from nuclear disintegrations; there is no natural supply. The only means we have of controlling free neutrons is to put nuclei in their way so that they will be slowed and deflected or absorbed by collisions. As we shall see, these effects are of the greatest practical importance.

The Positron and the Deuteron

1.21. The year 1932 brought the discovery not only of the neutron but also of the positron. The positron was first observed by C. D. Anderson at the California Institute of Technology. It has the same mass and the same magnitude of charge as the electron, but the charge is positive instead of negative. Except as a particle emitted by artificially radioactive nuclei, it is of little interest to us.

1.22. One other major discovery marked the year 1932. H. C. Urey, F. G. Brickwedde, and G. M. Murphy found that hydrogen had an isotope of mass number 2, present in natural hydrogen to one part in 5,000. Because of its special importance this heavy species of hydrogen is given a name of its own, deuterium, and the corresponding nucleus is called the deuteron. Like the alpha particle the deuteron is not one of the fundamental particles but does play an important role in certain processes for producing nuclear disintegration.

Nuclear Structure

1.23. The idea that all elements are made out of a few fundamental particles is an old one. It is now firmly established. We believe that there are three fundamental particles—the neutron, the proton, and the electron. A complete treatise would also discuss the positron, which we have mentioned, the neutrino and the mesotron. The deuteron and alpha particle, which have already been mentioned, are important complex particles.

1.24. According to our present views the nuclei of all atomic species are made up of neutrons and protons. The number of protons is equal to the atomic number, Z. The number of neutrons, N, is equal to the difference between the mass number and the atomic number, or $A - Z$. There are two sets of forces acting on these particles, ordinary electric coulomb forces of repulsion between the positive charges and very short-range forces between all the particles. These last forces are only partly understood, and we shall not attempt to discuss them. Suffice it to say that combined effects of these attractive and repulsive forces are such that only certain combinations of neutrons and protons are stable. If the neutrons and protons are few in number, stability occurs when their numbers are about equal. For larger nuclei, the proportion of neutrons required for stability is greater. Finally, at the end of the periodic table, where the number of protons is over 90 and the number of neutrons nearly 150, there are no completely stable nuclei. (Some of the heavy nuclei are almost stable as evidenced by very long half-lives.) If an unstable nucleus is formed artificially by adding an extra neutron or proton, eventually a change to a stable form occurs. Strangely enough, this is not accomplished by ejecting a proton or a neutron but by ejecting a positron or an electron; apparently within the nucleus a proton converts itself into a neutron and positron (or a neutron converts itself into a proton and electron), and the light charged particle is ejected. In other words, the mass number remains the same but the atomic number changes. The stability conditions are not very critical so that for a given mass number, i.e., given total number of protons and neutrons, there may be several stable arrangements of protons and neutrons (at most three or five) giving several isobars. For a given atomic number, i.e., given number of protons, conditions can vary still more widely so that some of the heavy elements have as many as ten or twelve stable isotopes. Some two hundred and fifty different stable nuclei have been identified, ranging in mass number from one to two hundred and thirty-eight and in atomic number from one to ninety-two.

1.25. All the statements we have been making are based on experimental evidence. The theory of nuclear forces is still incomplete, but it has been developed on quantum-mechanical principles sufficiently to explain not only the above observations but more detailed empirical data on artificial radioactivity and on differences between nuclei with odd and even mass numbers.

ARTIFICIAL RADIOACTIVITY

1.26. We mentioned the emission of positrons or electrons by nuclei seeking stability. Electron emission (beta rays) was already familiar in the study of naturally radioactive substances, but positron emission was not found in the case of such substances. In fact, the general discussion presented above obviously was based in part on information that cannot be presented in this report. We shall, however, give a brief account of the discovery of "artificial" radioactivity and what is now known about it.

1.27. In 1934, Curie and Joliot reported that certain light elements (boron, magnesium, aluminum) which had been bombarded with alpha particles continued to emit positrons for some time after the bombardment was stopped. In other words, alpha-particle bombardment produced radioactive forms of boron, magnesium, and aluminum. Curie and Joliot actually measured half-lives of 14 minutes, 2.5 minutes, and 3.25 minutes, respectively, for the radioactive substances formed by the alpha-particle bombardment.

1.28. This result stimulated similar experiments all over the world. In particular, E. Fermi reasoned that neutrons, because of their lack of charge, should be effective in penetrating nuclei, especially those of high atomic number which repel protons and alpha particles strongly. He was able to verify his prediction almost immediately, finding that the nucleus of the bombarded atom captured the neutron and that there was thus produced an unstable nucleus which then achieved stability by emitting an electron. Thus, the final, stable nucleus was one unit higher in mass number and one unit higher in atomic number than the initial target nucleus.

1.29. As a result of innumerable experiments carried out since 1934, radioactive isotopes of nearly every element in the periodic table can now be produced. Some of them revert to stability by the emission of positrons, some by the emission of electrons, some by a process known as K-electron capture which we shall not discuss, and a small number (probably three) by alpha-particle emission. Altogether some five hundred unstable nuclear species have been observed, and in most cases their atomic numbers and mass numbers have been identified.

1.30. Not only do these artificially radioactive elements play an important role throughout the project with which we are concerned, but their future value in medicine, in "tracer" chemistry, and in many other fields of research can hardly be overestimated.

ENERGY CONSIDERATIONS

Nuclear Binding Energies

1.31. In describing radioactivity and atomic structure we have deliberately avoided quantitative data and have not mentioned any applications of the equivalence of mass and energy which we announced as the guiding principle of this report. Now we must speak of quantitative details, not merely of general principles.

1.32. We have spoken of stable and unstable nuclei made up of assemblages of protons and neutrons held together by nuclear forces. It is a general principle of physics that work must be done on a stable system to break it up. Thus, if an assemblage of neutrons and protons is stable, energy must be supplied to separate its constituent particles. If energy and mass are really equivalent, then the total mass of a stable nucleus should be less than the total mass of the separate protons and neutrons that go to make it up. This mass difference, then, should be equivalent to the energy required to disrupt the nucleus completely, which is called the binding energy. Remember that the masses of all nuclei were "approximately" whole numbers. It is the small differences from whole numbers that are significant.

1.33. Consider the alpha particle as an example. It is stable; since its mass number is four and its atomic number two it consists of two protons and two neutrons. The mass of a proton is 1.00758 and that of a neutron is 1.00893 (see Appendix 2), so that the total mass of the separate components of the helium nucleus is

$$2 \times 1.00758 + 2 \times 1.00893 = 4.03302$$

whereas the mass of the helium nucleus itself is 4.00280. Neglecting the last two decimal places we have 4.033 and 4.003, a difference of 0.030 mass units. This, then, represents the "binding energy" of the protons and neutrons in the helium nucleus. It looks small, but recalling Einstein's equation, $E = mc^2$, we remember that a small amount of mass is equivalent to a large amount of energy. Actually 0.030 mass units is equal to 4.5×10^{-5} ergs per nucleus or 2.7×10^{19} ergs per gram molecule of helium. In units more familiar to the engineer or chemist, this means that to break up the nuclei of all the helium atoms in a gram of helium would require 1.62×10^{11} gram calories or 190,000 kilowatt hours of energy. Conversely, if free protons and neutrons could be assembled into helium nuclei, this energy would be released.

1.34. Evidently it is worth exploring the possibility of getting energy by combining protons and neutrons or by transmuting one kind of nucleus into another. Let us begin by reviewing present-day knowledge of the binding energies of various nuclei.

Mass Spectra and Binding Energies

1.35. Chemical atomic-weight determinations give the average weight of a large number of atoms of a given element. Unless the element has only one isotope, the chemical atomic weight is not proportional to the mass of individual atoms. The mass spectrograph developed by F. W. Aston and others from the earlier apparatus of J. J. Thomson measures the masses of individual isotopes. Indeed, it was just such measurements that proved the existence of isotopes and showed that on the atomic-weight scale the masses of all atomic species were very nearly whole numbers. These whole numbers, discovered experimentally, are the mass numbers which we have already defined and which represent the sums of the numbers of the protons and neutrons; their discovery contributed largely to our present views that all nuclei are combinations of neutrons and protons.

1.36. Improved mass spectrograph data supplemented in a few cases by nuclear reaction data have given accurate figures for binding energies for many atomic species over the whole range of atomic masses. This binding energy, B, is the difference between the true nuclear mass, M, and the sum of the masses of all the protons and neutrons in the nucleus. That is,

$$B = (ZM_p + NM_n) - M$$

where M_p and M_n are the masses of the proton and neutron respectively, Z is the number of protons, $N = A - Z$ is the number of neutrons, and M is the true mass of the nucleus. It is more interesting to study the binding energy per particle, B/A, than B itself. Such a study shows that, apart from fluctuations in the light nuclei, the general trend of the binding energy per particle is to increase rapidly to a flat maximum around $A = 60$ (nickel) and then decrease again gradually. Evidently the nuclei in the middle of the periodic table—nuclei of mass numbers 40 to 100—are the most strongly bound. Any nuclear reaction where the particles in the resultant nuclei are more strongly bound than the particles in the initial nuclei will release energy. Speaking in thermochemical terms, such reactions are exothermic. Thus, in general, energy may be gained by combining light nuclei to form heavier ones or by breaking very heavy ones into two or three smaller fragments. Also, there are a number of special cases of exothermic nuclear disintegrations among the first ten or twelve elements of the periodic table, where the binding energy per particle varies irregularly from one element to another.

1.37. So far we seem to be piling one supposition on another. First we assumed that mass and energy were equivalent; now we are assuming that atomic nuclei can be rearranged with a consequent reduction in their total mass, thereby releasing energy which can then be put to use. It is time to talk about some experiments that convinced physicists of the truth of these statements.

EXPERIMENTAL PROOF OF THE EQUIVALENCE OF MASS AND ENERGY

1.38. As we have already said, Rutherford's work in 1919 on artificial nuclear disintegration was followed by many similar experiments. Gradual improvement in high-voltage technique made it possible to substitute artificially produced high-speed ions of hydrogen or helium for natural alpha particles. J. D. Cockcroft and E. T. S. Walton in Rutherford's laboratory were the first to succeed in producing nuclear changes by such methods. In 1932 they bombarded a target of lithium with protons of 700 kilovolts energy and found that alpha particles were ejected from the target as a result of the bombardment. The nuclear reaction which occurred can be written symbolically as

$$_3\text{Li}^7 + {}_1\text{H}^1 \rightarrow {}_2\text{He}^4 + {}_2\text{He}^4$$

where the subscript represents the positive charge on the nucleus (atomic number) and the superscript is the number of massive particles in the nucleus (mass number). As in a chemical equation, quantities on the left must add up to those on the right; thus the subscripts total four and the superscripts eight on each side.

1.39. Neither mass nor energy has been included in this equation. In general, the incident proton and the resultant alpha particles will each have kinetic energy. Also, the mass of two alpha particles will not be precisely the same as the sum of the masses of a proton and a lithium atom. According to our theory, the totals of mass and energy taken together should be the same before and after the reaction. The masses were known from mass spectra. On the left (Li^7 + H^1) they totalled 8.0241, on the right ($2He^4$) 8.0056, so that 0.0185 units of mass had disappeared in the reaction. The experimentally determined energies of the alpha particles were approximately 8.5 million electron volts each, a figure compared to which the kinetic energy of the incident proton could be neglected. Thus 0.0185 units of mass had disappeared and 17 Mev of kinetic energy had appeared. Now 0.0185 units of mass is 3.07 $\times$ 10^{-26} grams, 17 Mev is 27.2 $\times$ 10^{-6} ergs and c is 3 $\times$ 10^{10} cm/sec. (See Appendix 2.) If we substitute these figures into Einstein's equation, $E = mc^2$, on the left side we have 27.2 $\times$ 10^{-6} ergs and on the right side we have 27.6 $\times$ 10^{-6} ergs, so that the equation is found to be satisfied to a good approximation. In other words, these experimental results prove that the equivalence of mass and energy was correctly stated by Einstein.

NUCLEAR REACTIONS

METHODS OF NUCLEAR BOMBARDMENT

1.40. Cockcroft and Walton produced protons of fairly high energy by ionizing gaseous hydrogen and then accelerating the ions in a transformer-rectifier high-voltage apparatus. A similar procedure can be used to produce high-energy deuterons from deuterium or high-energy alpha particles from helium. Higher energies can be attained by accelerating the ions in cyclotrons or Van de Graaff machines. However, to obtain high-energy gamma radiation or—most important of all—to obtain neutrons, nuclear reactions themselves must be used as sources. Radiations of sufficiently high energy come from certain naturally radioactive materials or from certain bombardments. Neutrons are commonly produced by the bombardment of certain elements, notably beryllium or boron, by natural alpha particles, or by bombarding suitable targets with protons or deuterons. The most common source of neutrons is a mixture of radium and beryllium where the alpha particles from radium and its decay products penetrate the Be^9 nuclei, which then give off neutrons and become stable C^{12} nuclei (ordinary carbon). A frequently used "beam" source of neutrons results from accelerated deuterons impinging on "heavy water" ice. Here the high-speed deuterons strike the target deuterons to produce neutrons and He³ nuclei. Half a dozen other reactions are also used involving deuterium, lithium, beryllium, or boron as targets. Note that in all these reactions the total mass number and total charge number are unchanged.

1.41. To summarize, the agents that are found to initiate nuclear reactions are—in approximate order of importance—neutrons, deuterons, protons, alpha particles, gamma rays and, rarely, heavier particles.

RESULTS OF NUCLEAR BOMBARDMENT

1.42. Most atomic nuclei can be penetrated by at least one type of atomic projectile (or by gamma radiation). Any such penetration may result in a nuclear rearrangement in the course of which a fundamental particle is ejected or radiation is emitted or both. The resulting nucleus may be one of the naturally available stable species, or—more likely—it may be an atom of a different type which is radioactive, eventually changing to still a different nucleus. This may in turn be radioactive and, if so, will again decay. The process continues until all nuclei have changed to a stable type. There are two respects in which these artificially radioactive substances differ from the natural ones: many of them change by emitting positrons (unknown in natural radioactivity) and very few of them emit alpha particles. In every one of the cases where accurate measurements have been made, the equivalence of mass and energy has been demonstrated and the mass-energy total has remained constant. (Sometimes it is necessary to invoke neutrinos to preserve mass-energy conservation.)

NOTATION

1.43. A complete description of a nuclear reaction should include the nature, mass and energy of the incident particle, also the nature (mass number and atomic number), mass and energy (usually zero) of the target particle, also the nature, mass and energy of the ejected particles (or radiation), and finally the nature, mass and energy of the remainder. But all of these are rarely known and for many purposes their complete specification is unnecessary. A nuclear reaction is frequently described by a notation that designates first the target by chemical symbol and mass number if known, then the projectile, then the emitted particle, and then the remainder. In this scheme the neutron is represented by the letter n, the proton by p, the deuteron by d, the alpha particle by α, and the gamma ray by γ. Thus the radium-beryllium neutron reaction can be written Be^9 $(\alpha, n)C^{12}$ and the deuteron-deuteron reaction $H^2(d, n)He^3$.

TYPES OF REACTION

1.44. Considering the five different particles (n, p, d, α, γ) both as projectiles and emitted products, we might expect to find twenty-five combinations possible. Actually the deuteron very rarely occurs as a product particle, and the photon (gamma rays) initiates only two types of reaction. There are, however, a few other types of reaction, such as (n, 2n), (d, H^3), and fission, which bring the total known types to about twenty-five. Perhaps the (n, γ) reaction should be specifically mentioned as it is very important in one process which will concern us. It is often called "radiative capture" since the neutron remains in the nucleus and only a gamma ray comes out.

PROBABILITY AND CROSS SECTION

1.45. So far nothing has been said about the probability of nuclear reactions. Actually it varies widely. There is no guarantee that a neutron or proton headed straight for a nucleus will penetrate it at all. It depends on the nucleus and on the incident particle. In nuclear physics, it is found convenient to express probability of a particular event by a "cross section." Statistically, the centers of the atoms in a thin foil can be considered as points evenly distributed over a plane. The center of an atomic projectile striking this plane has geometrically a definite probability of passing within a certain distance (r) of one of these points. In fact, if there are n atomic centers in an area A of the plane, this probability is $n\pi r^2/A$, which is simply the ratio of the aggregate area of circles of radius r drawn around the points to the whole area. If we think of the atoms as impenetrable steel discs and the impinging particle as a bullet of negligible diameter, this ratio is the probability that the bullet will strike a steel disc, i.e., that the atomic projectile will be stopped by the foil. If it is the fraction of impinging atoms getting *through* the foil which is measured, the result can still be expressed in terms of the equivalent stopping cross section of the atoms. This notion can be extended to any interaction between the impinging particle and the atoms in the target. For example, the probability that an alpha particle striking a beryllium target will produce a neutron can be expressed as the equivalent cross section of beryllium for this type of reaction.

1.46. In nuclear physics it is conventional to consider that the impinging particles have negligible diameter. The technical definition of cross section for any nuclear process is therefore:

$$\frac{\text{number of processes occurring}}{\text{number of incident particles}} = (\text{number of target nuclei per cm}^2) \times (\text{nuclear cross section in cm}^2)$$

It should be noted that this definition is for the cross section per nucleus. Cross sections can be computed for any sort of process, such as capture scattering, production of neutrons, etc. In many cases, the number of particles emitted or scattered in nuclear processes is not measured directly; one merely measures the attenuation produced in a parallel beam of incident particles by the interposition of a known thickness of a particular material. The cross section obtained in this way is called the total cross section and is usually denoted by σ.

1.47. As indicated in paragraph 1.11, the typical nuclear diameter is of the order of 10^{-12} cm. We might therefore expect the cross sections for nuclear reactions to be of the order of $\pi d^2/4$ or roughly 10^{-24} cm^2 and this is the unit in which they are usually expressed. Actually the observed cross sections vary enormously. Thus for slow neutrons absorbed by the (n, γ) reaction the cross section in some cases is as much as $1,000 \times 10^{-24}$ cm^2, while the cross sections for transmutations by gamma-ray absorption are in the neighborhood of $(1/1,000) \times 10^{-24}$ cm^2.

PRACTICABILITY OF ATOMIC POWER
IN 1939

SMALL SCALE OF EXPERIMENTS

1.48. We have talked glibly about the equivalence of mass and energy and about nuclear reactions, such as that of protons on lithium, where energy was released in relatively large amounts. Now let us ask why atomic power plants did not spring up all over the world in the 'thirties. After all, if we can get 2.76×10^{-5} ergs from an atom of lithium struck by a proton, we might expect to obtain approximately half a million kilowatt hours by combining a gram of hydrogen with seven grams of lithium. It looks better than burning coal. The difficulties are in producing the high-speed protons and in controlling the energy produced. All the experiments we have been talking about were done with very small quantities of material, large enough in numbers of atoms, to be sure, but in terms of ordinary masses infinitesimal— not tons or pounds or grams, but fractions of micrograms. The amount of energy used up in the experiment was always far greater than the amount generated by the nuclear reaction.

1.49. Neutrons are particularly effective in producing nuclear disintegration. Why weren't they used? If their initial source was an ion beam striking a target, the limitations discussed in the last paragraph applied. If a radium and beryllium source was to be used, the scarcity of radium was a difficulty.

THE NEED OF A CHAIN REACTION

1.50. Our common sources of power, other than sunlight and water power, are chemical reactions—usually the combustion of coal or oil. They release energy as the result of rearrangements of the outer electronic structures of the atoms, the same kind of process that supplies energy to our bodies. Combustion is always self-propagating; thus lighting a fire with a match releases enough heat to ignite the neighboring fuel, which releases more heat which ignites more fuel, and so on. In the nuclear reactions we have described this is not generally true; neither the energy released nor the new particles formed are sufficient to maintain the reaction. But we can imagine nuclear reactions emitting particles of the same sort that initiate them and in sufficient numbers to propagate the reaction in neighboring nuclei. Such a self-propagating reaction is called a "chain reaction" and such conditions must be achieved if the energy of the nuclear reactions with which we are concerned is to be put to large-scale use.

PERIOD OF SPECULATION

1.51. Although there were no atomic power plants built in the 'thirties, there were plenty of discoveries in nuclear physics and plenty of speculation. A theory was advanced by H. Bethe to explain the heat of the sun by a cycle of nuclear changes involving carbon, hydrogen, nitrogen, and oxygen, and leading eventually to the formation of helium.* This theory is now generally accepted. The discovery of a few (n, 2n) nuclear reactions (i.e., neutron-produced and neutron-producing reactions) suggested that a self-multiplying chain reaction might be initiated under the right conditions. There was much talk of atomic power and some talk of atomic bombs. But the last great step in this preliminary period came after four years of stumbling. The effects of neutron bombardment of uranium, the most complex element known, had been studied by some of the ablest physicists. The results were striking but confusing. The story of their gradual interpretation is intricate and highly technical, a fascinating tale of theory and experiment. Passing by the earlier inadequate

---

* The series of reactions postulated was

$$(1) \quad {}_6C^{12} + {}_1H^1 \rightarrow {}_7N^{13}$$
$$(2) \quad {}_7N^{13} \rightarrow {}_6C^{13} + {}_1e^0$$
$$(3) \quad {}_6C^{13} + {}_1H^1 \rightarrow {}_7N^{14}$$
$$(4) \quad {}_7N^{14} + {}_1H^1 \rightarrow {}_8O^{15}$$
$$(5) \quad {}_8O^{15} \rightarrow {}_7N^{15} + {}_1e^0$$
$$(6) \quad {}_7N^{15} + {}_1H^1 \rightarrow {}_6C^{12} + {}_2He^4$$

The net effect is the transformation of hydrogen into helium and positrons (designated as ${}_1e^0$) and the release of about thirty million electron volts energy.

explanations, we shall go directly to the final explanation, which, as so often happens, is relatively simple.

DISCOVERY OF URANIUM FISSION

1.52. As has already been mentioned, the neutron proved to be the most effective particle for inducing nuclear changes. This was particularly true for the elements of highest atomic number and weight where the large nuclear charge exerts strong repulsive forces on deuteron or proton projectiles but not on uncharged neutrons. The results of the bombardment of uranium by neutrons had proved interesting and puzzling. First studied by Fermi and his colleagues in 1934, they were not properly interpreted until several years later.

1.53. On January 16, 1939, Niels Bohr of Copenhagen, Denmark, arrived in this country to spend several months in Princeton, N. J., and was particularly anxious to discuss some abstract problems with Einstein. (Four years later Bohr was to escape from Nazi-occupied Denmark in a small boat.) Just before Bohr left Denmark two of his colleagues, O. R. Frisch and L. Meitner (both refugees from Germany), had told him their guess that the absorption of a neutron by a uranium nucleus sometimes caused that nucleus to split into approximately equal parts with the release of enormous quantities of energy, a process that soon began to be called nuclear "fission." The occasion for this hypothesis was the important discovery of O. Hahn and F. Strassmann in Germany (published in *Naturwissenschaften* in early January 1939) which proved that an isotope of barium was produced by neutron bombardment of uranium. Immediately on arrival in the United States Bohr communicated this idea to his former student J. A. Wheeler and others at Princeton, and from them the news spread by word of mouth to neighboring physicists including E. Fermi at Columbia University. As a result of conversations among Fermi, J. R. Dunning, and G. B. Pegram, a search was undertaken at Columbia for the heavy pulses of ionization that would be expected from the flying fragments of the uranium nucleus. On January 26, 1939, there was a conference on theoretical physics at Washington, D. C., sponsored jointly by the George Washington University and the Carnegie Institution of Washington. Fermi left New York to attend this meeting before the Columbia fission experiments had been tried. At the meeting Bohr and Fermi discussed the problem of fission, and in particular Fermi mentioned the possibility that neutrons might be emitted during the process. Although this was only a guess, its implication of the possibility of a chain reaction was obvious. A number of sensational articles were pub-

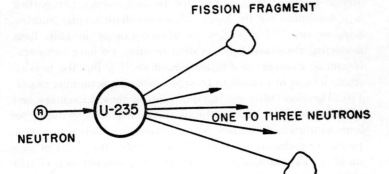

FISSION FRAGMENT

NEUTRON

ONE TO THREE NEUTRONS

FISSION FRAGMENT

lished in the press on this subject. Before the meeting in Washington was over, several other experiments to confirm fission had been initiated, and positive experimental confirmation was reported from four laboratories (Columbia University, Carnegie Institution of Washington, Johns Hopkins University, University of California) in the February 15, 1939, issue of the *Physical Review*. By this time Bohr had heard that similar experiments had been made in his laboratory in Copenhagen about January 15. (Letter by Frisch to *Nature* dated January 16, 1939, and appearing in the February 18 issue.) F. Joliot in Paris had also published his first results in the *Comptes Rendus* of January 30, 1939. From this time on there was a steady flow of papers on the subject of fission, so that by the time (December 6, 1939) L. A. Turner of Princeton wrote a review article on the subject in the *Reviews of Modern Physics* nearly one hundred papers had appeared. Complete analysis and discussion of these papers have appeared in Turner's article and elsewhere.

GENERAL DISCUSSION OF FISSION

1.54. Consider the suggestion of Frisch and Meitner in the light of the two general trends that had been discovered in nuclear structure: first, that the proportion of neutrons goes up with atomic number; second, that the binding energy per particle is a maximum for the nuclei of intermediate atomic number. Suppose the U-238 nucleus is broken exactly in half; then, neglecting the mass of the incident neutron, we have two nuclei of atomic number 46 and mass number 119. But the heaviest stable isotope of palladium (Z = 46) has a mass number of only 110. Therefore to reach stability each of these imaginary new nuclei must eject nine neutrons, becoming $_{46}Pd^{110}$ nuclei; or four neutrons in each nucleus must convert themselves to protons by emitting electrons, thereby forming stable tin nuclei of mass number 119 and atomic number 50; or a combination of such ejections and conversions must occur to give some other pair of stable nuclei. Actually, as was suggested by Hahn and Strassmann's identification of barium (Z = 56, A = 135 to 140) as a product of fission, the split occurs in such a way as to produce two unequal parts of mass numbers about 140 and 90 with the emission of a few neutrons and subsequent radioactive decay by electron emission until stable nuclei are formed. Calculations from binding-energy data show that any such rearrangement gives an aggregate resulting mass considerably less than the initial mass of the uranium nucleus, and thus that a great deal of energy must be released.

1.55. Evidently, there were three major implications of the phenomenon of fission: the release of energy, the production of radioactive atomic species and the possibility of a neutron chain reaction. The energy release might reveal itself in kinetic energy of the fission fragments and in the subsequent radioactive disintegration of the products. The possibility of a neutron chain reaction depended on whether neutrons were in fact emitted—a possibility which required investigation.

1.56. These were the problems suggested by the discovery of fission, the kind of problem reported in the journals in 1939 and 1940 and since then investigated largely in secret. The study of the fission process itself, including production of neutrons and fast fragments, has been largely carried out by physicists using counters, cloud chambers, etc. The study and identification of the fission products has been carried out largely by chemists, who have had to perform chemical separations rapidly even with submicroscopic quantities of material and to make repeated determinations of the half-lives of unstable isotopes. We shall summarize the state of knowledge as of June 1940. By that time the principal facts about fission had been discovered and revealed to the scientific world. A chain reaction had not been obtained, but its possibility—at least in principle—was clear and several paths that might lead to it had been suggested.

STATE OF KNOWLEDGE IN JUNE 1940

DEFINITE AND GENERALLY KNOWN INFORMATION ON FISSION

1.57. All the following information was generally known in June 1940, both here and abroad:

(1) That three elements—uranium, thorium, and protoactinium—when bombarded by neutrons sometimes split into approximately equal fragments, and that these fragments were isotopes of elements in the middle of the periodic table, ranging from selenium ($Z = 34$) to lanthanum ($Z = 57$).

(2) That most of these fission fragments were unstable, decaying radioactively by successive emission of beta particles through a series of elements to various stable forms.

(3) That these fission fragments had very great kinetic energy.

(4) That fission of thorium and protoactinum was caused only

by fast neutrons (velocities of the order of thousands of miles per second).

(5) That fission in uranium could be produced by fast or slow (so-called thermal velocity) neutrons; specifically, that thermal neutrons caused fission in one isotope, U-235, but not in the other, U-238, and that fast neutrons had a lower probability of causing fission in U-235 than thermal neutrons.

(6) That at certain neutron speeds there was a large capture cross section in U-238 producing U-239 but not fission.

(7) That the energy released per fission of a uranium nucleus was approximately 200 million electron volts.

(8) That high-speed neutrons were emitted in the process of fission.

(9) That the average number of neutrons released per fission was somewhere between one and three.

(10) That high-speed neutrons could lose energy by inelastic collision with uranium nuclei without any nuclear reaction taking place.

(11) That most of this information was consistent with the semi-empirical theory of nuclear structure worked out by Bohr and Wheeler and others; this suggested that predictions based on this theory had a fair chance of success.

SUGGESTION OF PLUTONIUM FISSION

1.58. It was realized that radiative capture of neutrons by U-238 would probably lead by two successive beta-ray emissions to the formation of a nucleus for which $Z = 94$ and $A = 239$. Consideration of the Bohr-Wheeler theory of fission and of certain empirical relations among the nuclei by L. A. Turner and others suggested that this nucleus would be a fairly stable alpha emitter and would probably undergo fission when bombarded by thermal neutrons. Later the importance of such thermal fission to the maintenance of the chain reaction was foreshadowed in private correspondence and discussion. In terms of our present knowledge and notation the particular reaction suggested is as follows:

$$_{92}U^{238} + _{0}n^{1} \rightarrow _{92}U^{239} \rightarrow _{93}Np^{239} + _{-1}e^{0}$$
$$_{93}Np^{239} \rightarrow _{94}Pu^{239} + _{-1}e^{0}$$

where Np and Pu are the chemical symbols now used for the two new elements, neptunium and plutonium; $_{0}n^{1}$ represents the neutron, and $_{-1}e^{0}$ represents an ordinary (negative) electron. Plutonium 239 is the nucleus rightly guessed to be fissionable by thermal neutrons. It will be discussed fully in later chapters.

GENERAL STATE OF NUCLEAR PHYSICS

1.59. By 1940 nuclear reactions had been intensively studied for over ten years. Several books and review articles on nuclear physics had been published. New techniques had been developed for producing and controlling nuclear projectiles, for studying artificial radioactivity, and for separating submicroscopic quantities of chemical elements produced by nuclear reactions. Isotope masses had been measured accurately. Neutron-capture cross sections had been measured. Methods of slowing down neutrons had been developed. Physiological effects of neutrons had been observed; they had even been tried in the treatment of cancer. All such information was generally available; but it was very incomplete. There were many gaps and many inaccuracies. The techniques were difficult and the quantities of materials available were often submicroscopic. Although the fundamental principles were clear, the theory was full of unverified assumptions and calculations were hard to make. Predictions made in 1940 by different physicists of equally high ability were often at variance. The subject was in all too many respects an art, rather than a science.

SUMMARY

1.60. Looking back on the year 1940, we see that all the prerequisites to a serious attack on the problem of producing atomic bombs and controlling atomic power were at hand. It had been proved that mass and energy were equivalent. It had been proved that the neutrons initiating fission of uranium reproduced themselves in the process and that therefore a multiplying chain reaction might occur with explosive force. To be sure, no one knew whether the required conditions could be achieved, but many scientists had clear ideas as to the problems involved and the directions in which solutions might be sought. The next chapter of this report gives a statement of the problems and serves as a guide to the developments of the past five years.

CHAPTER II. STATEMENT OF THE PROBLEM

INTRODUCTION

2.1. From the time of the first discovery of the large amounts of energy released in nuclear reactions to the time of the discovery of uranium fission, the idea of atomic power or even atomic bombs was discussed off and on in scientific circles. The discovery of fission made this talk seem much less speculative, but realization of atomic power still seemed in the distant future and there was an instinctive feeling among many scientists that it might not, in fact, ever be realized. During 1939 and 1940 many public statements, some of them by responsible scientists, called attention to the enormous energy available in uranium for explosives and for controlled power, so that U-235 became a familiar byword indicating great things to come. The possible military importance of uranium fission was called to the attention of the government (see Chapter III), and in a conference with representatives of the Navy Department in March 1939 Fermi suggested the possibility of achieving a controllable reaction using slow neutrons or a reaction of an explosive character using fast neutrons. He pointed out, however, that the data then available might be insufficient for accurate predictions.

2.2. By the summer of 1940 it was possible to formulate the problem fairly clearly, although it was still far from possible to answer the various questions involved or even to decide whether a chain reaction ever could be obtained. In this chapter we shall give a statement of the problem in its entirety. For purposes of clarification we may make use of some knowledge which actually was not acquired until a later date.

THE CHAIN-REACTION PROBLEM

2.3. The principle of operation of an atomic bomb or power plant utilizing uranium fission is simple enough. If one neutron causes a fission that produces more than one new neutron, the number of fissions may increase tremendously with the release of enormous amounts of energy. It is a question of probabilities. Neutrons produced in the fission process may escape entirely from the uranium, may be captured by uranium in a process not resulting in fission, or may be captured by an impurity. Thus the question of whether a chain reaction does or does not go depends on the result of a competition among four processes:

(1) escape,
(2) non-fission capture by uranium,
(3) non-fission capture by impurities,
(4) fission capture.

If the loss of neutrons by the first three processes is less than the surplus produced by the fourth, the chain reaction occurs; otherwise it does not. Evidently any one of the first three processes may have such a high probability in a given arrangement that the extra neutrons created by fission will be insufficient to keep the reaction going. For example, should it turn out that process (2)—non-fission capture by uranium—has a much higher probability than fission capture, there would presumably be no possibility of achieving a chain reaction.

2.4. An additional complication is that natural uranium contains three isotopes: U-234, U-235, and U-238, present to the extent of approximately 0.006, 0.7, and 99.3 per cent, respectively. We have already seen that the probabilities of processes (2) and (4) are different for different isotopes. We have also seen that the probabilities are different for neutrons of different energies.

2.5. We shall now consider the limitations imposed by the first three processes and how their effects can be minimized.

Neutron Escape; Critical Size

2.6. The relative number of neutrons which escape from a quantity of uranium can be minimized by changing the size and shape. In a sphere any surface effect is proportional to the square of the radius, and any volume effect is proportional to the cube of the radius. Now the escape of neutrons from a quantity of uranium is a surface effect depending on the area of the surface, but fission capture occurs throughout the material and is therefore a volume effect. Consequently the greater the amount of uranium, the less probable it is that neutron escape will predominate over fission capture and prevent a chain reaction. Loss of neutrons by non-fission capture is a volume effect like neutron production by fission capture, so that increase in size makes no change in its relative importance.

2.7. The critical size of a device containing uranium is defined as the size for which the production of free neutrons by fission is just equal to their loss by escape and by non-fission capture. In other words, if the size is smaller than critical, then—by definition—no chain reaction will sustain itself. In principle it was possible in 1940 to calculate the critical size, but in practice the uncertainty of the constants involved was so great that the various estimates differed widely. It seemed not improbable that the critical size might be too large for practical purposes. Even now estimates for untried arrangements vary somewhat from time to time as new information becomes available.

USE OF A MODERATOR TO REDUCE NON-FISSION CAPTURE

2.8. In Chapter I we said that thermal neutrons have the highest probability of producing fission of U-235 but we also said that the neutrons emitted in the process of fission had high speeds. Evidently it was an oversimplification to say that the chain reaction might maintain itself if more neutrons were created by fission than were absorbed. For the probability both of fission capture and of non-fission capture depends on the speed of the neutrons. Unfortunately, the speed at which non-fission capture is most probable is intermediate between the average speed of neutrons emitted in the fission process and the speed at which fission capture is most probable.

2.9. For some years before the discovery of fission, the customary way of slowing down neutrons was to cause them to pass through material of low atomic weight, such as hydrogenous material. The process of slowing down or moderation is simply one of elastic collisions between high-speed particles and particles practically at rest. The more nearly identical the masses of neutron and struck particle the greater the loss of kinetic energy by the neutron. Therefore the light elements are most effective as "moderators," i.e., slowing down agents, for neutrons.

2.10. It occurred to a number of physicists that it might be possible to mix uranium with a moderator in such a way that the high-speed fission neutrons, after being ejected from uranium and before re-encountering uranium nuclei, would have their speeds reduced below the speeds for which non-fission capture is highly probable. Evidently the characteristics of a good moderator are that it should be of low atomic weight and that it should have little or no tendency to absorb neutrons. Lithium and boron are excluded on the latter count. Helium is difficult to use because it is a gas and forms no compounds. The choice of moderator therefore lay among hydrogen, deuterium, beryllium, and carbon. Even now no one of these substances can be excluded from the list of practical possibilities. It was E. Fermi and L. Szilard who proposed the use of graphite as a moderator for a chain reaction.

Use of a Lattice to Reduce Non-fission Capture

2.11. The general scheme of using a moderator mixed with the uranium was pretty obvious. A specific manner of using a moderator was first suggested in this country, so far as we can discover, by Fermi and Szilard. The idea was to use lumps of uranium of considerable size imbedded in a matrix of moderator material. Such a lattice can be shown to have real advantages over a homogeneous mixture. As the constants were more accurately determined, it became possible to calculate theoretically the type of lattice that would be most effective.

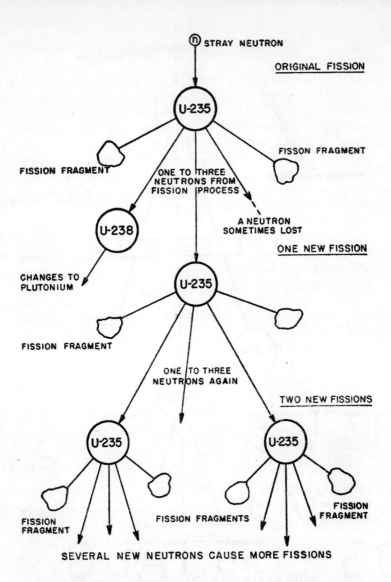

SCHEMATIC DIAGRAM OF CHAIN REACTION FROM FISSION, NEGLECTING EFFECT OF NEUTRON SPEED. IN AN EXPLOSIVE REACTION THE NUMBER OF NEUTRONS MULTIPLIES INDEFINITELY. IN A CONTROLLED REACTION THE NUMBER OF NEUTRONS BUILDS UP TO A CERTAIN LEVEL AND THEN REMAINS CONSTANT.

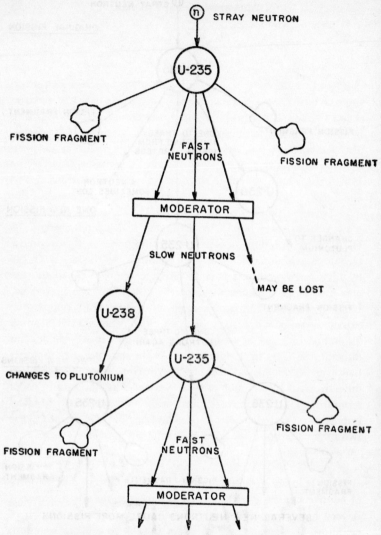

SCHEMATIC DIAGRAM OF FISSION CHAIN REACTION USING A
MODERATOR TO SLOW NEUTRONS TO SPEEDS MORE LIKELY TO
CAUSE FISSION

REDUCTION OF NON-FISSION CAPTURE BY
ISOTOPE SEPARATION

2.12. In Chapter I it was stated that for neutrons of certain intermediate speeds (corresponding to energies of a few electron volts) U-238 has a large capture cross section for the production of U-239 but not for fission. There is also a considerable probability of inelastic (i.e., non-capture-producing) collisions between high-speed neutrons and U-238 nuclei. Thus the presence of the U-238 tends both to reduce the speed of the fast neutrons and to effect the capture of those of moderate speed. Although there may be some non-fission capture by U-235, it is evident that if we can separate the U-235 from the U-238 and discard the U-238, we can reduce non-fission capture and can thus promote the chain reaction. In fact, the probability of fission of U-235 by high-speed neutrons may be great enough to make the use of a moderator unnecessary once the U-238 has been removed. Unfortunately, U-235 is present in natural uranium only to the extent of about one part in 140. Also, the relatively small difference in mass between the two isotopes makes separation difficult. In fact, in 1940 no large-scale separation of isotopes had ever been achieved except for hydrogen, whose two isotopes differ in mass by a factor of two. Nevertheless, the possibility of separating U-235 was recognized early as being of the greatest importance, and such separation has, in fact, been one of the two major lines of Project effort during the past five years.

PRODUCTION AND PURIFICATION OF MATERIALS

2.13. It has been stated above that the cross section for capture of neutrons varies greatly among different materials. In some it is very high compared to the maximum fission cross section of uranium. If, then, we are to hope to achieve a chain reaction, we must reduce effect (3)—non-fission capture by impurities— to the point where it is not serious. This means very careful purification of the uranium metal and very careful purification of the moderator. Calculations show that the maximum permissible concentrations of many impurity elements are a few parts per million—in either the uranium or the moderator. When it is recalled that up to 1940 the total amount of uranium metal produced in this country was not more than a few grams and even this was of doubtful purity, that the total amount of metallic beryllium produced in this country was not more than a few pounds, that the total amount of concentrated deuterium produced was not more than a few pounds, and that carbon had never been produced in quantity with anything like the purity required of a moderator, it is clear that the problem of producing and purifying materials was a major one.

CONTROL OF THE CHAIN REACTION

2.14. The problems that have been discussed so far have to do merely with the realization of the chain reaction. If such a reaction is going to be of use, we must be able to control it. The problem of control is different depending on whether we are interested in steady production of power or in an explosion. In general, the steady production of atomic power requires a slow-neutron-induced fission chain reaction occurring in a mixture or lattice of uranium and moderator, while an atomic bomb requires a fast-neutron-induced fission chain reaction in U-235 or Pu-239, although both slow- and fast-neutron fission may contribute in each case. It seemed likely, even in 1940, that by using neutron absorbers a power chain reaction could be controlled. It was also considered likely, though not certain, that such a chain reaction would be self-limiting by virtue of the lower probability of fission-producing capture when a higher temperature was reached. Nevertheless, there was a possibility that a chain-reacting system might get out of control, and it therefore seemed necessary to perform the chain-reaction experiment in an uninhabited location.

PRACTICAL APPLICATION OF THE CHAIN REACTION

2.15. Up to this point we have been discussing how to produce and control a nuclear chain reaction but not how to make use of it. The technological gap between producing a controlled chain reaction and using it as a large-scale power source or an explosive is comparable to the gap between the discovery of fire and the manufacture of a steam locomotive.

2.16. Although production of power has never been the principal object of this project, enough attention has been given to the matter to reveal the major difficulty: the attainment of high-temperature operation. An effective heat engine must not only develop heat but must develop heat at a high temperature. To run a chain-reacting system at a high temperature and to convert the heat generated to useful work is very much more difficult than to run a chain-reacting system at a low temperature.

2.17. Of course, the proof that a chain reaction is possible does not itself insure that nuclear energy can be effective in a bomb. To have an effective explosion it is necessary that the chain reaction build up extremely rapidly; otherwise only a small amount of the nuclear energy will be utilized before the bomb flies apart and the reaction stops. It is also necessary that no premature explosion occur. This entire "detonation" problem was and still remains one of the most difficult problems in designing a high-efficiency atomic bomb.

Possibility of Using Plutonium

2.18. So far, all our discussion has been primarily concerned with the use of uranium itself. We have already mentioned the suggestion that the element of atomic number 94 and mass 239, commonly referred to as plutonium, might be very effective. Actually, we now believe it to be of value comparable to pure U-235. We have mentioned the difficulty of separating U-235 from the more abundant isotope U-238. These two isotopes are, of course, chemically identical. But plutonium, although produced from U-238, is a different chemical element. Therefore, if a process could be worked out for converting some of the U-238 to plutonium, a *chemical* separation of the plutonium from uranium might prove more practicable than the *isotopic* separation of U-235 from U-238.

2.19. Suppose that we have set up a controllable chain reaction in a lattice of natural uranium and a moderator—say carbon, in the form of graphite. Then as the chain reaction proceeds, neutrons are emitted in the process of fission of the U-235 and many of these neutrons are absorbed by U-238. This produces U-239, each atom of which then emits a beta particle, becoming neptunium ($_{93}Np^{239}$). Neptunium, in turn, emits another beta particle, becoming plutonium ($_{94}Pu^{239}$), which emits an alpha particle, decaying again to U-235, but so slowly that in effect it is a stable element. (See figure on p. 8.) If, after the reaction has been allowed to proceed for a considerable time, the mixture of metals is removed, it may be possible to extract the plutonium by chemical methods and purify it for use in a subsequent fission chain reaction of an explosive nature.

COMBINED EFFECTS AND ENRICHED PILES

2.20. Three ways of increasing the likelihood of a chain reaction have been mentioned: use of a moderator; attainment of high purity of materials; use of special material, either U-235 or Pu. The three procedures are not mutually exclusive, and many schemes have been proposed for using small amounts of separated U-235 or Pu-239 in a lattice composed primarily of ordinary uranium or uranium oxide and of a moderator or two different moderators. Such proposed arrangements are usually called "enriched piles."

USE OF THORIUM OR PROTOACTINIUM OR OTHER MATERIAL

2.21. All our previous discussion has centered on the direct or indirect use of uranium, but it was known that both thorium and protoactinium also underwent fission when bombarded by high-speed neutrons. The great advantage of uranium, at least for preliminary work, was its susceptibility to slow neutrons. There was not very much consideration given to the other two substances. Protoactinium can be eliminated because of its scarcity in nature. Thorium is relatively plentiful but has no apparent advantage over uranium.

2.22. It is not to be forgotten that theoretically many nuclear reactions might be used to release energy. At present we see no way of initiating or controlling reactions other than those involving fission, but some such synthesis as has already been mentioned as a source of solar energy may eventually be produced in the laboratory.

AMOUNTS OF MATERIALS NEEDED

2.23. Obviously it was impossible in the summer of 1940 to make more than guesses as to what amounts of materials would be needed to produce:

(1) a chain reaction with use of a moderator:
(2) a chain-reaction bomb in pure, or at least enriched, U-235 or plutonium.

A figure of one to one hundred kilograms of U-235 was commonly given at this time for the critical size of a bomb. This would, of course, have to be separated from at least 140 times as much natural uranium. For a slow-neutron chain reaction using a moderator and unseparated uranium it was almost certain that tons of metal and of moderator would be required.

AVAILABILITY OF MATERIALS

2.24. Estimates of the composition of the earth's crust show uranium and thorium both present in considerable quantities (about 4 parts per million of uranium and 12 parts per million of thorium in the earth's crust). Deposits of uranium ore are known to exist in Colorado, in the Great Bear Lake region of northern Canada, in Joachimstal in Czechoslovakia, and in the Belgian Congo. Many other deposits of uranium ore are known, but their extent is in many cases unexplored. Uranium is always found with radium although in much larger quantity. Both are often found with vanadium ores. Small quantities of uranium oxide have been used for many years in the ceramics industry.

2.25. Thorium is also rather widely distributed, occurring as thorium oxide in fairly high concentration in monazite sands. Such sands are found to some extent in this country but particularly in Brazil and in British India.

2.26. Early rough estimates, which are probably optimistic, were that the nuclear energy available in known deposits of uranium was adequate to supply the total power needs of this country for 200 years (assuming utilization of U-238 as well as U-235).

2.27. As has already been mentioned, little or no uranium metal had been produced up to 1940 and information was so scant that even the melting point was not known. (For example, the *Handbook of Physics and Chemistry* for 1943–1944 says only that the melting point is below 1850° C. whereas we now know it to be in the neighborhood of 1150°.) Evidently, as far as uranium was concerned, there was no insurmountable difficulty as regards obtaining raw materials or producing the metal, but there were very grave questions as to how long it would take and how much it would cost to produce the necessary quantities of pure metal.

2.28. Of the materials mentioned above as being suitable for moderators, deuterium had the most obvious advantages. It is present in ordinary hydrogen to the extent of about one part in 5,000. By 1940 a number of different methods for separating it from hydrogen had been developed, and a few liters had been produced in this country for experimental purposes. The only large-scale production had been in a Norwegian plant, from which several hundred liters of heavy water (D_2O, deuterium oxide) had come. As in the case of uranium, the problem was one of cost and time.

2.29. Beryllium in the form of beryllium silicates is widely found but only in small quantities of ore. Its use as an alloying agent has become general in the last few years; for such use, however, it is not necessary to produce the beryllium in metallic form. In 1940 only 700 pounds of the metal were produced in this country.

2.30. As far as carbon was concerned, the situation was obviously quite different. There were many hundreds of tons of graphite produced every year in this country. This was one of the reasons why graphite looked very desirable as a moderator. The difficulties lay in obtaining sufficient quantities of graphite of the required purity, particularly in view of the expanding needs of war industry.

TIME AND COST ESTIMATES

2.31. Requirements of time and money depended not only on many unknown scientific and technological factors but also on policy decisions. Evidently years of time and millions of dollars might be required to achieve the ultimate objective. About all that was attempted at this time was the making of estimates as to how long it would take and how much it would cost to clarify the scientific and technological prospects. It looked as if it would not be a very great undertaking to carry along the development of the thermal-neutron chain reaction in a graphite-uranium lattice to the point of finding out whether the reaction would in fact go. Estimates made at the time were that approximately a year and $100,000 would be required to get an answer. These estimates applied to a chain-reacting system of very low power without a cooling system or any means for using the energy released.

HEALTH HAZARDS

2.32. It had been known for a long time that radioactive materials were dangerous. They give off very penetrating radiations—gamma rays—which are much like X-rays in their physiological effects. They also give off beta and alpha rays which, although less penetrating, can still be dangerous. The amounts of radium used in hospitals and in ordinary physical measurements usually comprise but a few milligrams. The amounts of radioactive material produced by the fission of uranium in a relatively small chain-reacting system may be equivalent to hundreds or thousands of grams of radium. A chain-reacting system also gives off intense neutron radiation known to be comparable to gamma rays as regards health hazards. Quite apart from its radioactive properties, uranium is poisonous chemically. Thus, nearly all work in this field is hazardous— particularly work on chain reactions and the resulting radioactive products.

METHOD OF APPROACH TO THE PROBLEM

2.33. There were two ways of attacking the problem. One was to conduct elaborate series of accurate physical measurements on absorption cross sections of various materials for various neutron-induced processes and various neutron energies. Once such data were available, calculations as to what might be done in the way of a chain reaction could be made with fair accuracy. The other approach was the purely empirical one of mixing uranium or uranium compounds in various ways with various moderators and observing what happened. Similar extremes of method were possible in the case of the isotope-separation problem. Actually an intermediate or compromise approach was adopted in both cases.

POWER VS. BOMB

2.34. The expected military advantages of uranium bombs were far more spectacular than those of a uranium power plant. It was conceivable that a few uranium bombs might be decisive in winning the war for the side first putting them into use. Such thoughts were very much in the minds of those working in this field, but the attainment of a slow-neutron chain reaction seemed a necessary preliminary step in the development of our knowledge and became the first objective of the group interested in the problem. This also seemed an important step in convincing military authorities and the more skeptical scientists that the whole notion was not a pipe dream. Partly for these reasons and partly because of the extreme secrecy imposed about this time, the idea of an atomic bomb does not appear much in the records between the summer of 1940 and the fall of 1941.

MILITARY USEFULNESS

2.35. If all the atoms in a kilogram of U-235 undergo fission, the energy released is equivalent to the energy released in the explosion of about 20,000 short tons of TNT. If the critical size of a bomb turns out to be practical—say, in the range of one to one hundred kilograms—and all the other problems can be solved, there remain two questions. First, how large a percentage of the fissionable nuclei can be made to undergo fission before the reaction stops; i.e., what is the efficiency of the explosion? Second, what is the effect of so concentrated a release of energy? Even if only 1 per cent of the theoretically available energy is released, the explosion will still be of a totally different order of magnitude from that produced by any previously known type of bomb. The value of such a bomb was thus a question for military experts to consider very carefully.

SUMMARY

2.36. It had been established (1) that uranium fission did occur with release of great amounts of energy; and (2) that in the process extra neutrons were set free which might start a chain reaction. It was not contrary to any known principle that such a reaction should take place and that it should have very important military application as a bomb. However, the idea was revolutionary and therefore suspect; it was certain that many technical operations of great difficulty would have to be worked out before such a bomb could be produced. Probably the only materials satisfactory for a bomb were either U-235, which would have to be separated from the 140-times more abundant isotope U-238, or Pu-239, an isotope of the hitherto unknown element plutonium, which would have to be generated by a controlled chain-reacting process itself hitherto unknown. To achieve such a controlled chain reaction it was clear that uranium metal and heavy water or beryllium or carbon might have to be produced in great quantity with high purity. Once bomb material was produced a process would have to be developed for using it safely and effectively. In some of the processes, health hazards of a new kind would be encountered.

POLICY PROBLEM

2.37. By the summer of 1940 the National Defense Research Committee had been formed and was asking many of the scientists in the country to work on various urgent military problems. Scientific personnel was limited although this was not fully realized at the time. It was, therefore, really difficult to decide at what rate work should be carried forward on an atomic bomb. The decision had to be reviewed at frequent intervals during the subsequent four years. An account of how these policy decisions were made is given in Chapters III and V.

CHAPTER III. ADMINISTRATIVE HISTORY UP TO DECEMBER 1941

INTEREST IN MILITARY POSSIBILITIES

3.1. The announcement of the hypothesis of fission and its experimental confirmation took place in January 1939, as has already been recounted in Chapter I. There was immediate interest in the possible military use of the large amounts of energy released in fission. At that time American-born nuclear physicists were so unaccustomed to the idea of using their science for military purposes that they hardly realized what needed to be done. Consequently the early efforts both at restricting publication and at getting government support were stimulated largely by a small group of foreign-born physicists centering on L. Szilard and including E. Wigner, E. Teller, V. F. Weisskopf, and E. Fermi.

RESTRICTION OF PUBLICATION

3.2. In the spring of 1939 the group mentioned above enlisted Niels Bohr's cooperation in an attempt to stop publication of further data by voluntary agreement. Leading American and British physicists agreed, but F. Joliot, France's foremost nuclear physicist, refused, apparently because of the publication of one letter in the *Physical Review* sent in before all Americans had been brought into the agreement. Consequently publication continued freely for about another year although a few papers were withheld voluntarily by their authors.

3.3. At the April 1940 meeting of the Division of Physical Sciences of the National Research Council, G. Breit proposed formation of a censorship committee to control publication in all American scientific journals. Although the reason for this suggestion was primarily the desire to control publication of papers on uranium fission, the "Reference Committee" as finally set up a little later that spring (in the National Research Council) was a general one, and was organized to control publication policy in all fields of possible military interest. The chairman of the committee was L. P. Eisenhart; other members were G. Breit, W. M. Clark, H. Fletcher, E. B. Fred, G. B. Pegram, H. C. Urey, L. H. Weed, and E. G. Wever. Various subcommittees were appointed, the first one of which had to do with uranium fission. G. Breit served as chairman of this subcommittee; its other members were J. W. Beams, L. J. Briggs, G. B. Pegram, H. C. Urey, and E. Wigner. In general, the procedure followed was to have the editors of various journals send copies of papers in this field, in cases where the advisability of publication was in doubt, either directly to Breit or indirectly to him through Eisenhart. Breit then usually circulated them to all members of the subcommittee for consideration as to whether or not they should be published, and informed the editors as to the outcome. This arrangement was very successful in preventing publication and was still nominally in effect, in modified form, in June 1945. Actually the absorption of most physicists in this country into war work of one sort or another soon reduced the number of papers referred to the committee practically to the vanishing point. It is of interest to note that this whole arrangement was a purely voluntary one; the scientists of the country are to be congratulated on their complete cooperation. It is to be hoped that it will be possible after the war to publish these papers at least in part so that their authors may receive proper professional credit for their contributions.

Initial Approaches to the Government
The First Committee

3.4. On the positive side—government interest and support of research in nuclear physics—the history is a much more complicated one. The first contact with the government was made by Pegram of Columbia in March 1939. Pegram telephoned to the

Navy Department and arranged for a conference between representatives of the Navy Department and Fermi. The only outcome of this conference was that the Navy expressed interest and asked to be kept informed. The next attempt to interest the government was stimulated by Szilard and Wigner. In July 1939 they conferred with A. Einstein, and a little later Einstein, Wigner, and Szilard discussed the problem with Alexander Sachs of New York. In the fall Sachs, supported by a letter from Einstein, explained to President Roosevelt the desirability of encouraging work in this field. The President appointed a committee, known as the "Advisory Committee on Uranium" and consisting of Briggs (director of the Bureau of Standards) as chairman, Colonel K. F. Adamson of the Army Ordnance Department, and Commander G. C. Hoover of the Navy Bureau of Ordnance, and requested this committee to look into the problem. This was the only committee on uranium that had official status up to the time of organization of the National Defense Research Committee in June 1940. The committee met very informally and included various additional scientific representatives in its meetings.

3.5. The first meeting of the Uranium Committee was on October 21, 1939 and included, besides the committee members, F. L. Mohler, Alexander Sachs, L. Szilard, E. Wigner, E. Teller, and R. B. Roberts. The result of this meeting was a report dated November 1, 1939, and transmitted to President Roosevelt by Briggs, Adamson, and Hoover. This report made eight recommendations, which need not be enumerated in detail. It is interesting, however, that it specifically mentions both atomic power and an atomic bomb as possibilities. It specifically recommended procurement of 4 tons of graphite and 50 tons of uranium oxide for measurements of the absorption cross section of carbon. Others of the recommendations either were of a general nature or were never carried out. Apparently a memorandum prepared by Szilard was more or less the basis of the discussion at this meeting.

3.6. The first transfer of funds ($6,000) from the Army and Navy to purchase materials in accordance with the recommendation of November 1 is reported in a memorandum from Briggs to General E. M. Watson (President Roosevelt's aide) on February 20, 1940. The next meeting of the "Advisory Committee on Uranium" was on April 28, 1940 and was attended by Sachs, Wigner, Pegram, Fermi, Szilard, Briggs, Admiral H. G. Bowen, Colonel Adamson, and Commander Hoover. By the time of this meeting two important new factors had come into the picture. First, it had been discovered that the uranium fission caused by neutrons of thermal velocities occurred in the U-235 isotope only. Second, it had been reported that a large section of the Kaiser Wilhelm Institute in Berlin had been set aside for research on uranium. Although the general tenor of the discussion at this meeting seems to have been that the work should be pushed more vigorously, no definite recommendations were made. It was pointed out that the critical measurements on carbon already under way at Columbia should soon give a result, and the implication was that definite recommendations should wait for such a result.

3.7. Within the next few weeks a number of people concerned, particularly Sachs, urged the importance of greater support and of better organization. Their hand was strengthened by the Columbia results (as reported, for example, in a letter from Sachs to General Watson on May 15, 1940) showing that the carbon absorption was appreciably lower than had been previously thought and that the probability of carbon being satisfactory as a moderator was therefore considerable. Sachs was also active in looking into the question of ore supply. On June 1, 1940, Sachs, Briggs, and Urey met with Admiral Bowen to discuss approaching officials of the Union Minière of the Belgian Congo. Such an approach was made shortly afterwards by Sachs.

3.8. The general status of the problem was discussed by a special advisory group called together by Briggs at the National Bureau of Standards on June 15, 1940. This meeting was attended by Briggs, Urey, M. A. Tuve, Wigner, Breit, Fermi, Szilard, and Pegram. "After full discussion, the recommendation of the group to the Uranium Committee was that funds should be sought to support research on the uranium-carbon experiment along two lines:

(A) further measurements of the nuclear constants involved in the proposed type of reaction;

(B) experiments with amounts of uranium and carbon equal to about one fifth to one quarter of the amount that could be estimated as the minimum in which a chain reaction would sustain itself.

"It was estimated that about $40,000 would be necessary for further measurements of the fundamental constants and that approximately $100,000 worth of metallic uranium and pure graphite would be needed for the intermediate experiment." (Quotations from memorandum of Pegram to Briggs, dated August 14, 1940.)

THE COMMITTEE RECONSTITUTED UNDER NDRC

3.9. Before any decisions made at this meeting could be put into effect, the organization of the National Defense Research Committee was announced in June 1940, and President Roosevelt gave instructions that the Uranium Committee should be reconstituted as a subcommittee of the NDRC, reporting to Vannevar Bush (chairman, NDRC). The membership of this reconstituted Uranium Committee was as follows: Briggs, Chairman; Pegram, Urey, Beams, Tuve, R. Gunn and Breit. On authorization from Briggs, Breit consulted Wigner and Teller frequently although they were not members of the committee. From that time until the summer of 1941 this committee continued in control with approximately the same membership. Its recommendations were transmitted by Briggs to the NDRC, and suitable contracts were made between the NDRC and various research institutions. The funds, however, were first supplied by the Army and Navy, not from regular NDRC appropriations.

SUPPORT OF RESEARCH

3.10. The first contract let under this new set-up was to Columbia University for the two lines of work recommended at the June 15 meeting as described above. The project was approved by the NDRC and the first NDRC contract (NDCrc-32) was signed November 8, 1940, being effective from November 1, 1940, to November 1, 1941. The amount of this contract was $40,000.

3.11. Only very small expenditures had been made before the contract went into effect. For example, about $3,200 had been spent on graphite and cadmium, this having been taken from the $6,000 allotted by the Army and Navy in February, 1940.

3.12. We shall not attempt to review in detail the other contracts that were arranged prior to December 1941. Their number and total amount grew gradually. Urey began to work on isotope separation by the centrifuge method under a Navy contract in the fall of 1940. Other contracts were granted to Columbia University, Princeton University, Standard Oil Development Company, Cornell University, Carnegie Institution of Washington, University of Minnesota, Iowa State College, Johns Hopkins University, National Bureau of Standards, University of Virginia, University of Chicago, and University of California in the course of the winter and spring of 1940–1941 until by November 1941 the total number of projects approved was sixteen, totalling about $300,000.

3.13. Scale of expenditure is at least a rough index of activity. It is therefore interesting to compare this figure with those in other branches of war research. By November 1941 the total budget approved by NDRC for the Radiation Laboratory at the Massachusetts Institute of Technology was several million dollars. Even a relatively small project like that of Section S of Division A of the NDRC had spent or been authorized to spend $136,000 on work that proved valuable but was obviously not potentially of comparable importance to the uranium work.

COMMITTEE REORGANIZED IN SUMMER OF 1941

3.14. The Uranium Committee as formed in the summer of 1940 continued substantially unchanged until the summer of

1941. At that time the main committee was somewhat enlarged and subcommittees formed on isotope separation, theoretical aspects, power production and heavy water.* It was thereafter called the Uranium Section or the S-1 Section of NDRC. Though not formally disbanded until the summer of 1942, this revised committee was largely superseded in December 1941 (see Chapter V).

THE NATIONAL ACADEMY REVIEWING COMMITTEE

3.15. In the spring of 1941, Briggs, feeling that an impartial review of the problem was desirable, requested Bush to appoint a reviewing committee. Bush then formally requested F. B. Jewett, president of the National Academy of Sciences, to appoint such a committee. Jewett complied, appointing A. H. Compton, chairman; W. D. Coolidge, E. O. Lawrence, J. C. Slater, J. H. Van Vleck, and B. Gherardi. (Because of illness, Gherardi was unable to serve.) This committee was instructed to evaluate the military importance of the uranium problem and to recommend the level of expenditure at which the problem should be investigated.

3.16. This committee met in May and submitted a report. (This report and the subsequent ones will be summarized in the next chapter.) On the basis of this report and the oral exposition by Briggs before a meeting of the NDRC, an appropriation of $267,000 was approved by the NDRC at its meeting of July 18, 1941, and the probability that much larger expenditures would be necessary was indicated. Bush asked for a second report with emphasis on engineering aspects, and in order to meet this request O. E. Buckley of the Bell Telephone Laboratories and

---

* Uranium Section: Briggs, chairman; Pegram, vice-chairman; S. K. Allison, Beams, Breit, E. U. Condon, H. D. Smyth, Urey.

Separation Subsection: Urey, chairman; Beams.

Power Production Subsection: Pegram, chairman; Allison, Fermi, Smyth, Szilard.

Heavy Water Subsection: Urey, chairman; T. H. Chilton.

Theoretical Aspects Subsection: Fermi, chairman; Breit, C. H. Eckart, Smyth, Szilard, J. A. Wheeler.

L. W. Chubb of the Westinghouse Electrical and Manufacturing Company were added to the committee. (Compton was in South America during the summer and therefore did not participate in the summer meetings of the committee.) The second report was submitted by Coolidge. As a result of new measurements of the fission cross section of U-235 and of increasing conviction that isotope separation was possible, in September 1941, Compton and Lawrence suggested to J. B. Conant of NDRC, who was working closely with Bush, that a third report was desirable. Since Bush and Conant had learned during the summer of 1941 that the British also felt increasingly optimistic, the committee was asked to make another study of the whole subject. For this purpose the committee was enlarged by the addition of W. K. Lewis, R. S. Mulliken, and G. B. Kistiakowsky. This third report was submitted by Compton on November 6, 1941.

INFORMATION RECEIVED FROM THE BRITISH

3.17. Beginning in 1940 there was some interchange of information with the British and during the summer of 1941 Bush learned that they had been reviewing the whole subject in the period from April to July. They too had been interested in the possibility of using plutonium; in fact, a suggestion as to the advisability of investigating plutonium was contained in a letter from J. D. Cockcroft to R. H. Fowler dated December 28, 1940. Fowler, who was at that time acting as British scientific liaison officer in Washington, passed Cockcroft's letter on to Lawrence. The British never pursued the plutonium possibility, since they felt their limited manpower should concentrate on U-235. Chadwick, at least, was convinced that a U-235 bomb of great destructive power could be made, and the whole British group felt that the separation of U-235 by diffusion was probably feasible.

3.18. Accounts of British opinion, including the first draft of the British report reviewing the subject, were made available to Bush and Conant informally during the summer of 1941, although the official British report of July 15 was first transmitted to Conant by G. P. Thomson on October 3. Since, however, the British review was not made available to the committee of the National Academy of Sciences, the reports by the Academy committee and the British reports constituted independent evaluations of the prospects of producing atomic bombs.

3.19. Besides the official and semi-official conferences, there were many less formal discussions held, one of these being stimulated by M. L. E. Oliphant of England during his visit to this country in the summer of 1941. As an example of such informal discussion we might mention talks among Conant, Compton, and Lawrence at the University of Chicago semicentennial celebration in September 1941. The general conclusion was that the program should be pushed; and this conclusion in various forms was communicated to Bush by a number of persons.

3.20. In the fall of 1941 Urey and Pegram were sent to England to get first-hand information on what was being done there. This was the first time that any Americans had been to England specifically in connection with the uranium problem. The report prepared by Urey and Pegram confirmed and extended the information that had been received previously.

DECISION TO ENLARGE AND REORGANIZE

3.21. As a result of the reports prepared by the National Academy committee, by the British, and by Urey and Pegram, and of the general urging by a number of physicists, Bush, as Director of the Office of Scientific Research and Development (of which NDRC is a part), decided that the uranium work should be pushed more aggressively.

3.22. Before the National Academy issued its third report and before Pegram and Urey visited England, Bush had taken up the whole uranium question with President Roosevelt and Vice-President Wallace. He summarized for them the British views, which were on the whole optimistic, and pointed out the uncertainties of the predictions. The President agreed that it was desirable to broaden the program, to provide a different organization, to provide funds from a special source, and to effect complete interchange of information with the British. It was agreed to confine discussions of general policy to the following group: The President, Vice-President, Secretary of War, Chief of Staff, Bush, and Conant. This group was often referred to as the Top Policy Group.

3.23. By the time of submission of the National Academy's third report and the return of Urey and Pegram from England, the general plan of the reorganization was beginning to emerge. The Academy's report was more conservative than the British report, as Bush pointed out in his letter of November 27, 1941, to President Roosevelt. It was, however, sufficiently optimistic to give additional support to the plan of enlarging the work. The proposed reorganization was announced at a meeting of the Uranium Section just before the Pearl Harbor attack and will be described in Chapter V.

SUMMARY

3.24. In March 1939, only a few weeks after the discovery of uranium fission, the possible military importance of fission was called to the attention of the government. In the autumn of 1939 the first government committee on uranium was created. In the spring of 1940 a mechanism was set up for restricting publication of significant articles in this field. When the NDRC was set up in June 1940, the Uranium Committee was reconstituted under the NDRC. However, up to the autumn of 1941 total expenditures were relatively small. In December 1941, after receipt of the National Academy report and information from the British, the decision was made to enlarge and reorganize the program.

CHAPTER IV. PROGRESS UP TO DECEMBER 1941

THE IMMEDIATE QUESTIONS

4.1. In Chapter II the general problems involved in producing a chain reaction for military purposes were described. Early in the summer of 1940 the questions of most immediate importance were:

(1) Could any circumstances be found under which the chain reaction would go?

(2) Could the isotope U-235 be separated on a large scale?

(3) Could moderator and other materials be obtained in sufficient purity and quantity?

Although there were many subsidiary problems, as will appear in the account of the progress made in the succeeding eighteen months, these three questions determined the course of the work.

THE CHAIN REACTION

PROGRAM PROPOSED JUNE 15, 1940

4.2. In June 1940, nearly all work on the chain reaction was concentrated at Columbia under the general leadership of Pegram, with Fermi and Szilard in immediate charge. It had been concluded that the most easily produced chain reaction was probably that depending on thermal neutron fission in a heterogeneous mixture of graphite and uranium. In the spring of 1940 Fermi, Szilard and H. L. Anderson had improved the accuracy of measurements of the capture cross section of carbon for neutrons, of the resonance (intermediate-speed) absorption of neutrons by U-238, and of the slowing down of neutrons in carbon.

4.3. Pegram, in a memorandum to Briggs on August 14, 1940, wrote, "It is not very easy to measure these quantities with accuracy without the use of large quantities of material. The net results of these experiments in the spring of 1940 were that the possibility of the chain reaction was not definitely proven, while it was still further from being definitely disproven. On the whole, the indications were more favorable than any conclusions that could fairly have been claimed from previous results."

4.4. At a meeting on June 15 (see Chapter III) these results were discussed and it was recommended that (A) further measurements be made on nuclear constants, and (B) experiments be made on lattices of uranium and carbon containing amounts of uranium from one fifth to one quarter the estimated critical amounts.

Progress up to February 15, 1941

4.5. Pegram's report of February 15, 1941 shows that most of the work done up to that time was on (A), while (B), the so-called intermediate experiment, was delayed by lack of materials.

4.6. Paraphrasing Pegram's report, the main progress was as follows:

(a) *The slowing down of neutrons* in graphite was investigated by studying the intensity of activation of various detectors (rhodium, indium, iodine) placed at various positions inside a rectangular graphite column of dimensions $3 \times 3 \times 8$ feet when a source of neutrons was placed therein. By suitable choice of cadmium screens the effects of resonance* and thermal neutrons were investigated separately.† A mathematical analysis, based on dif-

---

* See footnote p. 58.

† The presence of neutrons can be detected by ionization chambers or counters or by the artificial radioactivity induced in various metal foils. (See Appendix 1.) The response of each of these detectors depends on the particular characteristics of the detector and on the speed of the neutrons (e.g., neutrons of about 1.5 volts energy are particularly effective in activating indium). Furthermore, certain materials have very large absorption

fusion theory, of the experimental data made it possible to predict the results to be expected in various other arrangements. These results, coupled with theoretical studies of the diffusion of thermal neutrons, laid a basis for future calculations of the number of thermal and resonance neutrons to be found at any point in a graphite mass of given shape when a given neutron source is placed at a specified position within or near the graphite.

(b) *The number of neutrons emitted in fission.* The experiments on slowing down neutrons showed that high-energy (high-speed) neutrons such as those from fission were practically all reduced to thermal energies (low speeds) after passing through 40 cm or more of graphite. A piece of uranium placed in a region where thermal neutrons are present absorbs the thermal neutrons and —as fission occurs—re-emits fast neutrons, which are easily distinguished from the thermal neutrons. By a series of measurements with and without uranium present and with various detectors and absorbers, it is possible to get a value for the constant η, the number of neutrons emitted per thermal neutron absorbed by uranium. This is not the number of neutrons emitted *per fission*, but is somewhat smaller than that number since not every absorption causes fission.

(c) *Lattice theory.* Extensive calculations were made on the probable number of neutrons escaping from lattices of various designs and sizes. This was fundamental for the so-called intermediate experiment, mentioned above as item (B).

INITIATION OF NEW PROGRAMS

4.7. Early in 1941 interest in the general chain-reaction problem by individuals at Princeton, Chicago, and California led to the approval of certain projects at those institutions. Thereafter the work of these groups was coordinated with the work at Columbia, forming parts of a single large program.

---

cross sections for neutrons of particular ranges of speed (e.g., cadmium for thermal neutrons). Thus measurements with different detectors with or without various absorbers give some indication of both the number of neutrons present and their energy distribution. However, the state of the art of such measurements is rather crude.

WORK ON RESONANCE ABSORPTION*

4.8. In Chapter II it is stated that there were advantages in a lattice structure or "pile" with uranium concentrated in lumps regularly distributed in a matrix of moderator. This was the system on which the Columbia group was working. As is so often the case, the fundamental idea is a simple one. If the uranium and the moderator are mixed homogeneously, the neutrons on the average will lose energy in small steps between passages through the uranium so that in the course of their reduction to thermal velocity the chance of their passing through uranium at any given velocity, e.g., at a velocity corresponding to resonance absorption, is great. But, if the uranium is in large lumps spaced at large intervals in the moderator, the amounts of energy lost by neutrons between passages from one lump of uranium to another will be large and the chance of their reaching a uranium lump with energy just equal to the energy of resonance absorption is relatively small. Thus the chance of absorption by U-238 to produce U-239, compared to the chance of absorption as thermal neutrons to cause fission, may be reduced sufficiently to allow a chain reaction to take place. If one knew the exact values of the cross sections of each uranium isotope for each type of absorption and every range of neutron speed, and had similar knowledge for the moderator, one could calculate the "optimum lattice," i.e., the best size, shape and spacing for the lumps of uranium in the matrix of moderator. Since such data were only partially known, a direct experimental approach appeared to be in order. Consequently it was proposed that the absorption of neutrons by uranium should be measured under conditions similar to those expected in a chain-reacting pile employing graphite as moderator.

4.9. Experiments of this type were initiated at Columbia, and were continued at Princeton in February 1941. Essentially the

---

* The term "resonance absorption" is used to describe the very strong absorption of neutrons by U-238 when the neutron energies are in certain definite portions of the energy region from 0 to 1,000 electron volts. Such resonance absorption demonstrates the existence of nuclear energy levels at corresponding energies. On some occasions the term resonance absorption is used to refer to the whole energy region in the neighborhood of such levels.

experiment consisted of studying the absorption of neutrons in the energy range extending from a few thousand electron volts down to a fraction of an electron volt (thermal energies), the absorption taking place in different layers of uranium or uranium oxide spheres embedded in a pile of graphite.

4.10. In these experiments, a source of neutrons was provided by a mean of protons (accelerated by a cyclotron) impinging on a beryllium target. (The resulting yield of neutrons was equivalent to the yield from a radium-beryllium source of about 3,500 curies strength.) The neutrons thus produced had a wide, continuous, velocity distribution. They proceeded from this source into a large block of graphite. By placing the various uranium or uranium-oxide spheres inside the graphite block at various positions representing increasing distances from the source, absorption of neutrons of decreasing average speeds down to thermal speeds was studied. It was found that the total absorption of neutrons by such spheres could be expressed in terms of a "surface" effect and a "mass" effect.

4.11. These experiments, involving a variety of sphere sizes, densities, and positions were continued until the spring of 1942, when most of the group was moved to Chicago. Similar experiments performed at a later date at the University of Indiana by A. C. G. Mitchell and his co-workers have verified and in some cases corrected the Princeton data, but the Princeton data were sufficiently accurate by the summer of 1941 to be used in planning the intermediate-pile experiments and the subsequent experiments on operating piles.

4.12. The experimental work on resonance absorption at Princeton was done by R. R. Wilson, E. C. Creutz, and their collaborators, under the general leadership of H. D. Smyth; they benefited from the constant help of Wigner and Wheeler and frequent conferences with the Columbia group.

THE FIRST INTERMEDIATE EXPERIMENTS

4.13. About July 1941 the first lattice structure of graphite and uranium was set up at Columbia. It was a graphite cube about

8 feet on an edge, and contained about 7 tons of uranium oxide in iron containers distributed at equal intervals throughout the graphite. A preliminary set of measurements was made on this structure in August 1941. Similar structures of somewhat larger size were set up and investigated during September and October, and the so-called exponential method (described below) of determining the multiplication factor was developed and first applied. This work was done by Fermi and his assistants, H. L. Anderson, B. Feld, G. Weil, and W. H. Zinn.

4.14. The multiplication-factor experiment is rather similar to that already outlined for the determination of η, the number of neutrons produced per thermal neutron absorbed. A radium-beryllium neutron source is placed near the bottom of the lattice structure and the number of neutrons is measured at various points throughout the lattice. These numbers are then compared with the corresponding numbers determined when no uranium is present in the graphite mass. Evidently the absorption of neutrons by U-238 to produce U-239 tends to reduce the number of neutrons, while the fissions tend to increase the number. The question is: Which predominates? or, more precisely, Does the fission production of neutrons predominate over all neutron-removal processes other than escape? Interpretation of the experimental data on this crucial question involves many corrections, calculations, and approximations, but all reduce in the end to a single number, the multiplication factor k.

THE MULTIPLICATION FACTOR k

4.15. The whole success or failure of the uranium project depended on the multiplication factor k, sometimes called the reproduction factor. If k could be made greater than 1 in a practical system, the project would succeed; if not, the chain reaction would never be more than a dream. This is clear from the following discussion, which applies to any system containing fissionable material. Suppose that there is a certain number of free neutrons present in the system at a given time. Some of these neutrons will themselves initiate fissions and will thus directly produce new neutrons. The multiplication factor k is the ratio of the number of these new neutrons to the number of free neutrons originally present. Thus, if in a given pile comprising uranium, carbon, impurities, containers, etc., 100 neutrons are produced by fission, some will escape, some will be absorbed in the uranium without causing fission, some will be absorbed in the carbon, in the containers or in impurities, and some will cause fission, thereby producing more neutrons.* If the fissions are sufficiently numerous and sufficiently effective individually, more than 100 new neutrons will be produced and the system is chain reacting. If the number of new neutrons is 105, k = 1.05. But if the number of new neutrons per 100 initial ones is 99, k = .99 and no chain reaction can maintain itself.

4.16. Recognizing that the intermediate or "exponential" experiment described above was too small to be chain reacting, we see that it was a matter of great interest whether any larger pile of the same lattice structure would be chain reacting. This could be determined by calculating what the value of k would be for an infinitely large lattice of this same type. In other words, the problem was to calculate what the value of k would be if no neutrons leaked away through the sides of the pile. Actually it is found that, once a chain-reacting system is well above the critical size—say two or three times as great—and is surrounded by what is called a reflector, the effective value of k differs very little from that for infinite size provided that k is near 1.00. Consequently, it has become customary to characterize the chain-reaction potentialities of different mixtures of metal and moderator by the value of k_∞ the multiplication constant obtained by assuming infinite size of pile.

4.17. The value of k_∞ as reported by Fermi to the Uranium Section in the fall of 1941 was about 0.87. This was based on results from the second Columbia intermediate experiment. All agreed that the multiplication factor could be increased by greater purity of materials, different lattice arrangements, etc. None could say with certainty that it could be made greater than one.

* See drawing facing p. 35.

EXPERIMENTS ON BERYLLIUM

4.18. At about the same time that the work on resonance absorption was started at Princeton, S. K. Allison, at the suggestion of A. H. Compton, began work at Chicago under a contract running from January 1, 1941 to August 1, 1941. The stated objectives of the work were to investigate (a) the increase in neutron production when the pile is enclosed in a beryllium envelope or "reflector," and (b) the cross sections of beryllium. A new contract was authorized on July 18, 1941, to run to June 30, 1942. This stated the somewhat broader objective of investigating uranium-beryllium-carbon systems generally. The appropriations involved were modest: $9,500 for the first contract, and $30,000 for the second contract.

4.19. As has already been pointed out in Chapter II, beryllium has desirable qualities as a moderator because of its low atomic weight and low neutron-absorption cross section; there was also the possibility that a contribution to the number of neutrons would be realized from the (n, 2n) reaction in beryllium. The value of the cross section was not precisely known; furthermore it was far from certain that any large amount of pure beryllium could be obtained. Allison's problem was essentially similar to the Columbia problem, except for the use of beryllium in place of graphite. Because of the scarcity of beryllium it was suggested that it might be used in conjunction with graphite or some other moderator, possibly as a reflector.

4.20. In the Chicago experiments, neutrons produced with the aid of a cyclotron were caused to enter a pile of graphite and beryllium. Allison made a number of measurements on the slowing down and absorption by graphite which were valuable checks on similar experiments at Columbia. He finally was able to obtain enough beryllium to make significant measurements which showed that beryllium was a possible moderator comparable to graphite. However, beryllium was not in fact used at all extensively in view of the great difficulty of producing it in quantity in the required structural forms.

4.21. This Chicago project as described above became part of the Metallurgical Laboratory project established at the University of Chicago early in 1942.

THEORETICAL WORK

4.22. Both the intermediate experiments at Columbia and the continued resonance-absorption work at Princeton required skilful theoretical interpretation. Fermi worked out the theory of the "exponential" pile and Wigner the theory of resonance absorption; both these men were constantly conferring and contributing to many problems. Wheeler of Princeton, Breit of Wisconsin, and Eckart of Chicago—to mention only a few—also made contributions to general pile theory and related topics. Altogether one can say that by the end of 1941 the general theory of the chain reaction for slow neutrons was almost completely understood. It was the numerical constants and technological possibilities that were still uncertain.

4.23. On the theory of a fast-neutron reaction in U-235 a good deal of progress had also been made. In particular, new estimates of the critical size were made, and it was predicted that possibly 10 per cent of the total energy might be released explosively. On this basis one kilogram of U-235 would be equivalent to 2,000 tons of TNT. The conclusions are reviewed below in connection with the National Academy Report. It is to be remembered that there are two factors involved: (1) how large a fraction of the available fission energy will be released before the reaction stops; (2) how destructive such a highly concentrated explosion will be.

WORK ON PLUTONIUM

4.24. In Chapter I mention is made of the suggestion that the element 94, later christened plutonium, would be formed by beta-ray disintegrations of U-239 resulting from neutron absorption by U-238 and that plutonium would probably be an alpha-particle emitter of long half-life and would undergo fission when bombarded by neutrons. In the summer of 1940 the nuclear physics group at the University of California in Berkeley was urged to use neutrons from its powerful cyclotron for the production of plutonium, and to separate it from uranium and investigate its fission properties. Various pertinent experiments were performed by E. Segré, G. T. Seaborg, J. W. Kennedy, and A. C. Wahl at Berkeley prior to 1941 and were reported by E. O. Lawrence to the National Academy Committee (see below) in May 1941 and also in a memorandum that was incorporated in the Committee's second report dated July 11, 1941. It will be seen that this memorandum includes one important idea not specifically emphasized by others (paragraph 1.58), namely, the production of large quantities of plutonium for use in a bomb.

4.25. We quote from Lawrence's memorandum as follows: "Since the first report of the National Academy of Sciences Committee on Atomic Fission, an extremely important new possibility has been opened for the exploitation of the chain reaction with unseparated isotopes of uranium. Experiments in the Radiation Laboratory of the University of California have indicated (a) that element 94 is formed as a result of capture of a neutron by uranium 238 followed by two successive beta-transformations, and furthermore (b) that this transuranic element undergoes slow neutron fission and therefore presumably behaves like uranium 235.

"It appears accordingly that, if a chain reaction with unseparated isotopes is achieved, it may be allowed to proceed violently for a period of time for the express purpose of manufacturing element 94 in substantial amounts. This material could be extracted by ordinary chemistry and would presumably be the equivalent of uranium 235 for chain reaction purposes.

"If this is so, the following three outstanding important possibilities are opened:

"1. Uranium 238 would be available for energy production, thus increasing about one hundred fold the total atomic energy obtainable from a given quantity of uranium.

"2. Using element 94 one may envisage preparation of small chain reaction units for power purposes weighing perhaps a hundred pounds instead of a hundred tons as probably would be necessary for units using natural uranium.

"3. If large amounts of element 94 were available it is likely that a chain reaction with fast neutrons could be produced. In such a reaction the energy would be released at an explosive rate which might be described as 'super bomb.' "

RADIOACTIVE POISONS

4.26. As previously stated, the fragments resulting from fission are in most cases unstable nuclei, that is, artificially radioactive materials. It is common knowledge that the radiations from radioactive materials have deadly effects akin to the effects of X-rays.

4.27. In a chain-reacting pile these radioactive fission products build up as the reaction proceeds. (They have, in practice, turned out to be the most troublesome feature of a reacting pile.) Since they differ chemically from the uranium, it should be possible to extract them and use them like a particularly vicious form of poison gas. This idea was mentioned in the National Academy report (see paragraph 4.48) and was developed in a report written December 10, 1941, by E. Wigner and H. D. Smyth, who concluded that the fission products produced in one day's run of a 100,000 kw chain-reacting pile might be sufficient to make a large area uninhabitable.

4.28. Wigner and Smyth did not recommend the use of radioactive poisons nor has such use been seriously proposed since by the responsible authorities, but serious consideration was given to the possibility that the Germans might make surprise use of radioactive poisons, and accordingly defensive measures were planned.

ISOTOPE SEPARATION

SMALL-SCALE SEPARATION BY THE MASS SPECTROGRAPH

4.29. In Chapter I the attribution of thermal-neutron fission of uranium to the U-235 isotope was mentioned as being experimentally established. This was done by partly separating minute quantities of the uranium isotopes in A. O. Nier's mass spectograph and then studying the nuclear properties of the samples. Additional small samples were furnished by Nier in the summer of 1941 and studied by N. P. Heydenburg and others at M. A. Tuve's laboratory at the Department of Terrestrial Magnetism of the Carnegie Institution of Washington. But results of such experiments were still preliminary, and it was evident that further study of larger and more completely separated samples was desirable.

4.30. The need of larger samples of U-235 stimulated E. O. Lawrence at Berkeley to work on electromagnetic separation. He was remarkably successful and by December 6, 1941 reported that he could deposit in one hour one microgram of U-235 from which a large proportion of the U-238 had been removed.

4.31. Previously, at a meeting of the Uranium Committee, Smyth of Princeton had raised the question of possible large-scale separation of isotopes by electromagnetic means but had been told that it had been investigated and was considered impossible. Nevertheless, Smyth and Lawrence at a chance meeting in October 1941 discussed the problem and agreed that it might yet be possible. Smyth again raised the question at a meeting of the Uranium Committee on December 6 and at the next meeting (December 18, 1941) there was a general discussion of large-scale electromagnetic methods in connection with Lawrence's report of his results already mentioned. The consequences of this discussion are reported in Chapter XI.

The Centrifuge and Gaseous Diffusion Methods

4.32. Though we have made it clear that the separation of U-235 from U-238 might be fundamental to the whole success of the project, little has been said about work in this field. Such work had been going on since the summer of 1940 under the general direction of H. C. Urey at Columbia. Since this part of the uranium work was not very much affected by the reorganization in

December 1941, a detailed account of the work is reserved for Chapters IX and X. Only a summary is presented here.

4.33. After careful review and a considerable amount of experimenting on other methods, it had been concluded that the two most promising methods of separating large quantities of U-235 from U-238 were by the use of centrifuges and by the use of diffusion through porous barriers. In the centrifuge, the forces acting on the two isotopes are slightly different because of their differences in mass. In the diffusion through barriers, the rates of diffusion are slightly different for the two isotopes, again because of their differences in mass. Each method required the uranium to be in gaseous form, which was an immediate and serious limitation since the only suitable gaseous compound of uranium then known was uranium hexafluoride. In each method the amount of enrichment to be expected in a single production unit or "stage" was very small; this indicated that many successive stages would be necessary if a high degree of enrichment was to be attained.

4.34. By the end of 1941 each method had been experimentally demonstrated in principle; that is, single-stage separators had effected the enrichment of the U-235 on a laboratory scale to about the degree predicted theoretically. K. Cohen of Columbia and others had developed the theory for the single units and for the series or "cascade" of units that would be needed. Thus it was possible to estimate that about 5,000 stages would be necessary for one type of diffusion system and that a total area of many acres of diffusion barrier would be required in a plant separating a kilogram of U-235 each day. Corresponding cost estimates were tens of millions of dollars. For the centrifuge the number of stages would be smaller, but it was predicted that a similar production by centrifuges would require 22,000 separately driven, extremely high-speed centrifuges, each three feet in length at a comparable cost.

4.35. Of course, the cost estimates could not be made accurately since the technological problems were almost completely unsolved, but these estimates as to size and cost of plant did serve to emphasize the magnitude of the undertaking.

4.36. In September 1940, P. H. Abelson submitted to Briggs a 17-page memorandum suggesting the possibility of separating the isotopes of uranium by thermal diffusion in liquid uranium hexafluoride. R. Gunn of the Naval Research Laboratory was also much interested in the uranium problem and was appointed a member of the Uranium Committee when it was reorganized under the NDRC in the summer of 1940. As a result of Abelson's suggestion and Gunn's interest, work was started on thermal diffusion at the National Bureau of Standards. This work was financed by funds from the Navy Department and in 1940 was transferred to the Naval Research Laboratory, still under the direction of Abelson, where it was continued.

4.37. We shall discuss the thermal-diffusion work further in a later chapter, but we may mention here that significant results had already been obtained by the end of 1941 and that in January 1942, using a single separation column, a separation factor had been obtained which was comparable or superior to the one obtained up to that time in preliminary tests on the diffusion and centrifuge methods.

THE PRODUCTION OF HEAVY WATER

4.38. It was pointed out in Chapter II that deuterium appeared very promising as a moderator because of its low absorption and good slowing-down property but unpromising because of its scarcity. Interest in a deuterium moderator was stimulated by experimental results obtained in Berkeley demonstrating that the deuterium absorption cross section for neutrons was, in fact, almost zero. Since oxygen has a very low absorption coefficient for neutrons, it was usually assumed that the deuterium would be used combined with oxygen, that is, in the very convenient material: heavy water. Work at Columbia on possible methods of large-scale concentration of heavy water was initiated in February 1941 under the direction of H. C. Urey (under an OSRD contract). Early in 1941, R. H. Fowler of England reported the interest of the British group in a moderator of deuterium in the form of heavy water and their conviction that a chain reaction would go in relatively small units of uranium and heavy water.

4.39. Urey and A. von Grosse had already been considering the concentration of heavy water by means of a catalytic exchange reaction between hydrogen gas and liquid water. This process depends on the fact that, when isotopic equilibrium is established between hydrogen gas and water, the water contains from three to four times as great a concentration of deuterium as does the hydrogen gas. During 1941, this exchange reaction between water and hydrogen was investigated at Columbia and in the Frick Chemical Laboratory at Princeton and extensive work was done toward developing large-scale methods of producing materials suitable for catalyzing the reaction.

4.40. The further development of this work and of other methods of producing heavy water are discussed in Chapter IX. Like the other isotope-separation work at Columbia, this work was relatively unaffected by the reorganization in December 1941. It is mentioned in preliminary fashion here to indicate that all the principal lines of approach were under investigation in 1941.

PRODUCTION AND ANALYSIS OF MATERIALS

4.41. By the end of 1941 not very much progress had been made in the production of materials for use in a chain-reacting system. The National Bureau of Standards and the Columbia group were in contact with the Metal Hydrides Company of Beverly, Massachusetts. This company was producing some uranium in powdered form, but its production of solid ingots was still in the development stage.

4.42. Similarly, no satisfactory arrangement had been made for obtaining large amounts of highly purified graphite. The graphite in use at Columbia had been obtained from the U. S. Graphite Company of Saginaw, Michigan. It was of high purity for a commercial product, but it did contain about one part in 500,000 of boron, which was undesirable.

4.43. Largely through the interest of Allison the possibility of increasing the production of beryllium had been investigated to the extent of ascertaining that it would be difficult and expensive, but probably possible.

4.44. Though little progress had been made on procurement, much progress had been made on analysis. The development of sufficiently accurate methods of chemical analysis of the materials used has been a problem of the first magnitude throughout the history of the project, although sometimes overshadowed by the more spectacular problems encountered. During this period C. J. Rodden and others at the National Bureau of Standards were principally responsible for analyses; H. T. Beans of Columbia also cooperated. By 1942 several other groups had started analytical sections which have been continuously active ever since.

4.45. To summarize, by the end of 1941 there was no evidence that procurement of materials in sufficient quantity and purity was impossible, but the problems were far from solved.

EXCHANGE OF INFORMATION
WITH THE BRITISH

4.46. Prior to the autumn of 1941 there had been some exchange of reports with the British and some discussion with British scientific representatives who were here on other business. In September 1941, it was decided that Pegram and Urey should get first-hand information by a trip to England. They completed their trip in the first week of December 1941.

4.47. In general, work in England had been following much the same lines as in this country. As to the chain-reaction problem, their attention had focussed on heavy water as a moderator rather than graphite; as to isotope separation, they had done extensive work on the diffusion process including the general theory of cascades. Actually the principal importance of this visit and other interchanges during the summer of 1941 lay not in accurate scientific data but in the general scientific impressions. The British, particularly J. Chadwick, were convinced that a U-235 chain reaction could be achieved. They knew that several kilograms of heavy water a day were being produced in Norway, and that Germany had ordered considerable quantities of paraffin to be made using heavy hydrogen; it was difficult to imagine a use for these materials other than in work on the uranium problem. They feared that if the Germans got atomic bombs before the Allies did, the war might be over in a few weeks. The sense of urgency which Pegram and Urey brought back with them was of great importance.

THE NATIONAL ACADEMY COMMITTEE REPORT

4.48. The appointment of a National Academy committee was mentioned in Chapter III. The committee's first report in May 1941 mentioned (a) radioactive poisons, (b) atomic power, and (c) atomic bombs, but the emphasis was on power. The second report stressed the importance of the new results on plutonium, but was not specific about the military uses to which the fission process might be put. Both these reports urged that the project be pushed more vigorously.

4.49. The third report (November 6, 1941) was specifically concerned with the "possibilities of an explosive fission reaction with U-235." Although neither of the first two National Academy reports indicated that uranium would be likely to be of decisive importance in the present war, this possibility was emphasized in the third report. We can do no better than quote portions of this report.

"Since our last report, the progress toward separation of the isotopes of uranium has been such as to make urgent a consideration of (1) the probability of success in the attempt to produce a fission bomb, (2) the destructive effect to be expected from such a bomb, (3) the anticipated time before its development can be completed and production be underway, and (4) a preliminary estimate of the costs involved."

"1. *Conditions for a fission bomb. A fission bomb of superlatively destructive power will result from bringing quickly together a sufficient mass of element U-235.* This seems to be as sure as any untried prediction based upon theory and experiment can be. Our calculations indicate further that the required masses can be brought together quickly enough for the reaction to become efficient . . .

"2. *Destructive effect of fission bombs.* (a) *Mass of the bomb. The mass of U-235 required to produce explosive fission under appropriate conditions can hardly be less than 2 kg nor greater than 100 kg.* These wide limits reflect chiefly the experimental uncertainty in the capture cross section of U-235 for fast neutrons . . . (b) *Energy released by explosive fission.* Calculations for the case of masses properly located at the initial instant indicate that between 1 and 5 per cent of the fission energy of the uranium should be released at a fission explosion. This means from 2 to 10×10^8 kilocalories per kg of uranium 235. *The available explosive energy per kg of uranium is thus equivalent to about 300 tons of TNT.*

"3. *Time required for development and production of the necessary U-235.* (a) *Amount of uranium needed.* Since the destructiveness of present bombs is already an important factor in warfare, it is evident that, if the destructiveness of the bombs is thus increased 10,000-fold, they should become of decisive importance.

"The amount of uranium required will, nevertheless, be large. If the estimate is correct that 500,000 tons of TNT bombs would be required to devastate Germany's military and industrial objectives, *from 1 to 10 tons of U-235 will be required to do the same job.*

"(b) *Separation of U-235. The separation of the isotopes of uranium can be done in the necessary amounts.* Several methods are under development, at least two of which seem definitely adequate, and are approaching the stage of practical test. These are the methods of the centrifuge and of diffusion through porous barriers. Other methods are being investigated or need study which may ultimately prove superior, but are now farther from the engineering stage.

"(c) *Time required for production of fission bombs.* An estimate of time required for development, engineering and production of fission bombs can be made only very roughly at this time.

"If all possible effort is spent on the program, one might however expect fission bombs to be available in significant quantity within three or four years.

"4. *Rough estimate of costs.* (The figures given in the Academy report under this heading were recognized as only rough estimates since the scientific and engineering data to make them more precise were not available. They showed only that the undertaking would be enormously expensive but still in line with other war expenditures.)"

4.50. The report then goes on to consider immediate requirements and desirable reorganization.

SUMMARY

4.51. At the end of Chapter I we summarized the knowledge of nuclear fission as of June 1940, and in Chapter II we stated the outstanding problems as of the same date. In the light of these statements we wish to review the eighteen months' progress that has just been recounted. The tangible progress was not great. No chain reaction had been achieved; no appreciable amount of U-235 had been separated from U-238; only minute amounts of Pu-239 had been produced; the production of large quantities of uranium metal, heavy water, beryllium, and pure graphite was still largely in the discussion stage. But there had been progress. Constants were better known; calculations had been checked and extended; guesses as to the existence and nuclear properties of Pu-239 had been verified. Some study had been made of engineering problems, process effectiveness, costs, and time schedules. Most important of all, the critical size of the bomb had been shown to be almost certainly within practical limits. Altogether the likelihood that the problems might be solved seemed greater in every case than it had in 1940. Perhaps more important than the actual change was the psychological change. Possibly Wigner, Szilard, and Fermi were no more thoroughly convinced that atomic bombs were possible than they had been in 1940, but many other people had become familiar with the idea and its possible consequences. Apparently, the British and the Germans, both grimly at war, thought the problem worth undertaking. Furthermore, the whole national psychology had changed. Although the attack at Pearl Harbor was yet to come, the impending threat of war was much more keenly felt than before, and expenditures of effort and money that would have seemed enormous in 1940 were considered obviously necessary precautions in December 1941. Thus it was not surprising that Bush and his associates felt it was time to push the uranium project vigorously. For this purpose, there was created an entirely new administrative organization which will be described in the next chapter.

CHAPTER V. ADMINISTRATIVE
HISTORY 1942–1945

5.1. In Chapter III the administrative history of the uranium work up to December 1941 was reviewed. Chapter IV reported the progress of the scientific work up to the same date. The present chapter describes the administrative reorganization that took place in December 1941 and various changes that occurred after that time.

REORGANIZATION OF NDRC URANIUM SECTION
TRANSFER TO OSRD

5.2. Two major decisions were required in the further planning of the uranium or atomic-bomb program. These decisions were made by Vannevar Bush, Director of the Office of Scientific Research and Development (which included NDRC), after conference with various scientists and administrators concerned. (See Chapter III.) The decisions were: first, that the possibility of obtaining atomic bombs for use in the present war was great enough to justify an "all out" effort for their development; second, that the existing organization, the NDRC Uranium Section (known as the S-1 Section, and consisting of L. J. Briggs, chairman; G. B. Pegram, vice-chairman; H. T. Wensel, technical aide; S. K. Allison, J. W. Beams, G. Breit, E. U. Condon, R. Gunn, H. D. Smyth, and H. C. Urey) was not properly organized for such an effort.

5.3. At a meeting of the National Defense Research Committee on November 28, 1941, Dr. Bush explained why he felt that it was desirable to set up the uranium program outside NDRC. The members of NDRC agreed to a transfer. Accordingly, the NDRC as an organization had no further connection with the uranium program, which was administered for some time thereafter by the OSRD directly through an OSRD S-1 Section, and later through an OSRD S-1 Executive Committee.

5.4. At a meeting of the S-1 Section of OSRD on December 6, 1941, J. B. Conant, speaking for Bush, announced the proposed "all out" effort and the reorganization of the group. The S-1 Section itself had not been formally consulted on the proposed reorganization, but there is no doubt that most of its members were strongly in favor of the new proposals. The membership of the reorganized S-1 Section was as follows: J. B. Conant, representative of V. Bush; L. J. Briggs, chairman; G. B. Pegram, vice-chairman; A. H. Compton, program chief; E. O. Lawrence, program chief; H. C. Urey, program chief; E. V. Murphree, chairman of the separately organized Planning Board; H. T. Wensel, technical aid; S. K. Allison, J. W. Beams, G. Breit, E. U. Condon, H. D. Smyth.

FORMATION OF THE PLANNING BOARD

5.5. At the time the S-1 Section was reorganized, Bush also set up a Planning Board to be responsible for the technical and engineering aspects of the work, for procurement of materials and for construction of pilot plants and full-size production plants. This Planning Board consisted of E. V. Murphree (chairman), W. K. Lewis, L. W. Chubb, G. O. Curme, Jr., and P. C. Keith.

FUNCTIONS OF THE PLANNING BOARD AND OSRD S-1 SECTION

5.6. It was arranged that contracts for the scientific parts of the work would be recommended to Bush not by the full S-1 Section but by Briggs and Conant after conferences with the program chiefs involved and that recommendations on engineering contracts would be made to Bush by the Planning Board. (The contracts which had been made on behalf of the old Uranium Section had been administered through the NDRC.)

Contracts for the development of diffusion and centrifuge separation processes were to be recommended by the Planning Board, which would be responsible for the heavy-water production program also. Bush stated that the Planning Board "will be responsible for seeing to it that we have plans on which to proceed with the next step as expeditiously as possible."

5.7. The scientific aspects of the work were separated from the procurement and engineering phases. The Program Chiefs—H. C. Urey, E. O. Lawrence, and A. H. Compton—were to have charge of the scientific aspects. Initially it was proposed that Urey should have charge of the separation of isotopes by the diffusion and the centrifuge methods and of the research work on the production of heavy water. Lawrence was to have charge of the initial production of small samples of fissionable elements, of quantity production by electromagnetic-separation methods, and of certain experimental work relating to the properties of the plutonium nucleus. Compton was to have charge of fundamental physical studies of the chain reaction and the measurement of nuclear properties with especial reference to the explosive chain reaction. As an afterthought, he was authorized to explore also the possibility that plutonium might be produced in useful amounts by the controlled chain-reaction method. It was understood, however, that this division of responsibility was to be more precisely defined in later conferences. (The written records of that period do not always give adequate accounts of what was in the minds of the men concerned. In deference to security requirements, references to the importance of plutonium and even to the bomb itself were often omitted entirely.)

5.8. The effect of the reorganization was to put the direction of the projects in the hands of a small group consisting of Bush, Conant, Briggs, Compton, Urey, Lawrence, and Murphree. Theoretically, Compton, Lawrence, Urey, and Murphree were responsible only for their respective divisions of the program. Each met with Conant and Briggs or occasionally with Bush to discuss his specific problems, or even the overall program.

Meeting of Top Policy Group—Approval of Reorganization

5.9. A meeting of the Top Policy Group, consisting of Vice-President Henry A. Wallace, Secretary of War Henry L. Stimson, and Dr. V. Bush, was held on December 16, 1941. General George C. Marshall and Dr. J. B. Conant, also members of the group, were absent; Mr. H. L. Smith of the Budget Bureau attended. Bush described the reorganization that was in progress and his plans were approved. In a memorandum to Conant describing this meeting, Bush wrote, "It was definitely felt by the entire group that OSRD should press as fast as possible on the fundamental physics and on the engineering planning, and particularly on the construction of pilot plants." Bush estimated the cost of this aspect of the work would be four or five million dollars, and stated the Army should take over when full-scale construction was started, presumably when pilot plants were ready. He suggested the assignment of a technically trained Army officer to become familiar with the general nature of the uranium problem. It was made clear at this meeting that the international relations involved were in the hands of the President, with Bush responsible for liaison on technical matters only.

Meeting of OSRD S-1 Section on December 18, 1941

5.10. On December 18, 1941, a meeting of the reorganized S-1 Section was held. Conant was present and discussed the new policy, which called for an all-out effort. He emphasized that such an effort was justified only by the military value of atomic bombs and that all attention must be concentrated in the direction of bomb development. The whole meeting was pervaded by an atmosphere of enthusiasm and urgency. Several methods of electromagnetic separation were proposed and discussed, and a number of new contracts were recommended.

Meeting of OSRD S-1 Section on January 16, 1942

5.11. Another meeting of the OSRD S-1 Section was held on January 16, 1942. Informal discussions of the various production methods took place, and tentative estimates were made as to when each method would produce results. These forecasts actually were no more than guesses since at that time the scientific information available was very incomplete and the problems of applying such data as did exist to the construction and operation of production plants had hardly been approached.

REARRANGEMENT OF THE WORK EARLY IN 1942

5.12. In the middle of January 1942, Compton decided to concentrate the work for which he was responsible at the University of Chicago. The Columbia group under Fermi and its accumulated material and equipment and the Princeton group which had been studying resonance absorption were moved to Chicago in the course of the spring. Certain smaller groups elsewhere remained active under Compton's direction. Under Lawrence the investigation of large-scale electromagnetic separation was accelerated at the University of California at Berkeley and a related separation project was started at Princeton. Research and development on the diffusion process and on the production of heavy water continued at Columbia under Urey; under the general supervision of Murphree, the centrifuge work continued at the University of Virginia under Beams while the Columbia centrifuge work was transferred to the laboratories of the Standard Oil Development Co. at Bayway, New Jersey.

REPORT TO THE PRESIDENT BY BUSH
ON MARCH 9, 1942

5.13. In a report dated February 20, 1942, Conant recommended that all phases of the work be pushed at least until July 1, 1942. Similarly, on March 9, 1942, Dr. Bush sent a report to the President reflecting general optimism but placing proper emphasis on the tentative nature of conclusions. His report contemplated completion of the project in 1944. In addition, the report contained the suggestion that the Army be brought in during the summer of 1942 for construction of full-scale plants.

REVIEWS OF THE PROGRAM BY CONANT

5.14. The entire heavy-water program was under review in March and April 1942. The reviews followed a visit to the United States in February and March 1942 by F. Simon, H. Halban, and W. A. Akers from England. In a memorandum of April 1, 1942 addressed to Bush, Conant reviewed the situation and reported on conferences with Compton and Briggs. His report pointed out that extremely large quantities of heavy water would be required for a plutonium production plant employing heavy water instead of graphite as a moderator. For this reason, he reported adversely on the suggestion that Halban be invited to bring to this country the 165 liters of heavy water which he then had in England.

5.15. In a memorandum written to Bush on May 14, 1942 (shortly before a proposed meeting of Program Chiefs), Conant estimated that there were five separation or production methods which were about equally likely to succeed: the centrifuge, diffusion, and electromagnetic methods of separating U-235; the uranium-graphite pile and the uranium-heavy-water pile methods of producing plutonium. All were considered about ready for pilot plant construction and perhaps even for preliminary design of production plants. If the methods were to be pushed to the production stage, a commitment of five hundred million dollars would be entailed. Although it was too early to estimate the relative merits of the different methods accurately, it was presumed that some methods would prove to be more rapid and efficient than others. It was feared, however, that elimination of any one method might result in a serious delay. It was thought that the Germans might be some distance ahead of the United States in a similar program.

5.16. Conant emphasized a question that has been crucial throughout the development of the uranium project. The question was whether atomic bombs would be decisive weapons or merely supplementary weapons. If they were decisive, there was virtually no limit to the amount of effort and money that should be put into the work. But no one knew how effective the atomic bombs would be.

Change from OSRD S-1 Section to OSRD S-1 Executive Committee

5.17. In May 1942, Conant suggested to Bush that instead of encouraging members of the section individually to discuss their own phases of the work with Conant and Briggs, the OSRD S-1 Section should meet for general discussions of the entire program. Bush responded by terminating the OSRD S-1 Section and replacing it with the OSRD S-1 Executive Committee, consisting of the following: J. B. Conant, chairman, L. J. Briggs, A. H. Compton, E. O. Lawrence, E. V. Murphree, H. C. Urey. H. T. Wensel and I. Stewart were selected to sit with the Committee as technical aide and secretary respectively.

5.18. The following members of the old OSRD S-1 Section were appointed as consultants to the new Committee: S. K. Allison, J. W. Beams, G. Breit, E. U. Condon, H. D. Smyth.

5.19. The functions of the new OSRD S-1 Executive Committee were: (a) To report on the program and budget for the next eighteen months, for each method. (b) To prepare recommendations as to how many programs should be continued. (c) To prepare recommendations as to what parts of the program should be eliminated.

5.20. Recommendations relative to matters of OSRD S-1 policy and relative to the letting of OSRD S-1 contracts were made on the basis of a majority vote of the Committee. Conant refrained from voting except in case of a tie vote. While Bush alone had the authority to establish OSRD policies and commit OSRD funds, he ordinarily followed the recommendations of the S-1 Executive Committee.

Report to the President by Bush and Conant on June 17, 1942

5.21. On June 13, 1942, Bush and Conant sent to Vice-President Henry A. Wallace, Secretary of War Henry L. Stimson, and Chief of Staff General George C. Marshall a report recommending detailed plans for the expansion and continuation of the atomic-bomb program. All three approved the report. On June 17, 1942, the report was sent by Bush to the President, who also approved. The report, which is too long to present in full, contained four principal parts, which dealt with: (a) The status of the development as appraised by the senior scientists; (b) Recommendations by the program chiefs and Planning Board; (c) Comments by Bush, Conant, and Maj. Gen. W. D. Styer; (d) Recommendations by Bush and Conant. We may paraphrase parts (a) and (c) as follows:

(a) *The status of the program.* (1) It was clear that an amount of U-235 or plutonium comprising a number of kilograms would be explosive, that such an explosion would be equivalent to several thousand tons of TNT, and that such an explosion could be caused to occur at the desired instant. (2) It was clear that there were four methods of preparing the fissionable material and that all of these methods appeared feasible; but it was not possible to state definitely that any given one of these is superior to the others. (3) It was clear that production plants of considerable size could be designed and built. (4) It seemed likely that, granted adequate funds and priorities, full-scale plant operation could be started soon enough to be of military significance.

(c) *Comments by Bush, Conant, and General Styer.* Certain recommendations had been made by Lawrence, Urey, Compton, and Murphree. These recommendations had been reviewed by Bush, Conant, and General Styer (who was instructed by General Marshall to follow the progress of the program) and their comments concerning the program were as follows: (1) If four separate methods all appeared to a highly competent scientific group to be capable of successful application, it appeared certain that the desired end result could be attained by the enemy, provided he had sufficient time. (2) The program as proposed obviously could not be carried out rapidly without interfering with other important matters, as regards both scientific personnel and critical materials. A choice had to be made between the military result which appeared attainable and the certain interference with other war activities. (3) It was unsafe at that time, in view of the pioneering nature of the entire effort, to concentrate on only one means of obtaining the result. (4) It therefore appeared best to proceed at once with those phases of the program which interfered least with other important war activities. Work on other phases of the program could proceed after questions of interference were resolved.

5.22. The June 13, 1942, report to the President and Bush's transmittal letter dated June 17, 1942, were returned to Bush with the initialled approval of the President. A copy of the report was then sent by Bush to General Styer on June 19, 1942.

Selection of Colonel J. C. Marshall

5.23. On June 18, 1942, Colonel J. C. Marshall, Corps of Engineers, was instructed by the Chief of Engineers to form a new district in the Corps of Engineers to carry on special work (atomic bombs) assigned to it. This district was designated the Manhattan District and was officially established on August 13, 1942. The work with which it was concerned was labeled, for security reasons, the "DSM Project" (Development of Substitute Materials).

Selection of General L. R. Groves

5.24. On September 17, 1942, the Secretary of War placed Brigadier General L. R. Groves of the Corps of Engineers in complete charge of all Army activities relating to the DSM Project.

Military Policy Committee; Functioning of the OSRD Committees

5.25. A conference was held on September 23, 1942, among those persons designated by the President to determine the general policies of the project, and certain others. Those present were Secretary of War Henry L. Stimson, Chief of Staff General

George C. Marshall, Dr. J. B. Conant, Dr. V. Bush, Major General Brehon Somervell, Major General W. D. Styer, and Brigadier General L. R. Groves. (Vice-President Henry A. Wallace was unable to attend.) A Military Policy Committee was appointed consisting of Dr. V. Bush as Chairman with Dr. J. B. Conant as his alternate, Major General W. D. Styer, and Rear Admiral W. R. Purnell. General Groves was named to sit with the committee and act as Executive Officer to carry out the policies that were determined. The duties of this committee were to plan military policies relating to materials, research and development, production, strategy, and tactics, and to submit progress reports to the policy group designated by the President.

5.26. The appointment of the Military Policy Committee was approved by the Joint New Weapons Committee, established by the U. S. Joint Chiefs of Staff and consisting of Dr. V. Bush, Rear Admiral W. R. Purnell, and Brigadier General R. G. Moses.

5.27. The creation of the Military Policy Committee in effect placed all phases of the DSM Project under the control of Dr. Bush, Dr. Conant, General Styer, Admiral Purnell, and General Groves.

5.28. The OSRD S-1 Executive Committee held meetings about once every month from June 1942 to May 1943 and once after that time, in September 1943. These meetings were normally attended by General Groves, after September 1942, and Colonel Marshall, and frequently by representatives of the industrial companies concerned with the production plants. Recommendations of the Committee were not binding but were usually followed. Thus it served as an advisory body to Dr. Bush and General Groves, and as an initial liaison group between the scientific, industrial, and military parts of the DMS Project. The S-1 Executive Committee has never been formally dissolved, but it has been inactive since the fall of 1943.

5.29. The procurement and engineering functions of the Planning Board were taken over by the Manhattan District in the summer of 1942 and that board then became inactive.

5.30. By the spring of 1943 it was felt that the Manhattan

District was in a position to take over research and development contracts from the OSRD. Such a transfer was effected as of May 1, 1943, and marked the end of the formal connection of OSRD with the uranium project.

5.31. In July 1943 Conant and R. C. Tolman were formally asked by General Groves to serve as his scientific advisers. They had already been doing so informally and have continued to do so. Coordination of the various scientific and technical programs was accomplished by meetings between General Groves and the leaders of the various projects, in particular, Compton, Lawrence, Oppenheimer (see Chapter XII), and Urey.

SUBSEQUENT ORGANIZATION: THE
MANHATTAN DISTRICT

5.32. Since 1943 there have been no important changes in the form of the organization and few of importance in the operating personnel. General Groves has continued to carry the major responsibility for correlating the whole effort and keeping it directed toward its military objectives. It has been his duty to keep the various parts of the project in step, to see that raw materials were available for the various plants, to determine production schedules, to make sure that the development of bomb design kept up with production schedules, to arrange for use of the bombs when the time came, and to maintain an adequate system of security. In discharging these duties General Groves has had the help of his tremendous organization made up of civilian scientists and engineers and Engineer officers and enlisted men. Many of the civilians have been mentioned already or will be mentioned in later chapters dealing with particular projects. Brigadier General T. F. Farrell has acted as General Groves' deputy in the important later phases of the project. Colonel K. D. Nichols, the District Engineer of the Manhattan District with his headquarters at the Clinton Engineer Works, has been connected with the project since 1942. He has been concerned with the research and production problems of both U-235 and plutonium and has always shown exceptional understanding of the technical problems and their relative importance. Two other officers who should be mentioned are Colonel F. T. Matthias and Colonel S. L. Warren. Colonel Matthias has discharged major responsibilities at the Hanford Engineer Works in an extremely able manner; his duties have been concerned with both the construction and operational phases of the project. Colonel Warren is chief of the Medical Section of the Manhattan District and therefore has had ultimate responsibility for health problems in all parts of the project.

SUMMARY

5.33. By the end of 1941 an extensive review of the whole uranium situation had been completed. As a result of this review Bush and his advisers decided to increase the effort on the uranium project and to change the organization. This decision was approved by President Roosevelt. From January 1942 until early summer of 1942 the uranium work was directed by Bush and Conant working with the Program Chiefs and a Planning Board. In the summer of 1942 the Army, through the Corps of Engineers, was assigned an active part in the procurement and engineering phases, organizing the Manhattan District for the purpose. In September 1942, Dr. Bush, Dr. Conant, General Styer, and Admiral Purnell were appointed as a Military Policy Committee to determine the general policies of the whole project. Also in September, General Groves was appointed to take charge of all Army activities of the project. The period of joint OSRD and Army control continued through April 1943 with the Army playing an increasingly important role as the industrial effort got fully under way. In May 1943 the research contracts were transferred to the Corps of Engineers; the period of joint OSRD-Army control ended and the period of complete Army control began.

5.34. Since the earliest days of the project, President Roosevelt had followed it with interest and, until his death, continued to study and approve the broad programs of the Military Policy

Committee. President Truman, who as a United States Senator had been aware of the project and its magnitude, was given the complete up-to-date picture by the Secretary of War and General Groves at a White House conference immediately after his inauguration. Thereafter the President gave the program his complete support, keeping in constant touch with the progress.

CHAPTER VI. THE METALLURGICAL PROJECT AT CHICAGO IN 1942

INTRODUCTION

6.1. As has been made clear in Chapters IV and V, the information accumulated by the end of 1941 as to the possibility of producing an atomic bomb was such as to warrant expansion of the work, and this expansion called for an administrative reorganization. It was generally accepted that there was a very high probability that an atomic bomb of enormous destructive power could be made, either from concentrated U-235 or from the new element plutonium. It was proposed, therefore, to institute an intensive experimental and theoretical program including work both on isotope separation and on the chain-reaction problems. It was hoped that this program would establish definitely whether or not U-235 could be separated in significant quantities from U-238, either by electromagnetic or statistical methods; whether or not a chain reaction could be established with natural uranium or its compounds and could be made to yield relatively large quantities of plutonium; and whether or not the plutonium so produced could be separated from the parent material, uranium. It was hoped also that the program would provide the theoretical and experimental data required for the design of a fast-neutron chain-reacting bomb.

6.2. As has been explained in Chapter V, the problems of isotope separation had been assigned to groups under Lawrence and Urey while the remaining problems were assigned to Compton's group, which was organized under the cryptically named "Metallurgical Laboratory" of the University of Chicago. In this chapter and the following two chapters we shall describe the work of the Metallurgical Laboratory and the associated laboratories up to June 1945. In later chapters we shall discuss isotope-separation work and the work of the bomb development group, which was separated from the Metallurgical Laboratory early in 1943.

6.3. It would be futile to attempt an assessment of the relative importance of the contributions of the various laboratories to the overall success of the atomic-bomb project. This report makes no such attempt, and there is little correlation between the space devoted to the work of a given group and the ability or importance of that group. In deciding which subdivision of the atomic-bomb project should be discussed first and most fully, we have been governed by criteria of general interest and of military security. Some developments of great technical importance are of little general interest; others both interesting and important must still be kept secret. Such criteria, applied to the objectives and accomplishments of the various laboratories set up since large-scale work began, favor the Metallurgical Laboratory as the part of the project to be treated most completely.

OBJECTIVES

6.4. In accordance with the general objectives just outlined, the initial objectives of the Metallurgical Laboratory were: first, to find a system using normal uranium in which a chain reaction would occur; second, to show that, if such a chain reaction did occur, it would be possible to separate plutonium chemically from the other material; and, finally, to obtain the theoretical and experimental data for effecting an explosive chain reaction with either U-235 or with plutonium. The ultimate objective of the laboratory was to prepare plans for the large-scale production of plutonium and for its use in bombs.

ORGANIZATION OF THE WORK

6.5. The laboratory had not only to concern itself with its immediate objectives but simultaneously to bear in mind the ultimate objectives and to work toward them on the assumption that the immediate objectives would be attained. It could not wait for a chain reaction to be achieved before studying the chemistry of plutonium. It had to assume that plutonium would be separated and to go ahead with the formulation of plans for its production and use. Consequently problems were continually redefined as new information became available, and research programs were reassessed almost from week to week. In a general way the experimental nuclear physics group under E. Fermi was primarily concerned with getting a chain reaction going, the chemistry division organized by F. H. Spedding (later in turn under S. K. Allison, J. Franck, W. C. Johnson, and T. Hogness) with the chemistry of plutonium and with separation methods, and the theoretical group under E. Wigner with designing production piles. However, the problems were intertwined and the various scientific and technical aspects of the fission process were studied in whatever group seemed best equipped for the particular task. In March 1942, Thomas Moore was brought in to head the engineering group. Other senior men in this group were M. C. Leverett, J. A. Wheeler and C. M. Cooper, who later succeeded Moore as head of the Technical Division. In the summer of 1942 the importance of health problems became apparent and a Health Division was organized under Dr. R. S. Stone. The difficult task of organizing and administering a research laboratory growing in size and complexity with almost explosive violence was carried out by R. L. Doan as Laboratory Director.

6.6. We have chosen to confine this chapter to the work of 1942 because a self-sustaining chain reaction was first achieved on December 2 of that year, at a time when the whole Chicago project was being appraised by a reviewing committee with the members particularly selected for their engineering background.* That was a dramatic coincidence and also a convenient one for purposes of this report since either incident might be considered to mark the end of an epoch at the Metallurgical Laboratory. Furthermore, in preparation for the reviewing committee's visit

---

* This committee was composed of W. K. Lewis, C. H. Greenewalt, T. C. Gary, and Roger Williams. E. V. Murphree was also a member but due to illness was unable to participate.

a comprehensive report had been prepared. That report was generally known as the "Feasibility Report" and has been used extensively in preparing this chapter.

PLAN OF THIS CHAPTER

6.7. In this chapter we shall present the material in the order of the objectives given above. In Part I we shall discuss progress towards the initial objectives, including (a) procurement of materials, (b) the experimental proof of the chain reaction, (c) the chemistry of plutonium and some of the problems of separation, (d) some of the types of auxiliary experiments that were performed, and finally (e) the "fast neutron" work. Necessarily the work described in detail is only a sampling of the large amount of theoretical and experimental work actually performed. In Part II we shall discuss the possibilities that were considered for production piles and separation methods, and the specific proposals made in November 1942.

PART I: PROGRESS TOWARD THE INITIAL OBJECTIVES

PROCUREMENT OF MATERIALS

General

6.8. It has been made clear in earlier chapters of this report that the procurement of materials of sufficient purity was a major part of the problem. As far as uranium was concerned, it seemed likely that it would be needed in highly purified metallic form or at least as highly purified uranium oxide. The other materials which were going to be needed were either graphite, heavy water, or possibly beryllium. It was clear at this time that, however advantageous heavy water might be as a moderator, no large quantities of it would be available for months or years. Beryllium seemed less advantageous and almost as difficult to get. Therefore the procurement efforts for a moderator were centered on graphite. As has been explained in Chapter V, procurement of uranium and graphite was not primarily the responsibility of the Metallurgical Laboratory but was handled through E. V. Murphree and others on the "planning board." In fact, the obvious interest of the Metallurgical Laboratory in the problem led to continual intervention by its representatives. A great deal of the credit for the eventual success in obtaining materials is due to N. Hilberry and later R. L. Doan, always supported by A. H. Compton.

URANIUM ORE

6.9. Obviously there would be no point in undertaking this whole project if it were not going to be possible to find enough uranium for producing the bombs. Early indications were favorable, and a careful survey made in November 1942 showed that immediate delivery could be made of adequate tonnages of uranium ores.

URANIUM OXIDE AND URANIUM METAL

6.10. At the end of 1941 the only uranium metal in existence was a few grams of good material made on an experimental basis by the Westinghouse Electric and Manufacturing Company and others and a few pounds of pyrophoric powder, made by Metal Hydrides Company, not of the high purity required for the chain-reaction. The only considerable amount of raw material then available in this country was in the form of a commercial grade of black uranium oxide, which could be obtained in limited quantities from the Canadian Radium and Uranium Corp. It contained 2 to 5 per cent of impurities and was the material which gave a neutron multiplication factor of only about 0.87 when used in an exponential pile.

6.11. By May 1942, deliveries averaging 15 tons a month of black oxide of higher purity and more uniform grade started coming in. Total impurities were less than 1 per cent, boron comprised a few parts per million, and the neutron multiplication factor (k) was about 0.98. (It is to be remembered that the multiplication factor depends also on the purity of the graphite.) Deliveries of this material reached a ton a day in September 1942.

6.12. Experiments at the National Bureau of Standards by J. I. Hoffman demonstrated that, by the use of an ether extraction method, all the impurities are removed by a single extraction of uranyl nitrate. The use of this method removed the great bulk of the difficulties in securing pure oxide and pure materials for the production of metal. Early in May 1942, arrangements were completed with the Mallinckrodt Chemical Works in St. Louis to put the new grade of oxide through an ether extraction process on a production basis for a further reduction in impurity content and to deliver the final product as brown dioxide. Deliveries started in July 1942 at a rate of 30 tons a month. This oxide is now used as a starting point for all metal production, and no higher degree of purity can be expected on a commercial scale. In fact, it was a remarkable achievement to have developed and put into production on a scale of the order of one ton per day a process for transforming grossly impure commercial oxide to oxide of a degree of purity seldom achieved even on a laboratory scale.

6.13. The process which Westinghouse had been using to produce the metal was the electrolysis of KUF_5 at a cost of about $1,000 a pound. Since the KUF_5 was produced photochemically under the action of sunlight this method constituted a potential bottleneck in production. It was found that uranium tetrafluoride could be used instead of KUF_5, and steps were taken to have this salt produced at the Harshaw Chemical Company in Cleveland and at the du Pont plant in Penns Grove, New Jersey. Production started in August 1942 and by October 1942 was up to 700 pounds per day at Harshaw and 300 pounds per day at du Pont, the method of manufacture in both cases being the hydrofluorination of Mallinckrodt-purified dioxide.

6.14. As the result of this supply of raw materials to Westinghouse, and as a result of plant expansion, deliveries from Westinghouse had accumulated to a total of more than 6,000 pounds by November 1942 and were expected to be at the rate of 500 pounds per day by January 1943. The purity of the metal was good, and the cost had dropped to $22 per pound.

6.15. Deliveries of acceptable metal from Metal Hydrides Co. were delayed for various reasons and were just beginning in November 1942. This company's production was scheduled to reach a thousand pounds per week thereafter.

6.16. Neither the Westinghouse process nor the Metal Hydrides Process was entirely satisfactory. Intensive activity designed to accelerate metal production, and carried out independently by F. H. Spedding and his associates at Iowa State College at Ames, Iowa, and by C. J. Rodden at the National Bureau of Standards, resulted in the development of a satisfactory method. Production facilities were set up at Ames in the fall of 1942 and had already produced more than one ton by the end of November. The process was extremely simple, rapid and low cost.

6.17. Further research indicated additional changes that could be made to advantage, and by the middle of 1943 Spedding at Iowa and other producers who entered the picture were using the final production method adopted.

6.18. By the end of 1942 arrangements had been made by the Manhattan District to increase metal production by making greater use of the Mallinckrodt Chemical Works, the Union Carbide and Carbon Corporation, and the du Pont Company.

6.19. To summarize, almost no metal was available during most of 1942, a fact that seriously delayed progress as we shall see, but the production problems had been nearly solved by the end of 1942 and some 6 tons of metal were incorporated in the pile built in November 1942. The whole problem of procurement of metal was taken over by the Manhattan District at the end of the year, under the general direction of Colonel Ruhoff, formerly with the Mallinckrodt Chemical Works. From the point of view of the Metallurgical Project no further serious delays or difficulty have occurred because of metal shortages.

Graphite Procurement

6.20. At the beginning of 1942 graphite production was still unsatisfactory but it was, of course, in quite a different condition from the metal production since the industrial production of graphite had already been very large. The problem was merely one of purity and priority. Largely through the efforts of N. Hilberry, the National Carbon Company and the Speer Carbon Company were both drawn into the picture. Following suggestions made by the experts of the National Bureau of Standards, these companies were able to produce highly purified graphite with a neutron absorption some 20 per cent less than the standard commercial materials previously used. Although efforts further to reduce the impurities have had some success, the purity problem was essentially solved by the middle of 1942 and large orders were placed with the cooperation of the War Production Board. As in the case of the metal, the graphite procurement problem was taken over by the Manhattan District.

THE CHAIN REACTION

Further Intermediate Experiments

6.21. At the time that the Metallurgical Project was organized, most of the physicists familiar with the problem believed that a chain-reacting pile probably could be built if sufficiently pure graphite and pure uranium metal could be obtained. Enough work had been done on resonance absorption, on the theory of absorption and diffusion of neutrons in a pile, and on intermediate experiments to make it possible to design a lattice structure that had a very good chance of maintaining a chain reaction. Nevertheless, there were uncertainties in the experimental data and in the approximations that had to be made in the theoretical calculations. There were two alternatives: (1) to build a pile according to the best possible design; (2) to make more accurate determinations of the pertinent nuclear constants, to perform intermediate experiments, and to improve the calculations. There is little doubt that the first alternative was the one likely to lead most rapidly to the production of plutonium. There were many important questions which could have been answered more rapidly by such an operating pile than by a series of small-scale experiments. Unfortunately, the necessary amounts of materials were not available and did not become available for nearly nine months. Consequently, it was necessary to choose the second alternative, that is, to accumulate all relevant or possibly relevant information by whatever means were available.

6.22. The major line of investigation was a series of intermediate experiments. The particular set-up for each intermediate experiment could be used to test calculations based on separate auxiliary experiments. For example, the proportion of uranium oxide to graphite was varied, oxides of different purities were used, oxide was used in lumps of various sizes and shapes and degrees of compression, the lattice spacing was varied, the effect of surrounding the uranium oxide units with beryllium and with paraffin was tried; and, finally, piles of identical lattice type but of different total size were tried to see whether the values of the multiplication factor k (for infinite size) calculated from the different sets of results were identical. In general, E. Fermi had direct charge of investigations of effects of impurities, and S. K. Allison had charge of tests involving different lattice dimensions. All these experiments strengthened the confidence of the group in the calculated value of k and in the belief that a pile could be built with k greater than unity. In July enough purified uranium oxide from Mallinckrodt was available to permit building intermediate pile No. 9. As in previous experiments, a radium-beryllium neutron source was placed at the bottom of the lattice structure and the neutron density measured along the vertical axis of the pile. By this time it was known that the neutron density decreased exponentially with increasing distance from the neutron source (hence the name often used for experiments of this type, "exponential pile") and that, from such rates of decrease, the multiplication constant k for an infinitely large pile of the same lattice proportions could be calculated. For the first time the multiplication constant k so calculated from experimental results came out greater than one. (The actual value was 1.007.) Even before this experiment Compton predicted in his report of July 1 that a k value somewhere between 1.04 and 1.05 could be obtained in a pile containing highly purified uranium oxide and graphite, provided that the air was removed from the pile to avoid neutron absorption by nitrogen.

AN AUXILIARY EXPERIMENT; DELAYED NEUTRONS

6.23. We shall not mention a majority of the various auxiliary experiments done during this period. There was one, however,—the study of delayed neutrons—that we shall discuss because it is a good example of the kind of experiment that had to be performed and because it concerned one effect, not heretofore mentioned, that is of great importance in controlling a chain-reacting pile.

6.24. From previous investigations, some of which were already published, it was known that about 1 per cent of the neutrons emitted in fission processes were not ejected immediately but were given off in decreasing quantity over a period of time, a fact reminiscent of the emission of beta rays from shortlived radioactive substances. Several half-lives had been observed, the longest being of the order of a minute.

6.25. It was realized early that this time delay gave a sort of inertia to the chain reaction that should greatly facilitate control. If the effective multiplication factor of a pile became slightly greater than 1, the neutron density would not rise to harmfully large values almost instantly but would rise gradually so that there would be a chance for controls to operate. (Other time intervals involved, such as those between collisions, are too small to be useful.)

6.26. Because of the importance of this effect of delayed neutrons for control it was decided to repeat and improve the earlier measurements. (The fact that this was a repetition rather than a new measurement is also typical of much of the work in physics at this period.) A description of the experiment is given in Appendix 3. The results indicated that 1.0 per cent of the neutrons emitted in uranium fission are delayed by at least 0.01 second and that about 0.07 per cent are delayed by as much as a minute. By designing a pile such that the effective value of k, the multiplication factor, is only 1.01 the number of delayed neutrons is sufficient to allow easy control.

THE FIRST SELF-SUSTAINING CHAIN-REACTING PILE

6.27. By the fall of 1942 enough graphite, uranium oxide, and uranium metal were available at Chicago to justify an attempt to build an actual self-sustaining chain-reacting pile. But the amount of metal available was small—only about 6 tons—and other materials were none too plentiful and of varying quality. These conditions rather than optimum efficiency controlled the design.

6.28. The pile was constructed on the lattice principle with graphite as a moderator and lumps of metal or oxide as the reacting units regularly spaced through the graphite to form the lattice. Instruments situated at various points in the pile or near it indicated the neutron intensity, and movable strips of absorbing material served as controls. (For a more complete description of the pile, see Appendix 4.) Since there were bound to be some neutrons present from spontaneous fission or other sources, it was anticipated that the reaction would start as soon as the structure had reached critical size if the control strips were not set in "retard" position. Consequently, the control strips were placed in a suitable "retard" position from the start and the neutron intensity was measured frequently. This was fortunate since the approach to critical condition was found to occur at an earlier stage of assembly than had been anticipated.

6.29. The pile was first operated as a self-sustaining system on December 2, 1942. So far as we know, this was the first time that human beings ever initiated a self-maintaining nuclear chain reaction. Initially the pile was operated at a power level of $\frac{1}{2}$ watt, but on December 12 the power level was raised to 200 watts.

ENERGY DEVELOPED BY THE PILE

6.30. In these experiments no direct measurements of energy release were made. The number of neutrons per second emitted by the pile was estimated in terms of the activity of standardized indium foils. Then, from a knowledge of the number of neutrons produced per fission, the resultant rate of energy release (wattage) was calculated.

CONCLUSION

6.31. Evidently this experiment, performed on December 2 just as a reviewing committee was appraising the Chicago project, answered beyond all shadow of doubt the first question before the Metallurgical Laboratory; a self-sustaining nuclear chain reaction had been produced in a system using normal uranium. This experiment had been performed under the general direction of E. Fermi, assisted principally by the groups headed by W. H. Zinn and H. L. Anderson. V. C. Wilson and his group had been largely responsible for developing the instruments and controls, and a great many others in the laboratory had contributed to the success of the enterprise.

RELATION BETWEEN POWER AND PRODUCTION OF PLUTONIUM

6.32. The immediate object of building a uranium-graphite pile was to prove that there were conditions under which a chain reaction would occur, but the ultimate objective of the laboratory was to produce plutonium by a chain reaction. Therefore we are interested in the relation between the power at which a pile operates and the rate at which it produces plutonium. The relation may be evaluated to a first approximation rather easily. A pile running stably must be producing as many neutrons as it is losing. For every thermal neutron absorbed in U-235 a certain number of neutrons, η, is emitted. One of these neutrons is required to maintain the chain. Therefore, assuming the extra neutrons all are absorbed by U-238 to form plutonium, there will be $\eta - 1$ atoms of Pu^{239} formed for every fission. Every fission releases roughly 200 Mev of energy. Therefore the formation of $\eta - 1$ atoms of plutonium accompanies the release of about 200 Mev. Since $\eta - 1$ is a small number, we can guess that to produce a kilogram a day of plutonium a chain-reacting pile must be releasing energy at the rate of 500,000 to 1,500,000 kilowatts. The first chain-reacting pile that we have just described operated at a maximum of 200 watts. Assuming that a single bomb will require the order of one to 100 kilograms of plutonium, the pile that has been described would have to be kept going at least 70,000 years to produce a single bomb. Evidently the problem of quantity production of plutonium was not yet solved.

THE CHEMISTRY OF PLUTONIUM

6.33. The second specific objective of the Metallurgical Laboratory was to show that, if a chain reaction did occur, it would be feasible to separate the plutonium chemically from the other material with which it is found. Progress toward this objective was necessarily slower than toward the attainment of a chain reaction. Initially little was done at the Metallurgical Laboratory on chemical problems although the extraction problem was discussed in a conference soon after the project was organized and the work of Seaborg's group at the University of California on plutonium was encouraged. On April 22–23, 1942, a general conference on chemistry was held at Chicago, attended by F. H. Spedding, E. W. Thiele, G. T. Seaborg, J. W. Kennedy, H. C. Urey, E. Wigner, N. Hilberry, G. E. Boyd, I. B. Johns, H. A. Wilhelm, I. Perlman, A. C. Wahl, and J. A. Wheeler. Spedding, in opening the meeting, pointed out that there were two main tasks for the chemists: first, to separate plutonium in the amounts and purity required for war purposes; second, to obtain a good understanding of the chemistry necessary for the construction and maintenance of the pile. The separation problem was to be studied by a new group at Chicago under the direction of Seaborg, by Johns and Wilhelm at Ames, and by Wahl and Kennedy continuing the work at California. Other closely related groups at Chicago were to be C. D. Coryell's, working on the fission products, and Boyd's on analytical problems. The chemistry group at Chicago has grown speedily since that time. A new building had to be constructed to house it late in 1942, and this building was enlarged subsequently. Altogether, the solving of many of the chemical problems has been one of the most remarkable achievements of the Metallurgical Laboratory.

6.34. The first evidence of the actual existence of plutonium and neptunium (ruling out the original erroneous interpretation of the splitting of uranium as evidence for their existence) was obtained by E. McMillan and P. H. Abelson who isolated 93–239 from uranium bombarded with neutrons in the Berkeley cyclotron. This new element was identified as a beta emitter but the sample was too small for isolation of the daughter product 94–239. The first isotope of plutonum studied chemically was not the 239 isotope but the 238 isotope, which is an alpha-ray emitter with a half-life of about 50 years. U-238 bombarded with deuterons gives $_{93}Np^{238}$ which disintegrates to $_{94}Pu^{238}$ by beta emission.* Enough Pu-238 was prepared to permit Seaborg, Kennedy and Wahl to begin the study of its chemical properties in the winter of 1940–1941 by using tracer chemistry with carriers according to practice usual in radiochemistry. By such studies many chemical properties of plutonium were determined, and several possible chemical processes were evolved by which Pu-239 might be removed from the chain-reacting pile. The success of experiments on a tracer scale led to plans to produce enough Pu-239 to be treated as an ordinary substance on the ultra-microchemical scale. Such quantities were produced by prolonged bombardment of several hundred pounds of uranyl nitrate with neutrons obtained with the aid of cyclotrons, first at Berkeley and later at Washington University in St. Louis. By the end of 1942, something over 500 micrograms had been obtained in the form of pure plutonium salts. Although this amount is less than would be needed to make the head of a pin, for the micro-chemists it was sufficient to yield considerable information; for one microgram is considered sufficient to carry out weighing experiments, titrations, solubility studies, etc.

6.35. From its position in the periodic table, plutonium might be expected to be similar to the rare earths or to uranium.

* See drawing on p. 8.

thorium, or osmium. Which of these it will resemble most closely depends, of course, on the arrangement of the outermost groups of electrons and this arrangement could hardly have been predicted. On the whole, plutonium turned out to be more like uranium than like any of the other elements named and might even be regarded as the second member of a new rare-earth series beginning with uranium. It was discovered fairly early that there were at least two states of oxidation of plutonium. (It is now known that there are four, corresponding to positive valences of 3, 4, 5, and 6.) Successful microchemical preparation of some plutonium salts and a study of their properties led to the general conclusion that it was possible to separate plutonium chemically from the other materials in the pile. This conclusion represents the attainment of the second immediate objective of the Metallurgical Laboratory. Thus, by the end of 1942, plutonium, entirely unknown eighteen months earlier, was considered an element whose chemical behavior was as well understood as that of several of the elements of the old periodic table.

MISCELLANEOUS STUDIES

6.36. Besides the major problems we have mentioned, i.e., the chain reaction, the chemical separation, and the planning for a production plant, there were innumerable minor problems to be solved. Among the more important of these were the improvement of neutron counters, ionization chambers, and other instruments, the study of corrosion of uranium and aluminum by water and other possible coolants, the determination of the effects of temperature variation on neutron cross sections, the fabrication of uranium rods and tubes, the study of fission products, and the determination of the biological effects of radiation. As typical of this kind of work we can cite the development of methods of fabricating and coating uranium metal, under the direction of E. Creutz. Without the accomplishment of these secondary investigations the project could not have reached its goal. To give some further idea of the scope of the work, a list of twenty report titles is presented in Appendix 5, the 20 reports being selected from the 400 or so issued during 1942.

THE FAST-NEUTRON REACTION

6.37. The third initial objective of the Metallurgical Project was to obtain theoretical and experimental data on a "fast neutron" reaction, such as would be required in an atomic bomb. This aspect of the work was initially planned and coordinated by G. Breit of the University of Wisconsin and later continued by J. R. Oppenheimer of the University of California. Since the actual construction of the bomb was to be the final part of the program, the urgency of studying such reactions was not so great. Consequently, little attention was given to the theoretical problems until the summer of 1942, when a group was organized at Chicago under the leadership of Oppenheimer.

6.38. In the meantime experimental work initiated in most instances by G. Breit, had been in progress (under the general direction of the Metallurgical Project) at various institutions having equipment suitable for fast-neutron studies (Carnegie Institution of Washington, the National Bureau of Standards, Cornell University, Purdue University, University of Chicago, University of Minnesota, University of Wisconsin, University of California, Stanford University, University of Indiana, and Rice Institute). The problems under investigation involved scattering, absorption and fission cross section, the energy spectrum of fission neutrons, and the time delay in the emission of fission neutrons. For the most part this work represented an intermediate step in confirming and extending previous measurements but reached no new final conclusion. This type of work was subsequently concentrated at another site (see Chapter XII).

6.39. As indicated by the "Feasibility Report" (in a section written by J. H. Manley, J. R. Oppenheimer, R. Serber, and E. Teller) the picture had changed significantly in only one respect since the appearance of the National Academy Report a year earlier. Theoretical studies now showed that the effectiveness of the atomic bomb in producing damage would be greater than had been indicated in the National Academy report. However, critical size of the bomb was still unknown. Methods of detonating the bomb had been investigated somewhat, but on the whole no certain answers had been reached.

PART II: PROGRESS TOWARD THE ULTIMATE OBJECTIVE

PLANNING A PRODUCTION PLANT

PLANNING AND TECHNICAL WORK

6.40. As we have seen, the initial objectives of the Metallurgical Laboratory had been reached by the end of 1942, but the ultimate objectives, the production of large quantities of plutonium and the design and fabrication of bombs, were still far from attained. The responsibility for the design and fabrication of bombs was transferred to another group at about this time; its work is reported in Chapter XII. The production of Pu-239 in quantity has remained the principal responsibility of the Metallurgical Laboratory although shared with the du Pont Company since the end of 1942.

6.41. On the basis of the evidence available it was clear that a plutonium production rate somewhere between a kilogram a month and a kilogram a day would be required. At the rate of a kilogram a day, a 500,000 to 1,500,000 kilowatt plant would be required. (The ultimate capacity of the hydroelectric power plants at the Grand Coulee Dam is expected to be 2,000,000 kw.) Evidently the creation of a plutonium production plant of the required size was to be a major enterprise even without attempting to utilize the thermal energy liberated. Nevertheless, by November 1942 most of the problems had been well defined and tentative solutions had been proposed. Although these problems will be discussed in some detail in the next chapter, we will mention them here.

6.42. Since a large amount of heat is generated in any pile producing appreciable amounts of plutonium, the first problem of design is a cooling system. Before such a system can be designed, it is necessary to find the maximum temperature at which a pile can run safely and the factors—nuclear or structural—which determine this temperature. Another major problem is the method for loading and unloading the uranium, a problem complicated by the shielding and the cooling system. Shielding against radiation has to be planned for both the pile itself and the chemical separation plant. The nature of the separation plant depends on the particular separation process to be used, which has to be decided. Finally, speed of procurement and construction must be primary factors in the planning of both the pile and the chemical plant.

POSSIBLE TYPES OF PLANT

6.43. After examining the principal factors affecting plant design, i.e., cooling, efficiency, safety, and speed of construction, the "Feasibility Report" suggested a number of possible plant types in the following order of preference:

I. (a) Ordinary uranium metal lattice in a graphite moderator with helium cooling. (b) The same, with water cooling. (c) The same, with molten bismuth cooling.
II. Ordinary uranium metal lattice in a heavy-water moderator.
III. Uranium enriched in the 235 isotope using graphite, heavy water, or ordinary water as moderator.

Types II and III were of no immediate interest since neither enriched uranium nor heavy water was available. Development of both these types continued however, since if no other type proved feasible they might have to be used. Type I (c), calling for liquid bismuth cooling, seemed very promising from the point of view of utilization of the thermal energy released, but it was felt that the technical problems involved could not be solved for a long time.

The Pilot Plant at Clinton

6.44. During this period, the latter half of 1942, when production plants were being planned, it was recognized that a plant of intermediate size was desirable. Such a plant was needed for two reasons: first, as a pilot plant; second, as a producer of a few grams of plutonium badly needed for experimental purposes. Designed as an air-cooled plant of 1,000-kw capacity, the intermediate pile constructed at Clinton, Tennessee, might have served both purposes if helium cooling had been retained for the main plant. Although the plans for the main plant were shifted so that water cooling was called for, the pilot plant was continued with air cooling in the belief that the second objective would be reached more quickly. It thus ceased to be a pilot plant except for chemical separation. Actually the main plant was built without benefit of a true pilot plant, much as if the hydroelectric generators at Grand Coulee had been designed merely from experience gained with a generator of quite different type and of a small fraction of the power.

SPECIFIC PROPOSALS

6.45. As reviewed by Hilberry in the "Feasibility Report" of November 26, 1942, the prospects for a graphite pile with helium cooling looked promising as regards immediate production; the pile using heavy water for moderator and using heavy water or ordinary water as coolant looked better for eventual full-scale use. A number of specific proposals were made for construction of such plants and for the further study of the problems involved. These proposals were based on time and cost estimates which were necessarily little better than rough guesses. As the result of further investigation the actual program of construction—described in later chapters—has been quite different from that proposed.

SUMMARY

6.46. The procurement problem which had been delaying progress was essentially solved by the end of 1942. A small self-sustaining graphite-uranium pile was constructed in November 1942, and was put into operation for the first time on December 2, 1942, at a power level of $\frac{1}{2}$ watt and later at 200 watts. It was easily controllable thanks to the phenomenon of delayed neutron emission. A total of 500 micrograms of plutonium was made with the cyclotron and separated chemically from the uranium and fission products. Enough was learned of the chemistry of plutonium to indicate the possibility of separation on a relatively large scale. No great advance was made on bomb theory, but calculations were checked and experiments with fast neutrons extended. If anything, the bomb prospects looked more favorable than a year earlier.

6.47. Enough experimenting and planning were done to delineate the problems to be encountered in constructing and operating a large-scale production plant. Some progress was made in choice of type of plant, first choice at that time being a pile of metallic uranium and graphite, cooled either by helium or water. A specific program was drawn up for the construction of pilot and production plants. This program presented time and cost estimates.

CHAPTER VII. THE PLUTONIUM PRODUCTION PROBLEM AS OF FEBRUARY 1943

INTRODUCTION

NEED OF DECISIONS

7.1. By the first of January 1943, the Metallurgical Laboratory had achieved its first objective, a chain-reacting pile, and was well on the way to the second, a process for extracting the plutonium produced in such a pile. It was clearly time to formulate more definite plans for a production plant. The policy decisions were made by the Policy Committee (see Chapter V) on the recommendations from the Laboratory Director (A. H. Compton), from the S-1 Executive Committee, and from the Reviewing Committee that had visited Chicago in December 1942. The only decisions that had already been made were that the first chain-reacting pile should be dismantled and then reconstructed on a site a short distance from Chicago and that a 1,000-kilowatt plutonium plant should be built at Clinton, Tennessee.

THE SCALE OF PRODUCTION

7.2. The first decision to be made was on the scale of production that should be attempted. For reasons of security the figure decided upon may not be disclosed here. It was very large.

THE MAGNITUDE OF THE PROBLEM

7.3. As we have seen, the production of one gram of plutonium per day corresponds to a generation of energy at the rate of 500 to 1,500 kilowatts. Therefore a plant for large-scale production of plutonium will release a very large amount of energy.

The problem therefore was to design a plant of this capacity on the basis of experience with a pile that could operate at a power level of only 0.2 kilowatt. As regards the plutonium separation work, which was equally important, it was necessary to draw plans for an extraction and purification plant which would separate some grams a day of plutonium from some tons of uranium, and such planning had to be based on information obtained by microchemical studies involving only half a milligram of plutonium. To be sure, there was information available for the design of the large-scale pile and separation plant from auxiliary experiments and from large-scale studies of separation processes using uranium as a stand-in for plutonium, but even so the proposed extrapolations both as to chain-reacting piles and as to separation processes were staggering. In peacetime no engineer or scientist in his right mind would consider making such a magnification in a single stage, and even in wartime only the possibility of achieving tremendously important results could justify it.

Assignment of Responsibility

7.4. As soon as it had been decided to go ahead with large-scale production of plutonium, it was evident that a great expansion in organization was necessary. The Stone and Webster Engineering Corporation had been selected as the overall engineering and construction firm for the DSM Project soon after the Manhattan District was placed in charge of construction work in June 1942. By October 1942, it became evident that various component parts of the work were too far separated physically and were too complicated technically to be handled by a single company—especially in view of the rapid pace required. Therefore it was decided that it would be advantageous if Stone and Webster were relieved of that portion of the work pertaining to the construction of plutonium production facilities. This was done, and General Groves selected the E. I. du Pont de Nemours and Company as the firm best able to carry on this phase of the work. The arrangements made with various industrial companies by the Manhattan District took various forms. The arrangements with du Pont are discussed in detail as an example.

7.5. General Groves broached the question to W. S. Carpenter, Jr., president of du Pont, and after considerable discussion with him and other officials of the firm, du Pont agreed to undertake the work. In their acceptance, they made it plain and it was understood by all concerned that du Pont was undertaking the work only because the War Department considered the work to be of the utmost importance, and because General Groves stated that this view as to importance was one held personally by the President of the United States, the Secretary of War, the Chief of Staff, and General Groves, and because of General Groves' assertion that du Pont was by far the organization best qualified for the job. At the same time, it was recognized that the du Pont Company already had assumed all the war-connected activities which their existing organization could be expected to handle without undue difficulty.

7.6. The du Pont Company, in accepting the undertaking, insisted that the work be conducted without profit and without patent rights of any kind accruing to them. The du Pont Company did request, however, that in view of the unknown character of the field into which they were being asked to embark, and in view of the unpredictable hazards involved, the Government provide maximum protection against losses sustained by du Pont.

7.7. The cost-plus-a-fixed-fee contract between the Government and du Pont established a fixed fee of $1.00. The Government agreed to pay all costs of the work by direct reimbursement or through allowances provided by the contract to cover administrative and general expenses allocated to the work in accordance with normal du Pont accounting practices as determined by audit by certified public accountants. Under the terms of the contract, any portion of these allowances not actually expended by du Pont will, at the conclusion of the work, be returned to the United States. The contract also provided that no patent rights would accrue to the company.

7.8. The specific responsibilities assumed by du Pont were to engineer, design, and construct a small-scale semi-works at the Clinton Engineer Works in Tennessee and to engineer, design, construct, and operate a large-scale plutonium production plant of large capacity at the Hanford Engineer Works in the State of Washington. Because of its close connection with fundamental research, the Clinton semi-works was to be operated under the direction of the University of Chicago. A large number of key technical people from du Pont were to be used on a loan basis at Chicago and at Clinton, to provide the University with much needed personnel, particularly men with industrial experience, and to train certain of such personnel for future service at Hanford.

7.9. Inasmuch as du Pont was being asked to step out of its normal role in chemistry into a new field involving nuclear physics, it was agreed that it would be necessary for them to depend most heavily upon the Metallurgical Laboratory of the University of Chicago for fundamental research and development data and for advice. The du Pont Company had engineering and industrial experience, but it needed the Metallurgical Laboratory for nuclear-physics and radiochemistry experience. The Metallurgical Laboratory conducted the fundamental research on problems bearing on the design and operation of the semi-works and large-scale production plants. It proposed the essential parts of the plutonium production and recovery processes and equipment, answered the many specific questions raised by du Pont, and studied and concurred in the final du Pont decisions and designs.

7.10. The principal purpose of the Clinton semi-works was development of methods of operation for plutonium recovery. The semi-works had to include of course, a unit for plutonium production, in order to provide plutonium to be recovered experimentally. In the time and with the information available, the Clinton production unit could not be designed to be an early edition of the Hanford production units which, therefore, had to be designed, constructed and operated without major guidance from Clinton experience. In fact, even the Hanford recovery

units had to be far along in design and procurement of equipment before Clinton results became available. However, the
Clinton semi-works proved to be an extremely important tool in
the solution of the many completely new problems encountered
at Hanford. It also produced small quantities of plutonium
which, along with Metallurgical Laboratory data on the properties of plutonium, enabled research in the use of this material
to be advanced many months.

Choice of Plant Site

7.11. Once the scale of production had been agreed upon
and the responsibilities assigned, the nature of the plant and its
whereabouts had to be decided. The site in the Tennessee Valley,
known officially as the Clinton Engineer Works, had been acquired by the Army for the whole program as recommended in
the report to the President (see Chapter V).

7.12. Reconsideration at the end of 1942 led General Groves
to the conclusion that this site was not sufficiently isolated for a
large-scale plutonium production plant. At that time, it was
conceivable that conditions might arise under which a large pile
might spread radioactive material over a large enough area to
endanger neighboring centers of population. In addition to the
requirement of isolation, there remained the requirement of a
large power supply which had originally determined the choice
of the Tennessee site. To meet these two requirements a new site
was chosen and acquired on the Columbia River in the central
part of the State of Washington near the Grand Coulee power
line. This site was known as the Hanford Engineer Works.

7.13. Since the Columbia River is the finest supply of pure
cold river water in this country, the Hanford site was well suited
to either the helium-cooled plant originally planned or to the
water-cooled plant actually erected. The great distances separating the home office of du Pont in Wilmington, Delaware, the
pilot plant at Clinton, Tennessee, the Metallurgical Laboratory
at Chicago, and the Hanford site were extremely inconvenient,
but this separation could not be avoided. Difficulties also were

inherent in bringing workmen to the site and in providing living accommodations for them.

Choice of Type of Plant

7.14. It was really too early in the development to make a carefully weighed decision as to the best type of plutonium production plant. Yet a choice had to be made so that design could be started and construction begun as soon as possible. Actually a tentative choice was made and then changed.

7.15. In November 1942, the helium-cooled plant was the first choice of the Metallurgical Laboratory. Under the direction of T. Moore and M. C. Leverett, preliminary plans for such a plant had been worked out. The associated design studies were used as bases for choice of site, choice of accessory equipment, etc. Although these studies had been undertaken partly because it had been felt that they could be carried through more quickly for a helium-cooled plant than for a water-cooled plant, many difficulties were recognized. Meanwhile the theoretical group under Wigner, with the cooperation of the engineering personnel, had been asked to prepare a report on a water-cooled plant of high power output. This group had been interested in water-cooling almost from the beginning of the project and was able to incorporate the results of its studies in a report issued on January 9, 1943. This report contained many important ideas that were incorporated in the design of the production plant erected at Hanford.

7.16. When du Pont came into the picture, it at first accepted the proposal of a helium-cooled plant but after further study decided in favor of water cooling. The reasons for the change were numerous. Those most often mentioned were the hazard from leakage of a high-pressure gas coolant carrying radioactive impurities, the difficulty of getting large blowers quickly, the large amount of helium required, the difficulty of loading and unloading uranium from the pile, and the relatively low power output per kilogram of uranium metal. These considerations had to be balanced against the peculiar disadvantages of a water-cooled plant, principally the greater complexity of the pile itself and the dangers of corrosion.

7.17. Like so many decisions in this project, the choice between various types of plant had to be based on incomplete scientific information. The information is still incomplete, but there is general agreement that water cooling was the wise choice.

THE PROBLEMS OF PLANT DESIGN

SPECIFICATION OF THE OVERALL PROBLEM

7.18. In Chapter II of this report we attempted to define the general problem of the uranium project as it appeared in the summer of 1940. We now wish to give precise definition to the problem of the design of a large-scale plant for the production of plutonium. The objective had already been delimited by decisions as to scale of production, type of plant, and site. As it then stood, the specific problem was to design a water-cooled graphite-moderated pile (or several such piles) with associated chemical separation plant to produce a specified, relatively large amount of plutonium each day, the plant to be built at the Hanford site beside the Columbia River. Needless to say, speed of construction and efficiency of operation were prime considerations.

NATURE OF THE LATTICE

7.19. The lattices we have been describing heretofore consisted of lumps of uranium imbedded in the graphite moderator. There are two objections to such a type of lattice for production purposes: first, it is difficult to remove the uranium without disassembling the pile; second, it is difficult to concentrate the coolant at the uranium lumps, which are the points of maximum production of heat. It was fairly obvious that both these difficulties could be avoided if a rod lattice rather than a point lattice could be used, that is, if the uranium could be concentrated along lines passing through the moderator instead of being situated merely at points. There was little doubt that the rod arrangement would be excellent structurally and mechanically, but there was real doubt as to whether it was possible to build such a lattice which would still have a multiplication factor k greater than unity. This became a problem for both the theoretical and experimental physicists. The theoretical physicists had to compute what was the optimum spacing and diameter of uranium rods; the experimental physicists had to perform exponential experiments on lattices of this type in order to check the findings of the theoretical group.

LOADING AND UNLOADING

7.20. Once the idea of a lattice with cylindrical symmetry was accepted, it became evident that the pile could be unloaded and reloaded without disassembly since the uranium could be pushed out of the cylindrical channels in the graphite moderator and new uranium inserted. The decision had to be made as to whether the uranium should be in the form of long rods, which had advantages from the nuclear-physics point of view, or of relatively short cylindrical pieces, which had advantages from the point of view of handling. In either case, the materials would be so very highly radioactive that unloading would have to be carried out by remote control, and the unloaded uranium would have to be handled by remote control from behind shielding.

POSSIBLE MATERIALS; CORROSION

7.21. If water was to be used as coolant, it would have to be conveyed to the regions where heat was generated through channels of some sort. Since graphite pipes were not practical, some other kind of pipe would have to be used. But the choice of the material for the pipe, like the choice of all the materials to be used in the pile, was limited by nuclear-physics considerations. The pipes must be made of some material whose absorption cross section for neutrons was not large enough to bring the value of k below unity. Furthermore, the pipes must be made of material which would not disintegrate under the heavy density of neutron and gamma radiation present in the pile. Finally, the pipes must meet all ordinary requirements of cooling-system pipes: they must not leak; they must not corrode; they must not warp.

7.22. From the nuclear-physics point of view there were seven possible materials (Pb, Bi, Be, Al, Mg, Zn, Sn), none of which had high neutron-absorption cross sections. No beryllium tubing was available, and of all the other metals only aluminum was thought to be possible from a corrosion point of view. But it was by no means certain that aluminum would be satisfactory, and doubts about the corrosion of the aluminum pipe were not settled until the plant had actually operated for some time.

7.23. While the choice of material for the piping was very difficult, similar choices—involving both nuclear-physics criteria and radiation-resistance criteria—had to be made for all other materials that were to be used in the pile. For example, the electric insulating materials to be used in any instruments buried in the pile must not disintegrate under the radiation. In certain instances where control or experimental probes had to be inserted and removed from the pile, the likelihood had to be borne in mind that the probes would become intensely radioactive as a result of their exposure in the pile and that the degree to which this would occur would depend on the material used.

7.24. Finally, it was not known what effect the radiation fields in the pile would have on the graphite and the uranium. It was later found that the electric resistance, the elasticity, and the heat conductivity of the graphite all change with exposure to intense neutron radiation.

Protection of the Uranium from Corrosion

7.25. The most efficient cooling procedure would have been to have the water flowing in direct contact with the uranium in which the heat was being produced. Indications were that this was probably out of the question because the uranium would react chemically with the water, at least to a sufficient extent to put a dangerous amount of radioactive material into solution and probably to the point of disintegrating the uranium slugs. Therefore it was necessary to find some method of protecting the uranium from direct contact with the water. Two possibilities were considered: one was some sort of coating, either by electroplating or dipping; the other was sealing the uranium slug in a protective jacket or "can." Strangely enough, this "canning problem" turned out to be one of the most difficult problems encountered in such piles.

WATER SUPPLY

7.26. The problem of dissipating thousands of kilowatts of energy is by no means a small one. How much water was needed depended, of course, on the maximum temperature to which the water could safely be heated and the maximum temperature to be expected in the intake from the Columbia River; certainly the water supply requirement was comparable to that of a fair-sized city. Pumping stations, filtration and treatment plants all had to be provided. Furthermore, the system had to be a very reliable one; it was necessary to provide fast-operating controls to shut down the chain-reacting unit in a hurry in case of failure of the water supply. If it was decided to use "once-through" cooling instead of recirculation, a retention basin would be required so that the radioactivity induced in the water might die down before the water was returned to the river. The volume of water discharged was going to be so great that such problems of radioactivity were important, and therefore the minimum time that the water must be held for absolute safety had to be determined.

CONTROLS AND INSTRUMENTATION

7.27. The control problem was very similar to that discussed in connection with the first chain-reacting pile except that everything was on a larger scale and was, therefore, potentially more dangerous. It was necessary to provide operating controls which would automatically keep the pile operating at a determined power level. Such controls had to be connected with instruments in the pile which would measure neutron density or some other property which indicated the power level. There would also have to be emergency controls which would operate almost instantaneously if the power level showed signs of rapid increase or if there was any interruption of the water supply. It was highly desirable that there be some means of detecting incipient difficulties such as the plugging of a single water tube or a break in the coating of one of the uranium slugs. All these controls and instruments had to be operated from behind the thick shielding walls described below.

SHIELDING

7.28. As we have mentioned a number of times, the radiation given off from a pile operating at a high power level is so strong as to make it quite impossible for any of the operating personnel to go near the pile. Furthermore, this radiation, particularly the neutrons, has a pronounced capacity for leaking out through holes or cracks in barriers. The whole of a power pile therefore has to be enclosed in very thick walls of concrete, steel, or other absorbing material. But at the same time it has to be possible to load and unload the pile through these shields and to carry the water supply in and out through the shields. The shields should not only be radiation-tight but air-tight since air exposed to the radiation in the pile would become radioactive.

7.29. The radiation dangers that require shielding in the pile continue through a large part of the separation plant. Since the fission products associated with the production of the plutonium are highly radioactive, the uranium after ejection from the pile must be handled by remote control from behind shielding and must be shielded during transportation to the separation plant. All the stages of the separation plant, including analyses, must be handled by remote control from behind shields up to the point where the plutonium is relatively free of radioactive fission products.

MAINTENANCE

7.30. The problem of maintenance is very simply stated. There could not be any maintenance inside the shield or pile once the pile had operated. The same remark applies to a somewhat lesser extent to the separation unit, where it was probable that a shut-down for servicing could be effected, provided, of course, that adequate remotely-controlled decontamination processes were carried out in order to reduce the radiation intensity below the level dangerous to personnel. The maintenance problem for the auxiliary parts of the plant was normal except for the extreme importance of having stand-by pumping and power equipment to prevent a sudden accidental breakdown of the cooling system.

SCHEDULE OF LOADING AND UNLOADING

7.31. Evidently the amount of plutonium in an undisturbed operating pile increases with time of operation. Since Pu-239 itself undergoes fission its formation tends to maintain the chain reaction, while the gradual disappearance of the U-235 and the appearance of fission products with large neutron absorption cross sections tend to stop the reaction. The determination of when a producing pile should be shut down and the plutonium extracted involves a nice balancing of these factors against time schedules, material costs, separation-process efficiency, etc. Strictly speaking, this problem is one of operation rather than of design of the plant, but some thought had to be given to it in order to plan the flow of uranium slugs to the pile and from the pile to the separation plant.

SIZE OF UNITS

7.32. We have been speaking of the production capacity of the plant only in terms of overall production rate. Naturally, a given rate of production might be achieved in a single large pile or in a number of smaller ones. The principal advantage of the smaller piles would be the reduction in construction time for the first pile, the possibility of making alterations in later piles, and—perhaps most important—the improbability of simultaneous breakdown of all piles. The disadvantage of small piles is that they require disproportionately large amounts of uranium, moderator, etc. There is, in fact, a preferred "natural size" of pile which can be roughly determined on theoretical grounds.

General Nature of the Separation Plant

7.33. As we have already pointed out, the slugs coming from the pile are highly radioactive and therefore must be processed by remote control in shielded compartments. The general scheme to be followed was suggested in the latter part of 1942, particularly in connection with plans for the Clinton separation plant. This scheme was to build a "canyon" which would consist of a series of compartments with heavy concrete walls arranged in a line and almost completely buried in the ground. Each compartment would contain the necessary dissolving or precipitating tanks or centrifuges. The slugs would come into the compartment at one end of the canyon; they would then be dissolved and go through the various stages of solution, precipitation, oxidation, or reduction, being pumped from one compartment to the next until a solution of plutonium free from uranium and fission products came out in the last compartment. As in the case of the pile, everything would be operated by remote control from above ground, but the operations would be far more complicated than in the case of the pile. However, as far as the chemical operations themselves were concerned, their general nature was not so far removed from the normal fields of activity of the chemists involved.

Analytical Control

7.34. In the first stages of the separation process even the routine analysis of samples which was necessary in checking the operation of the various chemical processes had to be done by remote control. Such testing was facilitated, however, by use of radioactive methods of analysis as well as conventional chemical analyses.

Waste Disposal

7.35. The raw material (uranium) is not dangerously radioactive. The desired product (plutonium) does not give off penetrating radiation, but the combination of its alpha-ray activity and chemical properties makes it one of the most dangerous substances known if it once gets into the body. However, the really troublesome materials are the fission products, i.e., the major fragments into which uranium is split by fission. The fission products are very radioactive and include some thirty elements. Among them are radioactive xenon and radioactive iodine. These are released in considerable quantity when the slugs are dissolved and must be disposed of with special care. High stacks must be built which will carry off these gases along with the acid fumes from the first dissolving unit, and it must be established that the mixing of the radioactive gases with the atmosphere will not endanger the surrounding territory. (As in all other matters of health, the tolerance standards that were set and met were so rigid as to leave not the slightest probability of danger to the health of the community or operating personnel.)

7.36. Most of the other fission products can be retained in solution but must eventually be disposed of. Of course, possible pollution of the adjacent river must be considered. (In fact, the standards of safety set and met with regard to river pollution were so strict that neither people nor fish down the river can possibly be affected.)

RECOVERY OF URANIUM

7.37. Evidently, even if the uranium were left in the pile until all the U-235 had undergone fission, there would still be a large amount of U-238 which had not been converted to plutonium. Actually the process is stopped long before this stage is reached. Uranium is an expensive material and the total available supply is seriously limited. Therefore the possibility of recovering it after the plutonium is separated must be considered. Originally there was no plan for recovery, but merely the intention of storing the uranium solution. Later, methods of large-scale recovery were developed.

CORROSION IN THE SEPARATION PLANT

7.38. An unusual feature of the chemical processes involved was that these processes occur in the presence of a high density of radiation. Therefore the containers used may corrode more rapidly than they would under normal circumstances. Furthermore, any such corrosion will be serious because of the difficulty of access. For a long time, information was sadly lacking on these dangers.

EFFECT OF RADIATION ON CHEMICAL REACTIONS

7.39. The chemical reactions proposed for an extraction process were, of course, tested in the laboratory. However, they could not be tested with appreciable amounts of plutonium nor could they be tested in the presence of radiation of anything like the expected intensity. Therefore it was realized that a process found to be successful in the laboratory might not work in the plant.

CHOICE OF PROCESS

7.40. The description given above as to what was to happen in the successive chambers in the canyon was very vague. This was necessarily so, since even by January 1943 no decision had been made as to what process would be used for the extraction and purification of plutonium. The major problem before the Chemistry Division of the Metallurgical Laboratory was the selection of the best process for the plant.

THE HEALTH PROBLEM

7.41. Besides the hazards normally present during construction and operation of a large chemical plant, dangers of a new kind were expected here. Two types of radiation hazard were anticipated—neutrons generated in the pile, and alpha particles, beta particles, and gamma rays emitted by products of the pile. Although the general effects of these radiations had been proved to be similar to those of X-rays, very little detailed knowledge was available. Obviously the amounts of radioactive material to be handled were many times greater than had ever been encountered before.

7.42. The health group had to plan three programs: (1) provision of instruments and clinical tests to detect any evidence of dangerous exposure of the personnel; (2) research on the effects of radiation on persons, instruments, etc.; and (3) estimates of what shielding and safety measures must be incorporated in the design and plan of operation of the plant.

THE PROPERTIES OF PLUTONIUM

7.43. Although we were embarking on a major enterprise to produce plutonium, we still had less than a milligram to study and still had only limited familiarity with its properties. The study of plutonium, therefore, remained a major problem of the Metallurgical Laboratory.

THE TRAINING OF OPERATORS

7.44. Evidently the operation of a full-scale plant of the type planned would require a large and highly skilled group of operators. Although du Pont had a tremendous background of experience in the operation of various kinds of chemical plant, this was something new and it was evident that operating personnel would need special training. Such training was carried out partly in Chicago and its environs, but principally at the Clinton Laboratories.

THE NEED FOR FURTHER INFORMATION

7.45. In the preceding paragraphs of this chapter we have outlined the problems confronting the group charged with designing and building a plutonium production plant. In Chapter VI the progress in this field up to the end of 1942 was reviewed. Throughout these chapters it is made clear that a great deal more information was required to assure the success of the plant. Such answers as had been obtained to most of the questions were only tentative. Consequently research had to be pushed simultaneously with planning and construction.

THE RESEARCH PROGRAM

7.46. To meet the need for further information, research programs were laid out for the Metallurgical Laboratory and the Clinton Laboratory. The following passage is an excerpt from the 1943 program of the Metallurgical Project:

"*Product Production Studies.* These include all aspects of the research, development and semi-works studies necessary for the design, construction, and operation of chain-reacting piles to produce plutonium or other materials.

Pile Characteristics. Theoretical studies and experiments on lattice structures to predict behavior in high-level piles, such as temperature and barometric effects, neutron characteristics, pile poisoning, etc.

Control of Reacting Units. Design and experimental tests of devices for controlling rate of reaction in piles.

Cooling of Reacting Units. Physical studies of coolant material, engineering problems of circulation, corrosion, erosion, etc.

Instrumentation. Development of instruments and technique for monitoring pile and surveying radiation throughout plant area.

Protection. Shielding, biological effects of radiation at pile and clinical effects of operations associated with pile.

Materials. Study of physical (mechanical and nuclear) properties of construction and process materials used in pile construction and operation.

Activation Investigations. Production of experimental amounts of radioactive materials in cyclotron and in piles and study of activation of materials by neutrons, protons, electrons, gamma rays, etc.

Pile Operation. Study of pile operation procedures such as materials handling, instrument operation, etc.

Process Design. Study of possible production processes as a whole leading to detailed work in other categories.

"*Product Recovery Studies.* These include all aspects of the work necessary for the development of processes for the extraction of plutonium and possible by-products from the pile material and their preparation in purified form. Major effort at the Metallurgical Laboratory will be on a single process to be selected by June 1, 1943 for the production of plutonium, but alternatives will continue to be studied both at the Metallurgical Laboratory and Clinton with whatever manpower is available.

Separation. Processes for solution of uranium, extraction of plutonium and decontamination by removal of fission products.

Concentration, Purification and Product Reduction. Processes leading to production of plutonium as pure metal, and study of properties of plutonium necessary to its production.

Wastes. Disposal and possible methods of recovery of fission products and metal from wastes.

Instrumentation. Development and testing of instruments for monitoring chemical processes and surveying radiation throughout the area.

Protection. Shielding studies, determination of biological effects of radioactive dusts, liquids, solids, and other process materials, and protective measures.

Materials. Corrosion of equipment materials, and radiation stability. Necessary purity and purity analysis of process materials, etc.

Recovery of Activated Materials. Development of methods and actual recovery of activated material (tracers, etc.) from cyclotron and pile-activated materials.

Operations Studies. Equipment performance, process control, material handling operations, etc.

Process Design. Study of product recovery processes as a whole (wet processes, physical methods) leading to detailed work in other categories.

"*Fundamental Research.* Studies of the fundamental physical, chemical and biological phenomena occurring in chain-reacting piles, and basic properties of all materials involved. Although the primary emphasis at Clinton is on the semi-works level, much fundamental research will require Clinton conditions (high radiation intensity, large scale processes).

Nuclear Physics. Fundamental properties of nuclear fission such as cross section, neutron yield, fission species, etc. Other nuclear properties important to processes, such as cross sections, properties of moderators, neutron effect on materials, etc.

General Physics. Basic instrument (electronic, ionization, optical, etc.) research, atomic mass determinations, neutron, α, β, γ radiation studies, X-ray investigations, etc.

Radiation Chemistry. Effects of radiation on chemical processes and chemical reactions produced by radiation.

Nuclear Chemistry. Tracing of fission products, disintegration constants, chains, investigation of nuclei of possible use to project.

Product Chemistry. Chemical properties of various products and basic studies in separation and purification of products.

General Chemistry. Chemistry of primary materials and materials associated with process, including by-products.

General Biology. Fundamental studies of effects of radiation on living matter, metabolism of important materials, etc.

Clinical Investigations. Basic investigations, such as hematology, pathology, etc.

Metallurgical Studies. Properties of U, Pu, Be, etc.

Engineering Studies. Phenomena basic to corrosion and similar studies essential to continued engineering development of processes."

7.47. An examination of this program gives an idea of the great range of investigations which were considered likely to give relevant information. Many of the topics listed are not specific research problems such as might be solved by a small team of scientists working for a few months but are whole fields of investigation that might be studied with profit for years. It was necessary to pick the specific problems that were likely to give the most immediately useful results but at the same time it was desirable to try to uncover general principles. For example, the effect of radiation on the properties of materials ("radiation stability") was almost entirely unknown. It was necessary both to make empirical tests on particular materials that might be used in a pile and to devise general theories of the observed effects. Every effort was made to relate all work to the general objective: a successful production plant.

ORGANIZATION OF THE PROJECT

7.48. There have been many changes in the organization and personnel of the project. During most of the period of construction at Clinton and Hanford, A. H. Compton was director of the Metallurgical Project; S. K. Allison was director of the Metallurgical Laboratory at Chicago; and M. D. Whitaker was director of the Clinton Laboratory. The Chicago group was organized in four divisions: physics, chemistry, technology, and health. Later the Physics Division was split into general physics and nuclear physics. R. L. Doan was research director at Clinton but there was no corresponding position at Chicago. Among others who have been associate or assistant laboratory or project directors or have been division directors are S. T. Cantril, C. M. Cooper, F. Daniels, A. J. Dempster, E. Fermi, J. Franck, N. Hilberry, T. R. Hogness, W. C. Johnson, H. D. Smyth, J. C. Stearns, R. S. Stone, H. C. Vernon, W. W. Watson, and E.

Wigner. Beginning in 1943 C. H. Thomas of the Monsanto Chemical Company acted as chairman of a committee on the Chemistry and Metallurgy of Plutonium. This committee correlated the activities of the Metallurgical Laboratory with those at Los Alamos (see Chapter XII) and elsewhere. Later the Monsanto Chemical Company did some work on important special problems arising in connection with the Los Alamos work.

7.49. It was the responsibility of these men to see that the research program described above was carried out and that significant results were reported to du Pont. It was their responsibility also to answer questions raised by du Pont and to approve or criticize plans submitted by du Pont.

COOPERATION BETWEEN THE METALLURGICAL LABORATORY AND DU PONT

7.50. Since du Pont was the design and construction organization and the Metallurgical Laboratory was the research organization, it was obvious that close cooperation was essential. Not only did du Pont need answers to specific questions, but they could benefit by criticism and suggestions on the many points where the Metallurgical group was especially well-informed. Similarly, the Metallurgical group could profit by the knowledge of du Pont on many technical questions of design, construction, and operation. To promote this kind of cooperation du Pont stationed one of their physicists, J. B. Miles, at Chicago, and had many other du Pont men, particularly C. H. Greenewalt, spend much of their time at Chicago. Miles and Greenewalt regularly attended meetings of the Laboratory Council. There was no similar reciprocal arrangement although many members of the laboratory visited Wilmington informally. In addition, J. A. Wheeler was transferred from Chicago to Wilmington and became a member of the du Pont staff. There was, of course, constant exchange of reports and letters, and conferences were held frequently between Compton and R. Williams of du Pont. Whitaker spent much of his time at Wilmington during the period when the Clinton plant was being designed and constructed.

SUMMARY

7.51. By January 1943, the decision had been made to build a plutonium production plant with a large capacity. This meant a pile developing thousands of kilowatts and a chemical separation plant to extract the product. The du Pont Company was to design, construct, and operate the plant; the Metallurgical Laboratory was to do the necessary research. A site was chosen on the Columbia River at Hanford, Washington. A tentative decision to build a helium-cooled plant was reversed in favor of water-cooling. The principal problems were those involving lattice design, loading and unloading, choice of materials particularly with reference to corrosion and radiation, water supply, controls and instrumentation, health hazards, chemical separation process, and design of the separation plant. Plans were made for the necessary fundamental and technical research and for the training of operators. Arrangements were made for liaison between du Pont and the Metallurgical Laboratory.

CHAPTER VIII. THE PLUTONIUM PROBLEM
JANUARY 1943 TO JUNE 1945

INTRODUCTION

8.1. The necessity for pushing the design and construction of the full-scale plutonium plant simultaneously with research and development inevitably led to a certain amount of confusion and inefficiency. It became essential to investigate many alternative processes. It became necessary to investigate all possible causes of failure even when the probability of their becoming serious was very small. Now that the Hanford plant is producing plutonium successfully, we believe it is fair to say that a large percentage of the results of investigation made between the end of 1942 and the end of 1944 will never be used—at least not for the originally intended purposes. Nevertheless had the Hanford plant run into difficulties, any one of the now superfluous investigations might have furnished just the information required to convert failure into success. Even now it is impossible to say that future improvements may not depend on the results of researches that seem unimportant today.

8.2. It is estimated that thirty volumes will be required for a complete report of the significant scientific results of researches conducted under the auspices of the Metallurgical Project. Work was done on every item mentioned on the research program presented in the last chapter. In the present account it would be obviously impossible to give more than a brief abstract of all these researches. We believe this would be unsatisfactory and that it is preferable to give a general discussion of the chain-reacting units and separation plants as they now operate, with some discussion of the earlier developments.

THE CHAIN REACTION IN A PILE

8.3. In Chapter I and other early chapters we have given brief accounts of the fission process, pile operation, and chemical separation. We shall now review these topics from a somewhat different point of view before describing the plutonium production plants themselves.

8.4. The operation of a pile depends on the passage of neutrons through matter and on the nature of the collisions of neutrons with the nuclei encountered. The collisions of principal importance are the following:

I. Collisions in which neutrons are scattered and lose appreciable amounts of energy. (a) Inelastic collisions of fast neutrons with uranium nuclei. (b) Elastic collisions of fast or moderately fast neutrons with the light nuclei of the moderator material; these collisions serve to reduce the neutron energy to very low (so-called thermal) energies.

II. Collisions in which the neutrons are absorbed. (a) Collisions which result in fission of nuclei and give fission products and additional neutrons. (b) Collisions which result in the formation of new nuclei which subsequently disintegrate radioactively (e.g., $_{92}U^{239}$ which produces $_{94}Pu^{239}$).

8.5. Only the second class of collision requires further discussion. As regards collisions of Type II (a), the most important in a pile are the collisions between neutrons and U-235, but the high-energy fission of U-238 and the thermal fission of Pu-239 also take place. Collisions of Type II (b) are chiefly those between neutrons and U-238. Such collisions occur for neutrons of all energies, but they are most likely to occur for neutrons whose energies lie in the "resonance" region located somewhat above thermal energies. The sequence of results of the Type II (b) collision is represented as follows:

$$_{92}U^{238} + {}_{0}n^1 \rightarrow {}_{92}U^{239} + \text{gamma rays}$$
$$_{92}U^{239} \xrightarrow[23 \text{ min.}]{} {}_{93}Np^{239} + {}_{-1}e^0$$
$$_{93}Np^{239} \xrightarrow[2.3 \text{ days}]{} {}_{94}Pu^{239} + {}_{-1}e^0 + \text{gamma rays}$$

8.6. Any other non-fission absorption processes are important chiefly because they waste neutrons; they occur in the moderator, in U-235, in the coolant, in the impurities originally present, in the fission products, and even in plutonium itself.

8.7. Since the object of the chain reaction is to generate plutonium, we would like to absorb all excess neutrons in U-238, leaving just enough neutrons to produce fission and thus to maintain the chain reaction. Actually the tendency of the neutrons to be absorbed by the dominant isotope U-238 is so great compared to their tendency to produce fission in the 140-times-rarer U-235 that the principal design effort had to be directed toward favoring the fission (as by using a moderator, a suitable lattice, materials of high purity, etc.,) in order to maintain the chain reaction.

Life History of One Generation of Neutrons*

8.8. All the chain-reacting piles designed by the Metallurgical Laboratory or with its cooperation consist of four categories of material—the uranium metal, the moderator, the coolant, and the auxiliary materials such as water tubes, casings of uranium, control strips or rods, impurities, etc. All the piles depend on stray neutrons from spontaneous fission or cosmic rays to initiate the reaction.

8.9. Suppose that the pile were to be started by simultaneous release (in the uranium metal) of N high-energy neutrons. Most of these neutrons originally have energies above the threshold energy of fission of U-238. However, as the neutrons pass back and forth in the metal and moderator, they suffer numerous inelastic collisions with the uranium and numerous elastic collisions with the moderator, and all these collisions serve to reduce the energies below that threshold. Specifically, in a typical graphite-moderated pile a neutron that has escaped from the uranium into the graphite travels on the average about 2.5 cm between collisions and makes on the *average* about 200 elastic collisions before passing from the graphite back into the uranium. Since at each such collision a neutron loses on the average about one sixth of its energy, a one-Mev neutron is reduced to thermal

* See drawing facing p. 35.

energy (usually taken to be 0.025 electron volt) considerably before completing a single transit through the graphite. There are, of course, many neutrons that depart from this average behavior, and there will be enough fissions produced by fast neutrons to enhance slightly the number of neutrons present. The enhancement may be taken into account by multiplying the original number of neutrons N by a factor ϵ which is called the fast-fission effect or the fast-multiplication factor.

8.10. As the average energy of the Nϵ neutrons present continues to fall, inelastic collision in the uranium becomes unimportant, the energy being reduced essentially only in the moderator. However, the chance of non-fission absorption (resonance capture) in U-238 becomes significant as the intermediate or resonance energy region is reached. Actually quite a number of neutrons in this energy region will be absorbed regardless of choice of lattice design. The effect of such capture may be expressed by multiplying Nϵ by a factor p, (which is always less than one) called the "resonance escape probability" which is the probability that a given neutron starting with energy above the resonance region will reach thermal energies without absorption in U-238. Thus from the original N high-energy neutrons we obtain Nϵp neutrons of thermal energy.

8.11. Once a neutron has reached thermal energy the chance that it will lose more energy by collision is no greater than the chance that it will gain energy. Consequently the neutrons will remain at this average energy until they are absorbed. In the thermal-energy region the chance for absorption of the neutron by the moderator, the coolant and the auxiliary materials is greater than at higher energies. At any rate it is found that we introduce little error into our calculations by assuming all such unwanted absorption takes place in this energy region. We now introduce a factor f, called the thermal utilization factor, which is defined as the probability that a given thermal neutron will be absorbed in the uranium. Thus from the original N fast neutrons we have obtained Nϵpf thermal neutrons which are absorbed by uranium.

8.12. Although there are several ways in which the normal mixture of uranium isotopes can absorb neutrons, the reader may recall that we defined in a previous chapter a quantity η, which is the number of fission neutrons produced for each thermal neutron absorbed in uranium regardless of the details of the process. If, therefore, we multiply the number of thermal neutrons absorbed in uranium, Nϵpf, by η, we have the number of new high speed neutrons generated by the original N high speed neutrons in the course of their lives. If Nϵpfη is greater than N, we have a chain reaction and the number of neutrons is continually increasing. Evidently the product ϵpfη = k_∞, the multiplication factor already defined in Chapter IV.

8.13. Note that no mention has been made of neutrons escaping from the pile. Such mention has been deliberately avoided since the value of k_∞ as defined above applies to an infinite lattice. From the known values of k_∞ and the fact that these piles do operate, one finds that the percentage of neutrons escaping cannot be very great. As we saw in Chapter II, the escape of neutrons becomes relatively less important as the size of the pile increases. If it is necessary to introduce in the pile a large amount of auxiliary material such as cooling-system pipes, it is necessary to build a somewhat larger pile to counteract the increase in absorption.

8.14. To sum up, a pile operates by reducing high-energy neutrons to thermal energies by the use of a moderator-lattice arrangement, then allowing the thermal-energy neutrons to be absorbed by uranium, causing fission which regenerates further high-energy neutrons. The regeneration of neutrons is aided slightly by the fast neutron effect; it is impeded by resonance absorption during the process of energy reduction, by absorption in graphite and other materials, and by neutron escape.

THE EFFECTS OF REACTION PRODUCTS ON THE MULTIPLICATION FACTOR

8.15. Even at the high power level used in the Hanford piles, only a few grams of U-238 and of U-235 are used up per day per

Above: Administration Building for the Manhattan Engineer District at Oak Ridge, Tenn. *Below*: Hanford, near Pasco, Wash., which at one time housed thousands of workers who built the plants at the Hanford Engineer Works. Now a ghost town.

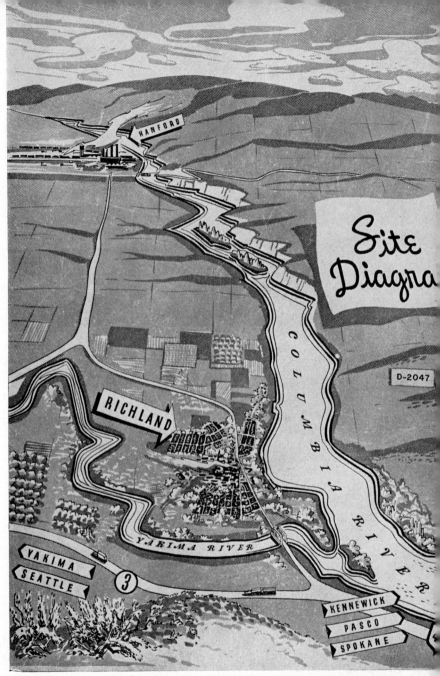

Site
Diagra

D-2047

HANFORD

RICHLAND

COLUMBIA RIVER

YAKIMA RIVER

YAKIMA
SEATTLE

③

KENNEWICK

PASCO

SPOKANE

Site diagram of the Hanford Engineer Works near Pasco, Wash.

A pilot plant at the Clinton Engineer Works at Oak Ridge, Tenn.

One of the production areas at the Clinton Engineer Works at Oak Ridge, Tenn.

One of the production areas at the Hanford Engineer Works near Pasco, Wash.

One of the production plants at the Clinton Engineer Works at Oak Ridge, Tenn.

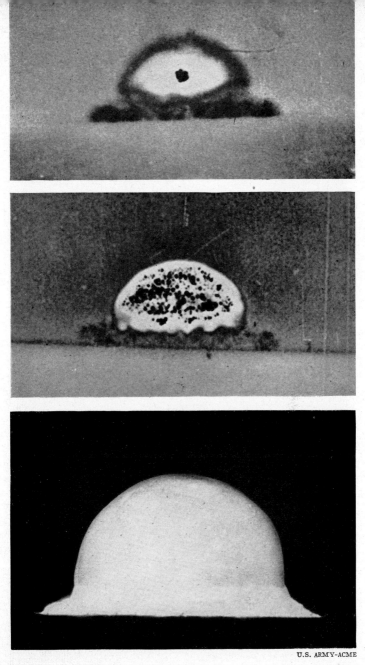

Initial test of the atomic bomb in New Mexico on July 16, from a distance of 6 miles. *Above*: The start of the explosion. This small cloud later rose to a height of 40,000 feet. *Center*: Multi-colored cloud from the explosion. Black areas were brighter than the sun itself, according to observers. *Below*: A later stage of the development of the cloud.

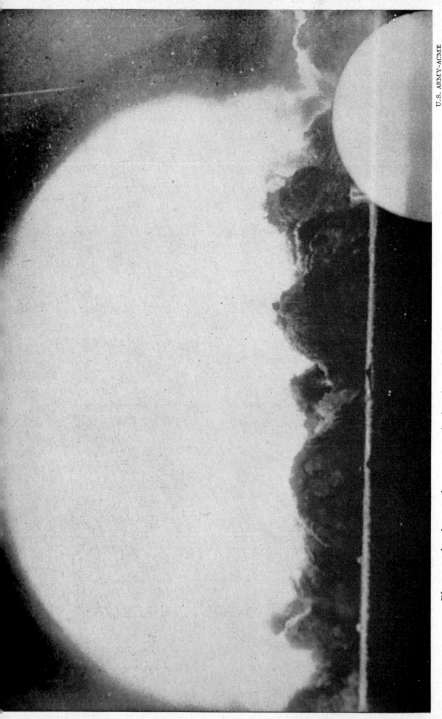

Photograph taken at the moment the bomb exploded, from a distance of 6 miles. It is believed

million grams of uranium present. Nevertheless the effects of these changes are very important. As the U-235 is becoming depleted, the concentration of plutonium is increasing. Fortunately, plutonium itself is fissionable by thermal neutrons and so tends to counterbalance the decrease of U-235 as far as maintaining the chain reaction is concerned. However, other fission products are being produced also. These consist typically of unstable and relatively unfamiliar nuclei so that it was originally impossible to predict how great an undesirable effect they would have on the multiplication constant. Such deleterious effects are called poisoning.

THE REACTION PRODUCTS AND THE SEPARATION PROBLEM

8.16. There are two main parts of the plutonium production process at Hanford: actual production in the pile, and separation of the plutonium from the uranium slugs in which it is formed. We turn now to a discussion of the second part, the separation process.

8.17. The uranium slugs containing plutonium also contain other elements resulting from the fission of U-235. When a U-235 nucleus undergoes fission, it emits one or more neutrons and splits into two fragments of comparable size and of total mass 235 or less. Apparently fission into precisely equal masses rarely occurs, the most abundant fragments being a fragment of mass number between 134 and 144 and a fragment of mass number between 100 and 90. Thus there are two groups of fission products: a heavy group with mass numbers extending approximately from 127 to 154, and a light group from approximately 115 to 83. These fission products are in the main unstable isotopes of the thirty or so known elements in these general ranges of mass number. Typically they decay by successive beta emissions accompanied by gamma radiation finally to form known stable nuclei. The half-lives of the various intermediate nuclei range from fractions of a second to a year or more; several of the important species have half-lives of the order of a month or so.

About twenty different elements are present in significant concentration. The most abundant of these comprises slightly less than 10 per cent of the aggregate.

8.18. In addition to radioactive fission products, U-239 and Np-239 (intermediate products in the formation of plutonium) are present in the pile and are radioactive. The concentrations of all these products begin to build up at the moment the pile starts operating. Eventually the rate of radioactive decay equals the rate of formation so that the concentrations become constant. For example, the number of atoms of U-239 produced per second is constant for a pile operating at a fixed power level. According to the laws of radioactive disintegration, the number of U-239 atoms disappearing per second is proportional to the number of such atoms present and is thus increasing during the first few minutes or hours after the pile is put into operation. Consequently there soon will be practically as many nuclei disintegrating each second as are formed each second. Equilibrium concentrations for other nuclei will be approached in similar manner, the equilibrium concentration being proportional to the rate of formation of the nucleus and to its half-life. Products which are stable or of extremely long half-life (e.g., plutonium) will steadily increase in concentration for a considerable time. When the pile is stopped, the radioactivity of course continues, but at a continually diminishing absolute rate. Isotopes of very short half-life may "drop out of sight" in a few minutes or hours; others of longer half-life keep appreciably active for days or months. Thus at any time the concentrations of the various products in a recently stopped pile depend on what the power level was, on how long the pile ran, and on how long it has been shut down. Of course, the longer the pile has run, the larger is the concentration of plutonium and (unfortunately) the larger is the concentration of long-lived fission products. The longer the "cooling" period, i.e., the period between removal of material from the pile and chemical treatment, the lower is the radiation intensity from the fission products. A compromise must be made between such considerations as the desire for a long running and cooling time on the one hand and the desire for early extraction of the plutonium on the other hand.

8.19. Tables can be prepared showing the chemical concentrations of plutonium and the various fission products as functions of power level, length of operation, and length of cooling period. The half-life of the U-239 is so short that its concentration becomes negligible soon after the pile shuts down. The neptunium becomes converted fairly rapidly to plutonium. Of course, the total weight of fission products, stable and unstable, remains practically constant after the pile is stopped. For the Clinton and Hanford operating conditions the maximum plutonium concentration attained is so small as to add materially to the difficulty of chemical separation.

THE CHOICE OF A CHEMICAL SEPARATION PROCESS

8.20. The problem then is to make a chemical separation at the daily rate of, say, several grams of plutonium from several thousand grams of uranium contaminated with large amounts of dangerously radioactive fission products comprising twenty different elements. The problem is especially difficult as the plutonium purity requirements are very high indeed.

8.21. Four types of method for chemical separation were examined: volatility, absorption, solvent extraction, and precipitation. The work on absorption and solvent extraction methods has been extensive and such methods may be increasingly used in the main process or in waste recovery, but the Hanford Plant was designed for a precipitation process.

8.22.* The phenomena of co-precipitation, i.e., the precipitation of small concentrations of one element along with a "carrier" precipitate of some other element, had been commonly used in radioactive chemistry, and was adopted for plutonium separation. The early work on plutonium chemistry, confined as it was to minute amounts of the element, made great use of precipitation

* Paragraphs 8.22–8.26 are quoted or paraphrased from a general report of the Metallurgical Laboratory prepared in the spring of 1945.

reactions from which solubility properties could be deduced. It was therefore natural that precipitation methods of separation were the most advanced at the time when the plant design was started. It was felt that, should the several steps in the separations process have to be developed partly by the empirical approach, there would be less risk in the scale-up of a precipitation process than, for example, of one involving solid-phase reactions. In addition, the precipitation processes then in mind could be broken into a sequence of repeated operations (called cycles), thereby limiting the number of different equipment pieces requiring design and allowing considerable process change without equipment change. Thus, while the basic plant design was made with one method in mind, the final choice of a different method led to no embarrassments.

8.23. Most of the precipitation processes which have received serious consideration made use of an alternation between the (IV) and (VI) oxidation states of plutonium. Such processes involve a precipitation of plutonium (IV) with a certain compound as a carrier, then dissolution of the precipitate, oxidation of the plutonium to the (VI) state, and reprecipitation of the carrier compound while the plutonium (VI) remains in solution. Fission products which are not carried by these compounds remain in solution when plutonium (IV) is precipitated. The fission products which carry are removed from the plutonium when it is in the (VI) state. Successive oxidation-reduction cycles are carried out until the desired decontamination is achieved. The process of elimination of the fission products is called decontamination and the degree of elimination is tested by measuring the change in radioactivity of the material.

COMBINATION PROCESSES

8.24. It is possible to combine or couple the various types of process. Some advantages may be gained in this way since one type of process may supplement another. For example, a process which gives good decontamination might be combined advantageously with one which, while inefficient for decontamination, would be very efficient for separation from uranium.

8.25. At the time when it became necessary to decide on the process to serve as the basis for the design of the Hanford plant (June 1943), the choice, for reasons given above, was limited to precipitation processes and clearly lay between two such processes. However, the process as finally chosen actually represented a combination of the two.

8.26. The success of the separation process at Hanford has exceeded all expectations. The high yields and decontamination factors and the relative ease of operation have amply demonstrated the wisdom of its choice as a process. This choice was based on a knowledge of plutonium chemistry which had been gleaned from less than a milligram of plutonium. Further developments may make the present Hanford process obsolete, but the principal goal, which was to have a workable and efficient process for use as soon as the Hanford piles were delivering plutonium, has been attained.

THE ARGONNE LABORATORY

8.27. The Argonne Laboratory was constructed early in 1943 outside Chicago. The site, originally intended for a pilot plant, was later considered to be too near the city and was used for reconstructing the so-called West Stands pile which was originally built on the University of Chicago grounds and which was certainly innocuous. Under the direction of E. Fermi and his colleagues, H. L. Anderson, W. H. Zinn, G. Weil, and others, this pile has served as a prototype unit for studies of thermal stability, controls, instruments, and shielding, and as a neutron source for materials testing and neutron-physics studies. Furthermore, it has proved valuable as a training school for plant operators. More recently a heavy-water pile (see below) has been constructed there.

8.28. The first Argonne pile, a graphite-uranium pile, need not be described in detail. The materials and lattice structure are nearly identical to those which were used for the original

West Stands pile. The pile is a cube; it is surrounded by a shield and has controls and safety devices somewhat similar to those used later at Clinton. It has no cooling system and is normally run at a power level of only a few kilowatts. It has occasionally been run at high-power levels for very brief periods. Considering that it is merely a reconstruction of the first chain-reacting unit ever built, it is amazing that it has continued in operation for more than two years without developing any major troubles.

8.29. One of the most valuable uses of the Argonne pile has been the measurement of neutron-absorption cross sections of a great variety of elements which might be used in piles as structural members, etc., or which might be present in pile materials as impurities. These measurements are made by observing the change in the controls necessary to make k_{eff} equal to 1.00 when a known amount of the substance under study is inserted at a definite position in the pile. The results obtained were usually expressed in terms of "danger coefficients."

8.30. An opening at the top of the pile lets out a very uniform beam of thermal neutrons that can be used for exponential-pile experiments, for direct measurements of absorption cross sections, for Wilson cloud chamber studies, etc.

8.31. An interesting phenomenon occurring at the top of the pile is the production of a beam or flow of "cold" neutrons. If a sufficient amount of graphite is interposed between the upper surface of the pile and an observation point a few yards above, the neutron energy distribution is found to correspond to a temperature much lower than that of the graphite. This is presumed to be the result of a preferential transmission by the crystalline graphite of the slowest ("coldest") neutrons, whose quantum-mechanical wave-length is great compared to the distance between successive planes in the graphite crystals.

8.32. More recently a pile using heavy water as moderator was constructed in the Argonne Laboratory. The very high intensity beam of neutrons produced by this pile has been found well-suited to the study of "neutron optics," e.g., reflection and refraction of neutron beams as by graphite.

8.33. A constant objective of the Argonne Laboratory has been a better understanding of nuclear processes in uranium, neptunium, and plutonium. Repeated experiments have been made to improve the accuracy of constants such as thermal-fission cross sections of U-235, U-238, and Pu-239, probabilities of non-fission neutron absorption by each of these nuclei, and number of neutrons emitted per fission.

THE CLINTON PLANT

8.34. In Chapter VI we mentioned plans for a "pilot" plant for production of plutonium to be built at the Clinton site in Tennessee. By January 1943, the plans for this project were well along; construction was started soon afterward. M. D. Whitaker was appointed director of the Clinton Laboratories. The pilot-plant plans were made cooperatively by du Pont and the Metallurgical Laboratory; construction was carried out by du Pont; plant operation was maintained by the University of Chicago as part of the Metallurgical Project.

8.35. The main purposes of the Clinton plant were to produce some plutonium and to serve as a pilot plant for chemical separation. As regards research, the emphasis at Clinton was on chemistry and on the biological effects of radiations. A large laboratory was provided for chemical analysis, for research on purification methods, for fission-product studies, for development of intermediate-scale extraction and decontamination processes, etc. Later a "hot laboratory," i.e., a laboratory for remotely-controlled work on highly radioactive material, was provided. There is also an instrument shop and laboratory that has been used very actively. There are facilities for both clinical and experimental work of the health division, which has been very active. There is a small physics laboratory in which some important work was done using higher neutron intensities than were available at the Argonne Laboratory. The principal installations constructed at the Clinton Laboratory site were the pile and the separation plant; these are briefly described below.

THE CLINTON PILE

8.36. In any steadily operating pile the effective multiplication factor k must be kept at 1, whatever the power level. The best k_∞ that had been observed in a uranium-graphite lattice could not be achieved in a practical pile because of neutron leakage, cooling system, cylindrical channels for the uranium, protective coating on the uranium, and other minor factors. Granted air-cooling and a maximum safe temperature for the surface of the uranium, a size of pile had to be chosen that could produce 1,000 kw. The effective k would go down with rising temperature but not sufficiently to be a determining factor. Though a sphere was the ideal shape, practical considerations recommended a rectangular block.

8.37. The Clinton pile consists of a cube of graphite containing horizontal channels filled with uranium. The uranium is in the form of metal cylinders protected by gas-tight casings of aluminum. The uranium cylinders or slugs may be slid into the channels in the graphite; space is left to permit cooling air to flow past, and to permit pushing the slugs out at the back of the pile when they are ready for processing. Besides the channels for slugs there are various other holes through the pile for control rods, instruments, etc.

8.38. The Clinton pile was considerably larger than the first pile at Chicago (see Chapter VI). More important than the increased size of the Clinton pile were its cooling system, heavier shields, and means for changing the slugs. The production goal of the Clinton plant was set at a figure which meant that the pile should operate at a power level of 1,000 kw.

8.39. The instrumentation and controls are identical in principle to those of the first pile. Neutron intensity in the pile is measured by a BF_3 ionization chamber and is controlled by boron steel rods that can be moved in and out of the pile, thereby varying the fraction of neutrons available to produce fission.

8.40. In spite of an impressive array of instruments and safety devices, the most striking feature of the pile is the simplicity of operation. Most of the time the operators have nothing to do except record the readings of various instruments.

THE SEPARATION PLANT

8.41. Here, as at Hanford, the plutonium processes have to be carried out by remote control and behind thick shields. The separation equipment is housed in a series of adjacent cells having heavy concrete walls. These cells form a continuous structure (canyon) which is about 100 feet long and is two-thirds buried in the ground. Adjacent to this canyon are the control rooms, analytical laboratories, and a laboratory for further purification of the plutonium after it has been decontaminated to the point of comparative safety.

8.42. Uranium slugs that have been exposed in the pile are transferred under water to the first of these cells and are then dissolved. Subsequent operations are performed by pumping solutions or slurries from one tank or centrifuge to another.

PERFORMANCE OF CLINTON PILE

8.43. The Clinton pile started operating on November 4, 1943, and within a few days was brought up to a power level of 500 kw at a maximum slug surface temperature of 110° C. Improvements in the air circulation and an elevation of the maximum uranium surface temperature to 150° C. brought the power level up to about 800 kw, where it was maintained until the spring of 1944. Starting at that time, a change was made in the distribution of uranium, the change being designed to level out the power distribution in the pile by reducing the amount of metal near the center relative to that further out and thereby to increase the average power level without anywhere attaining too high a temperature. At the same time improvements were realized in the sealing of the slug jackets, making it possible to operate the pile at higher temperature. As a result, a power level of 1,800 kw was attained in May 1944; this was further increased after the installation of better fans in June 1944.

8.44. Thus the pile performance of June 1944 considerably exceeded expectations. In ease of control, steadiness of operation, and absence of dangerous radiation, the pile has been most satisfactory. There have been very few failures attributable to mistakes in design or construction.

8.45. The pile itself was simple both in principle and in practice. Not so the plutonium-separation plant. The step from the first chain-reacting pile to the Clinton pile was reasonably predictable; but a much greater and more uncertain step was required in the case of the separation process, for the Clinton separation plant was designed on the basis of experiments using only microgram amounts of plutonium.

8.46. Nevertheless, the separation process worked! The first batch of slugs from the pile entered the separation plant on December 20, 1943. By the end of January 1944, metal from the pile was going to the separation plant at the rate of $\frac{1}{3}$ ton per day. By February 1, 1944, 190 mg of plutonium had been delivered and by March 1, 1944, several grams had been delivered. Furthermore, the efficiency of recovery at the very start was about 50 per cent, and by June 1944 it was between 80 and 90 per cent.

8.47. During this whole period there was a large group of chemists at Clinton working on improving the process and developing it for Hanford. The Hanford problem differed from that at Clinton in that much higher concentrations of plutonium were expected. Furthermore, though the chemists were to be congratulated on the success of the Clinton plant, the process was complicated and expensive. Any improvements in yield or decontamination or in general simplification were very much to be sought.

8.48. Besides the proving of the pile and the separation plant and the production of several grams of plutonium for experimental use at Chicago, Clinton, and elsewhere, the Clinton Laboratories have been invaluable as a training and testing center for Hanford, for medical experiments, pile studies, purification studies, and physical and chemical studies of plutonium and fission products.

8.49. As typical of the kind of problems tackled there and at

Chicago, the following problems—listed in a single routine report for May 1944—are pertinent:

Problems Closed Out during May 1944: Search for New Oxidizing Agent, Effect of Radiation on Water and Aqueous Solutions, Solubility of Plutonium Peroxide, Plutonium Compounds Suitable for Shipment, Fission Product Distribution in Plant Process Solutions, Preliminary Process Design for Adsorption Extraction, Adsorption Semi-Works Assistance, Completion of Adsorption Process Design.

New Problems Assigned during May 1944: New Product Analysis Method, Effect of Radiation on Graphite, Improvement in Yield, New Pile Explorations, Waste Uranium Recovery, Monitoring Stack Gases, Disposal of Active Waste Solutions, Spray Cooling of X Pile, Assay Training Program, Standardization of Assay Methods, Development of Assay Methods, Shielded Apparatus for Process Control Assays, Cloud Chamber Experiment, Alpha Particles from U-235, Radial Product Distribution, Diffraction of Neutrons.

THE HANFORD PLANT

8.50. It is beyond the scope of this report to give any account of the construction of the Hanford Engineer Works, but it is to be hoped that the full story of this extraordinary enterprise and the companion one, the Clinton Engineer Works, will be published at some time in the future. The Hanford site was examined by representatives of General Groves and of du Pont at the end of 1942, and use of the site was approved by General Groves after he had inspected it personally. It was on the west side of the Columbia River in central Washington north of Pasco. In the early months of 1943 a 200-square-mile tract in this region was acquired by the government (by lease or purchase) through the Real Estate Division of the Office of the Chief of Engineers. Eventually an area of nearly a thousand square miles was brought under government control. At the time of acquisition of the land there were a few farms and two small villages, Hanford and Richland, on the site, which was otherwise sage-brush plains and barren hills. On the 6th of April, 1943, ground was broken for the Hanford construction camp. At the peak of activity in 1944, this camp was a city of 60,000 inhabitants, the fourth largest city in the state. Now, however, the camp is practically deserted as the operating crew is housed at Richland.

8.51. Work was begun on the first of the Hanford production piles on June 7, 1943, and operation of the first pile began in September 1944. The site was originally laid out for five piles, but the construction of only three has been undertaken. Besides the piles, there are, of course, plutonium separation plants, pumping stations and water-treatment plants. There is also a low-power chain-reacting pile for material testing. Not only are the piles themselves widely spaced for safety—several miles apart —but the separation plants are well away from the piles and from each other. All three piles were in operation by the summer of 1945.

CANNING AND CORROSION

8.52. No one who lived through the period of design and construction of the Hanford plant is likely to forget the "canning" problem, i.e., the problem of sealing the uranium slugs in protective metal jackets. On periodic visits to Chicago the writer could roughly estimate the state of the canning problem by the atmosphere of gloom or joy to be found around the laboratory. It was definitely not a simple matter to find a sheath that would protect uranium from water corrosion, would keep fission products out of the water, would transmit heat from the uranium to the water, and would not absorb too many neutrons. Yet the failure of a single can might conceivably require shut-down of an entire operating pile.

8.53. Attempts to meet the stringent requirements involved experimental work on electroplating processes, hot-dipping processes, cementation-coating processes, corrosion-resistant alloys of uranium, and mechanical jacketing or canning processes. Mechanical jackets or cans of thin aluminum were feasible from the nuclear-physics point of view and were chosen early as the most likely solution of the problem. But the problem of getting a uniform, heat-conducting bond between the uranium and the surrounding aluminum, and the problem of effecting a gas-tight closure for the can both proved very troublesome. Development of alternative methods had to be carried along up to the last minute, and even up to a few weeks before it was time to load the uranium slugs into the pile there was no certainty that any of the processes under development would be satisfactory. A final minor but apparently important modification in the preferred canning process was adopted in October 1944, after the first pile had begun experimental operation. By the summer of 1945, there had been no can failure reported.

PRESENT STATUS OF THE HANFORD PLANTS

8.54. During the fall of 1944 and the early months of 1945 the second and third Hanford piles were finished and put into operation, as were the additional chemical separation plants. There were, of course, some difficulties; however, none of the fears expressed as to canning failure, film formation in the water tubes, or radiation effects in the chemical processes, have turned out to be justified. As of early summer 1945 the piles are operating at designed power, producing plutonium, and heating the Columbia River.* The chemical plants are separating the plutonium from the uranium and from the fission products with better efficiency than had been anticipated. The finished product is being delivered. How it can be used is the subject of Chapter XII.

THE WORK ON HEAVY WATER

8.55. In previous chapters there have been references to the advantages of heavy water as a moderator. It is more effective than graphite in slowing down neutrons and it has a smaller neutron absorption than graphite. It is therefore possible to build

---

* The actual rise in temperature is so tiny that no effect on fish life could be expected. To make doubly sure, this expectation was confirmed by an elaborate series of experiments.

a chain-reacting unit with uranium and heavy water and thereby to attain a considerably higher multiplication factor, k, and a smaller size than is possible with graphite. But one must have the heavy water.

8.56. In the spring of 1943 the Metallurgical Laboratory decided to increase the emphasis on experiments and calculations aimed at a heavy-water pile. To this end a committee was set up under E. Wigner, a group under H. C. Vernon was transferred from Columbia to Chicago, and H. D. Smyth, who had just become associate director of the Laboratory, was asked to take general charge.

8.57. The first function of this group was to consider in what way heavy water could best be used to insure the overall success of the Metallurgical Project, taking account of the limited production schedule for heavy water that had been already authorized.

8.58. It became apparent that the production schedule was so low that it would take two years to produce enough heavy water to "moderate" a fair-sized pile for plutonium production. On the other hand, there might be enough heavy water to moderate a small "laboratory" pile, which could furnish information that might be valuable. In any event, during the summer of 1943 so great were the uncertainties as to the length of the war and as to the success of the other parts of the DSM project that a complete study of the possibilities of heavy-water piles seemed desirable. Either the heavy-water production schedule might be stepped up or the smaller, experimental pile might be built. An intensive study of the matter was made during the summer of 1943 but in November it was decided to curtail the program and construction was limited to a 250-kw pile located at the Argonne site.

The Argonne Heavy-Water Pile

8.59. Perhaps the most striking aspect of the uranium and heavy-water pile at the Argonne is its small size. Even with its surrounding shield of concrete it is relatively small compared to the uranium-graphite piles.

8.60. By May 15, 1944, the Argonne uranium and heavy-water pile was ready for test. With the uranium slugs in place, it was found that the chain reaction in the pile became self sustaining when only three fifths of the heavy water had been added. The reactivity of the pile was so far above expectations that it would have been beyond the capacity of the control rods to handle if the remainder of the heavy water had been added. To meet this unusual and pleasant situation some of the uranium was removed and extra control rods were added.

8.61. With these modifications it was possible to fill the tank to the level planned. By July 4, 1944, W. H. Zinn reported that the pile was running satisfactorily at 190 kw, and by August 8, 1944, he reported that it was operating at 300 kw.

8.62. In general the characteristics of this pile differed slightly from those of comparable graphite piles. This pile takes several hours to reach equilibrium. It shows small (less than 1 per cent) but sudden fluctuations in power level, probably caused by bubbles in the water. It cannot be shut down as completely or as rapidly as the graphite pile because of the tendency of delayed gamma rays to produce (from the heavy water) additional neutrons. As anticipated, the neutron density at the center is high. The shields, controls, heat exchanger, etc., have operated satisfactorily.

THE HEALTH DIVISION

8.63. The major objective of the health group was in a sense a negative one, to insure that no one concerned suffered serious injury from the peculiar hazards of the enterprise. Medical case histories of persons suffering serious injury or death resulting from radiation were emphatically not wanted. The success of the health division in meeting these problems was remarkable. Even in the research group where control is most difficult, cases showing even temporary bad effects were extremely rare. Factors of safety used in plant design and operation are so great that the hazards of the home and the family car are far greater for the personnel than any arising from the plants.

8.64. To achieve its objective the health group worked along three major lines:

(1) Adoption of pre-employment physical examinations and frequent re-examinations, particularly of those exposed to radiation.

(2) Setting of tolerance standards for radiation doses and development of instruments measuring exposure of personnel; giving advice on shielding, etc.; continually measuring radiation intensities at various locations in the plants; measuring contamination of clothes, laboratory desks, waste water, the atmosphere, etc.

(3) Carrying out research on the effects of direct exposure of persons and animals to various types of radiation, and on the effects of ingestion and inhalation of the various radioactive or toxic materials such as fission products, plutonium and uranium.

ROUTINE EXAMINATIONS

8.65. The white blood-corpuscle count was used as the principal criterion as to whether a person suffered from overexposure to radiation. A number of cases of abnormally low counts were observed and correlated with the degree of overexposure. Individuals appreciably affected were shifted to other jobs or given brief vacations; none has shown permanent ill effects.

8.66. At the same time it was recognized that the white blood-corpuscle count is not an entirely reliable criterion. Some work on animals indicated that serious damage might occur before the blood count gave any indication of danger. Accordingly, more elaborate blood tests were made on selected individuals and on experimental animals in the hope of finding a test that would give an earlier warning of impending injury.

INSTRUMENTS FOR RADIATION MEASUREMENTS

8.67. The Health Division had principal responsibility for the development of pocket meters for indicating the extent of exposure of persons. The first of these instruments was a simple electroscope about the size and shape of a fountain pen. Such instruments were electrostatically charged at the start of each day and were read at the end of the day. The degree to which they became discharged indicated the total amount of ionizing radiation to which they had been exposed. Unfortunately they were none too rugged and reliable, but the error of reading was nearly always in the right direction—i.e., in the direction of over-stating the exposure. At an early date the practice was established of issuing two of these pocket meters to everyone entering a dangerous area. A record was kept of the readings at the time of issuance and also when the meters were turned in. The meters themselves were continually although gradually improved. The Health Division later introduced "film badges," small pieces of film worn in the identification badge, the films being periodically developed and examined for radiation blackening. These instruments for individuals such as the pocket meter and film badge were extra and probably unnecessary precautions. In permanent installations the shielding alone normally affords complete safety. Its effect is under frequent survey by either permanently installed or portable instruments.

8.68. The Health Division cooperated with the Physics Division in the development and use of various other instruments. There was "Sneezy" for measuring the concentration of radioactive dust in the air and "Pluto" for measuring α-emitting contamination (usually plutonium) of laboratory desks and equipment. Counters were used to check the contamination of laboratory coats before and after the coats were laundered. At the exit gates of certain laboratories concealed counters sounded an alarm when someone passed whose clothing, skin or hair was contaminated. In addition, routine inspections of laboratory areas were made.

8.69. One of the studies made involved meteorology. It became essential to know whether the stack gases (at Clinton and at Hanford) would be likely to spread radioactive fission products in dangerous concentrations. Since the behavior of these gases is very dependent on the weather, studies were made at both sites over a period of many months, and satisfactory stack operation was specified.

8.70. Since both the scale and the variety of the radiation hazards in this enterprise were unprecedented, all reasonable precautions were taken; but no sure means were at hand for determining the adequacy of the precautions. It was essential to supplement previous knowledge as completely as possible. For this purpose, an extensive program of animal experimentation was carried out along three main lines: (1) exposure to neutron, alpha, beta and gamma radiation; (2) ingestion of uranium, plutonium and fission products; (3) inhalation of uranium, plutonium and fission products. Under the general direction of Dr. Stone these experiments were carried out at Chicago, Clinton and the University of California principally by Dr. Cole and Dr. Hamilton. Extensive and valuable results were obtained.

SUMMARY

8.71. Both space and security restrictions prevent a detailed report on the work of the laboratories and plants concerned with plutonium production.

8.72. Two types of neutron absorption are fundamental to the operation of the plant: one, neutron absorption in U-235 resulting in fission, maintains the chain reaction as a source of neutrons; the other, neutron absorption in U-238 leads to the formation of plutonium, the desired product.

8.73. The course of a nuclear chain reaction in a graphite-moderated heterogeneous pile can be described by following a single generation of neutrons. The original fast neutrons are slightly increased in number by fast fission, reduced by resonance absorption in U-238 and further reduced by absorption at thermal energies in graphite and other materials and by escape; the remaining neutrons, which have been slowed in the graphite, cause fission in U-235, producing a new generation of fast neutrons similar to the previous generation.

8.74. The product, plutonium, must be separated by chemical processes from a comparable quantity of fission products and a much larger quantity of uranium. Of several possible separation processes the one chosen consists of a series of reactions including precipitating with carriers, dissolving, oxidizing and reducing.

8.75. The chain reaction was studied at low power at the Argonne Laboratory beginning early in 1943. Both chain reaction and chemical separation processes were investigated at the Clinton Laboratories beginning in November 1943, and an appreciable amount of plutonium was produced there.

8.76. Construction of the main production plant at Hanford, Washington, was begun in 1943 and the first large pile went into operation in September 1944. The entire plant was in operation by the summer of 1945 with all chain-reacting piles and chemical-separation plants performing better than had been anticipated.

8.77. Extensive studies were made on the use of heavy water as a moderator and an experimental pile containing heavy water was built at the Argonne Laboratory. Plans for a production plant using heavy water were given up.

8.78. The Health Division was active along three main lines: (1) medical examination of personnel; (2) advice on radiation hazards and constant check on working conditions; (3) research on the effects of radiation. The careful planning and exhaustive research work of this division have resulted in an outstanding health record at Hanford and elsewhere in the project.

CHAPTER IX. GENERAL DISCUSSION OF THE SEPARATION OF ISOTOPES

INTRODUCTORY NOTE

9.1. The possibility of producing an atomic bomb of U-235 was recognized before plutonium was discovered. Because it was appreciated at an early date that the separation of the uranium isotopes would be a direct and major step toward making such a bomb, methods of separating uranium isotopes have been under scrutiny for at least six years. Nor was attention confined to uranium since it was realized that the separation of deuterium was also of great importance. In the present chapter the general problems of isotope separation will be discussed; later chapters will take up the specific application of various processes.

FACTORS AFFECTING THE SEPARATION OF ISOTOPES

9.2. By definition, the isotopes of an element differ in mass but not in chemical properties. More precisely, although the nuclear masses and structures differ, the nuclear charges are identical and therefore the external electronic structures are practically identical. For most practical purposes, therefore, the isotopes of an element are separable only by processes depending on the nuclear mass.

9.3. It is well known that the molecules of a gas or liquid are in continual motion and that their average kinetic energy depends only on the temperature, not on the chemical properties of the molecules. Thus in a gas made up of a mixture of two isotopes the average kinetic energy of the light molecules and of the heavy ones is the same. Since the kinetic energy of a molecule is $\frac{1}{2} mv^2$, where m is the mass and v the speed of the molecule, it is apparent that on the average the speed of a lighter molecule must be greater than that of a heavier molecule. Therefore, at least in principle, any process depending on the average speed of molecules can be used to separate isotopes. Unfortunately, the average speed is inversely proportional to the *square root* of the mass so that the difference is very small for the gaseous compounds of the uranium isotopes. Also, although the *average* speeds differ, the ranges of speed show considerable overlap. In the case of the gas uranium hexafluoride, for example, over 49 per cent of the light molecules have speeds as low as those of 50 per cent of the heavy molecules.

9.4. Obviously there is no feasible way of applying mechanical forces directly to molecules individually; they cannot be poked with a stick or pulled with a string. But they are subject to gravitational fields and, if ionized, may be affected by electric and magnetic fields. Gravitational forces are, of course, proportional to the mass. In a very high vacuum U-235 atoms and U-238 atoms would fall with the same acceleration, but just as a feather and a stone fall at very different rates in air where there are frictional forces resisting motion, there may be conditions under which a combination of gravitational and opposing intermolecular forces will tend to move heavy atoms differently from light ones. Electric and magnetic fields are more easily controlled than gravitational fields or "pseudogravitational" fields (i.e., centrifugal-force fields) and are very effective in separating ions of differing masses.

9.5. Besides gravitational or electromagnetic forces, there are, of course, interatomic and intermolecular forces. These forces govern the interaction of molecules and thus affect the rates of chemical reactions, evaporation processes, etc. In general, such forces will depend on the outer electrons of the molecules and not on the nuclear masses. However, whenever the forces between separated atoms or molecules lead to the formation of new molecules, a mass effect (usually very small) does appear. In accordance with quantum-mechanical laws, the energy levels of the molecules are slightly altered, and differently for each isotope. Such effects do slightly alter the behavior of two isotopes in certain chemical reactions, as we shall see, although the difference in behavior is far smaller than the familiar differences of chemical behavior between one element and another.

9.6. These, then, are the principal factors that may have to be considered in devising a separation process: equality of average thermal kinetic energy of molecules at a given temperature, gravitational or centrifugal effects proportional to the molecular masses, electric or magnetic forces affecting ionized molecules, and interatomic or intermolecular forces. In some isotope-separation processes only one of these effects is involved and the overall rate of separation can be predicted. In other isotope-separation processes a number of these effects occur simultaneously so that prediction becomes difficult.

CRITERIA FOR APPRAISING A SEPARATION PROCESS

9.7. Before discussing particular processes suitable for isotope separation, we should know what is wanted. The major criteria to be used in judging an isotope-separation process are as follows.

SEPARATION FACTOR

9.8. The separation factor, sometimes known as the enrichment or fractionating factor of a process, is the ratio of the relative concentration of the desired isotope after processing to its relative concentration before processing. Defined more precisely: if, before the processing, the numbers of atoms of the isotopes of mass number m_1 and m_2 are n_1 and n_2 respectively (per gram of the isotope mixture) and if, after the processing, the corresponding numbers are n'_1 and n'_2, then the separation factor is:

$$r = \frac{n'_1/n'_2}{n_1/n_2}$$

This definition may be applied to one stage of a separation plant or to an entire plant consisting of many stages. We are usually interested either in the "single stage" separation factor or in the "overall" separation factor of the whole process. If r is only slightly greater than unity, as is often the case for a single stage, the number r — 1 is sometimes more useful than r. The quantity r — 1 is called the enrichment factor. In natural uranium $m_1 = 235$, $m_2 = 238$, and $n_1/n_2 = \frac{1}{140}$ approximately, but in 90 per cent U-235, $n_1'/n_2' = \frac{9}{1}$. Consequently in a process producing 90 per cent U-235 from natural uranium the overall value of r must be about 1,260.

YIELD

9.9. In nearly every process a high separation factor means a low yield, a fact that calls for continual compromise. Unless indication is given to the contrary, we shall state yields in terms of U-235. Thus a separation device with a separation factor of 2—that is, $n_1'/n_2' = \frac{1}{70}$—and a yield of one gram a day is one that, starting from natural uranium, produces, in one day, material consisting of 1 gram of U-235 mixed with 70 grams of U-238.

HOLD-UP

9.10. The total amount of material tied up in a separation plant is called the "hold-up." The hold-up may be very large in a plant consisting of many stages.

START-UP TIME

9.11. In a separation plant having large hold-up, a long time —perhaps weeks or months—is needed for steady operating conditions to be attained. In estimating time schedules this "start-up" or "equilibrium" time must be added to the time of construction of the plant.

EFFICIENCY

9.12. If a certain quantity of raw material is fed into a separation plant, some of the material will be enriched, some impoverished, some unchanged. Parts of each of these three fractions will be lost and parts recovered. The importance of highly efficient recovery of the enriched material is obvious. In certain processes the amount of unchanged material is negligible, but in others, notably in the electromagnetic method to be described below, it is the largest fraction and consequently the efficiency with which it can be recovered for recycling is very important. The importance of recovery of impoverished material varies widely, depending very much on the degree of impoverishment. Thus in general there are many different efficiencies to be considered.

Cost

9.13. As in all parts of the uranium project, cost in time was more important than cost in money. Consequently a number of large-scale separation plants for U-235 and deuterium were built at costs greater than would have been required if construction could have been delayed for several months or years until more ideal processes were worked out.

SOME SEPARATION PROCESSES

Gaseous Diffusion

9.14. As long ago as 1896 Lord Rayleigh showed that a mixture of two gases of different atomic weight could be partly separated by allowing some of it to diffuse through a porous barrier into an evacuated space. Because of their higher average speed the molecules of the light gas diffuse through the barrier faster so that the gas which has passed through the barrier (i.e., the "diffusate") is enriched in the lighter constituent and the residual gas which has not passed through the barrier is impoverished in the lighter constituent. The gas most highly enriched in the lighter constituent is the so-called "instantaneous diffusate"; it is the part that diffuses before the impoverishment of the residue has become appreciable. If the diffusion process is continued until nearly all the gas has passed through the barrier, the average enrichment of the diffusate naturally diminishes. In the next chapter we shall consider these phenomena more fully. Here we shall merely point out that, on the assumption that the diffusion rates are inversely proportional to the square roots of the molecular weights the separation factor for the instantaneous diffusate, called the "ideal separation factor" α, is given by

$$\alpha = \sqrt{\frac{M_2}{M_1}}$$

where M_1 is the molecular weight of the lighter gas and M_2 that of the heavier. Applying this formula to the case of uranium will illustrate the magnitude of the separation problem. Since uranium itself is not a gas, some gaseous compound of uranium must be used. The only one obviously suitable is uranium hexafluoride, UF_6, which has a vapor pressure of one atmosphere at a temperature of 56° C. Since fluorine has only one isotope, the two important uranium hexafluorides are $U^{235}F_6$ and $U^{238}F_6$; their molecular weights are 349 and 352. Thus, if a small fraction of a quantity of uranium hexafluoride is allowed to diffuse through a porous barrier, the diffusate will be enriched in $U^{235}F_6$ by a factor

$$\alpha = \sqrt{352/349} = 1.0043$$

which is a long way from the 1,260 required (see paragraph 9.8.).

9.15. Such calculations might make it seem hopeless to separate isotopes (except, perhaps, the isotopes of hydrogen) by diffusion processes. Actually, however, such methods may be used successfully—even for uranium. It was the gaseous diffusion method that F. W. Aston used in the first partial separation of isotopes (actually the isotopes of neon). Later G. Hertz and others, by operating multi-stage recycling diffusion units, were able to get practically complete separation of the neon isotopes. Since the multiple-stage recycling system is necessary for nearly all separation methods, it will be described in some detail immediately following introductory remarks on the various methods to which it is pertinent.

FRACTIONAL DISTILLATION

9.16. The separation of compounds of different boiling points, i.e., different vapor pressures, by distillation is a familiar industrial process. The separation of alcohol and water (between which the difference in boiling point is in the neighborhood of

20° C.) is commonly carried out in a simple still using but a single evaporator and condenser. The condensed material (condensate) may be collected and redistilled a number of times if necessary. For the separation of compounds of very nearly the same boiling point it would be too laborious to carry out the necessary number of successive evaporations and condensations as separate operations. Instead, a continuous separation is carried out in a fractionating tower. Essentially the purpose of a fractionating tower is to produce an upward-directed stream of vapor and a downward-directed stream of liquid, the two streams being in intimate contact and constantly exchanging molecules. The molecules of the fraction having the lower boiling point have a relatively greater tendency to get into the vapor stream and vice versa. Such counter-current distillation methods can be applied to the separation of light and heavy water, which differ in boiling point by 1.4° C.

GENERAL APPLICATION OF COUNTERCURRENT FLOW

9.17. The method of countercurrent flow is useful not only in two-phase (liquid-gas) distillation processes, but also in other separation processes such as those involving diffusion resulting from temperature variations (gradients) within one-phase systems or from centrifugal forces. The countercurrents may consist of two gases, two liquids, or one gas and one liquid.

THE CENTRIFUGE

9.18. We have pointed out that gravitational separation of two isotopes might occur since the gravitational forces tending to move the molecules downward are proportional to the molecular weights, and the intermolecular forces tending to resist the downward motion depend on the electronic configuration, not on the molecular weights. Since the centrifuge is essentially a method of applying pseudogravitational forces of large magnitude, it was early considered as a method for separating isotopes. However, the first experiments with centrifuges failed. Later development of the high speed centrifuge by J. W. Beams and others led to success. H. C. Urey suggested the use of tall cylindrical centrifuges with countercurrent flow; such centrifuges have been developed successfully.

9.19. In such a countercurrent centrifuge there is a downward flow of vapor in the outer part of the rotating cylinder and an upward flow of vapor in the central or axial region. Across the interface region between the two currents there is a constant diffusion of both types of molecules from one current to the other, but the radial force field of the centrifuge acts more strongly on the heavy molecules than on the light ones so that the concentration of heavy ones increases in the peripheral region and decreases in the axial region, and vice versa for the lighter molecules.

9.20. The great appeal of the centrifuge in the separation of heavy isotopes like uranium is that the separation factor depends on the difference between the masses of the two isotopes, not on the square root of the ratio of the masses as in diffusion methods.

Thermal Diffusion Method

9.21. The kinetic theory of gases predicts the extent of the differences in the rates of diffusion of gases of different molecular weights. The possibility of accomplishing practical separation of isotopes by thermal diffusion was first suggested by theoretical studies of the details of molecular collisions and of the forces between molecules. Such studies made by Enskog and by Chapman before 1920 suggested that if there were a temperature gradient in a mixed gas there would be a tendency for one type of molecule to concentrate in the cold region and the other in the hot region. This tendency depends not only on the molecular weights but also on the forces between the molecules. If the gas is a mixture of two isotopes, the heavier isotope may accumulate at the hot region or the cold region or not at all, depending on the nature of the intermolecular forces. In fact, the direction of separation may reverse as the temperature or relative concentration is changed.

9.22. Such thermal diffusion effects were first used to separate isotopes by H. Clusius and G. Dickel in Germany in 1938. They built a vertical tube containing a heated wire stretched along the axis of the tube and producing a temperature difference of about 600° C. between the axis and the periphery. The effect was twofold. In the first place, the heavy isotopes (in the substances they studied) became concentrated near the cool outer wall, and in the second place, the cool gas on the outside tended to sink while the hot gas at the axis tended to rise. Thus thermal convection set up a countercurrent flow, and thermal diffusion caused the preferential flow of the heavy molecules outward across the interface between the two currents.

9.23. The theory of thermal diffusion in gases is intricate enough; that of thermal diffusion in liquids is practically impossible. A separation effect does exist, however, and has been used successfully to separate the light and heavy uranium hexafluorides.

Chemical Exchange Method

9.24. In the introduction to this chapter we pointed out that there was some reason to hope that isotope separation might be accomplished by ordinary chemical reactions. It has in fact been found that in simple exchange reactions between compounds of two different isotopes the so-called equilibrium constant is not exactly one, and thus that in reactions of this type separation can occur. For example, in the catalytic exchange of hydrogen atoms between hydrogen gas and water, the water contains between three and four times as great a concentration of deuterium as the hydrogen gas in equilibrium with it. With hydrogen and water vapor the effect is of the same general type but equilibrium is more rapidly established. It is possible to adapt this method to a continuous countercurrent flow arrangement like that used in distillation, and such arrangements are actually in use for production of heavy water. The general method is well understood, and the separation effects are known to decrease in general with increasing molecular weight, so that there is but a small chance of applying this method successfully to heavy isotopes like uranium.

ELECTROLYSIS METHOD

9.25. The electrolysis method of separating isotopes resulted from the discovery that the water contained in electrolytic cells used in the regular commercial production of hydrogen and oxygen has an increased concentration of heavy water molecules. A full explanation of the effect has not yet been worked out. Before the war practically the entire production of heavy hydrogen was by the electrolysis method. By far the greatest production was in Norway, but enough for many experimental purposes had been made in the United States.

STATISTICAL METHODS IN GENERAL

9.26. The six methods of isotope separation we have described so far (diffusion, distillation, centrifugation, thermal diffusion, exchange reactions, and electrolysis) have all been tried with some degree of success on either uranium or hydrogen or both. Each of these methods depends on small differences in the *average* behavior of the molecules of different isotopes. Because an average is by definition a statistical matter, all such methods depending basically on average behavior are called statistical methods.

9.27. With respect to the criteria set up for judging separation processes the six statistical methods are rather similar. In every case the separation factor is small so that many successive stages of separation are required. In most cases relatively large quantities of material can be handled in plants of moderate size. The holdup and starting-time values vary considerably but are usually high. The similarity of the six methods renders it inadvisable to make final choice of method without first studying in detail the particular isotope, production rate, etc., wanted. Exchange reaction and electrolysis methods are probably unsuitable in the case of uranium, and no distillation scheme for uranium has survived. All of the other three methods have been developed with varying degrees of success for uranium, but are not used for hydrogen.

THE ELECTROMAGNETIC METHOD
AND ITS LIMITATIONS

9.28. The existence of non-radioactive isotopes was first demonstrated during the study of the behavior of ionized gas molecules moving through electric and magnetic fields. It is just

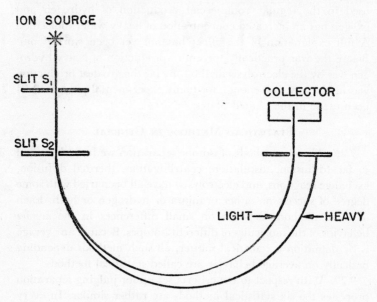

ION SOURCE

SLIT S$_1$

SLIT S$_2$

COLLECTOR

LIGHT→ ←HEAVY

**MAGNETIC FIELD PERPENDICULAR
TO PLANE OF DRAWING**

such fields that form the basis of the so-called mass spectrographic or electromagnetic method of separating isotopes. This method is the best available for determining the relative abundance of many types of isotope. The method is used constantly in checking the results of the uranium isotope separation methods we have already described. The reason the method is so valuable is that it can readily effect almost complete separation of the isotopes very rapidly and with small hold-up and short start-up time. If this is so, it may well be asked why any other method of separation is considered. The answer is that an ordinary mass spectrograph can handle only very minute quantities of material, usually of the order of fractions of a microgram per hour.

9.29. To understand the reasons for this limitation in the yield, we shall outline the principle of operation of a simple type of mass spectrograph first used by A. J. Dempster in 1918. Such an instrument is illustrated schematically in the drawing on p. 164. The gaseous compound to be separated is introduced in the ion source, where some of its molecules are ionized in an electric discharge. Some of these ions go through the slit s_1. Between s_1 and s_2 they are accelerated by an electric field which gives them all practically the same kinetic energy, thousands of times greater than their average thermal energy. Since they now all have practically the same kinetic energy, the lighter ions must have less momenta than the heavy ones. Entering the magnetic field at the slit s_2 all the ions will move perpendicular to the magnetic field in semi-circular paths of radii proportional to their momenta. Therefore the light ions will move in smaller semicircles than the heavy, and with proper positioning of the collector, only the light ions will be collected.

9.30. Postponing detailed discussion of such a separation device, we may point out the principal considerations that limit the amount of material that passes through it. They are three-fold: First, it is difficult to produce large quantities of gaseous ions. Second, a sharply limited ion beam is usually employed (as in the case shown) so that only a fraction of the ions produced are used. Third, too great densities of ions in a beam can cause space-charge effects which interfere with the separating action. Electromagnetic methods developed before 1941 had very high separation factors but very low yields and efficiencies. These were the reasons which—before the summer of 1941—led the Uranium Committee to exclude such methods for large-scale separation of U-235. (See Paragraph 4:31.) Since that time it has been shown that the limitations are not insuperable. In fact, the first appreciable-size samples of pure U-235 were produced by an electromagnetic separator, as will be described in a later chapter.

OTHER ISOTOPE-SEPARATION METHODS

9.31. In addition to the isotope-separation methods described above, several other methods have been tried. These include the ionic mobility method, which, as the name implies, depends on the following fact: In an electrolytic solution two ions which are chemically identical but of different mass progress through the solution at different rates under the action of an electric field. However, the difference of mobility will be small and easily obscured by disturbing effects. A. K. Brewer of the Bureau of Standards reported that he was able to separate the isotopes of potassium by this method. Brewer also obtained some interesting results with an evaporation method. Two novel electromagnetic methods, the isotron and the ionic centrifuge, are described in Chapter XI. The isotron produced a number of fair-size samples of partly separated uranium. The ionic centrifuge also produced some uranium samples showing separation, but its action was erratic.

CASCADES AND COMBINED PROCESSES

9.32. In all the statistical methods of separating isotopes many successive stages of separation are necessary to get material that is 90 per cent or more U-235 or deuterium. Such a series of successive separating stages is called a cascade if the flow is continuous from one stage to the next. (A fractionating tower of separate plates such as has been described is an example of a simple cascade of separating units.) A complete analysis of the problems of a cascade might be presented in general terms. Actually it has been worked out by R. P. Feynman of Princeton and others for a certain type of electromagnetic separator and by K. Cohen and I. Kaplan of Columbia, by M. Benedict and A. M. Squires of the Kellex Corporation and others for diffusion processes. At present we shall make only two points about multiple-stage or "cascade" plants.

9.33. The first point is that there must be recycling. Considering a U-235 separation plant, the material fed into any stage above the first has already been enriched in U-235. Part of this feed material may be further enriched in passing through the stage under consideration. The remainder will typically become impoverished but not so much impoverished as to be valueless. It must be returned to an earlier stage and recycled. Even the impoverished material from the first (least enriched) stage may be worth recycling; some of the U-235 it still contains may be recovered (stripped).

9.34. The second point is that the recycling problem changes greatly at the higher (more enriched) stages. Assuming steady stage operation, we see that the net flow of uranium through the first stage must be at least 140 times as great as through the last stage. The net flow in any given stage is proportional to the relative concentration of U-238 and thus decreases with the number of stages passed. Since any given sample of material is recycled many times, the amount of material processed in any stage is far greater than the net flow through that stage but is proportional to it.

9.35. We mention these points to illustrate a phase of the separation problem that is not always obvious, namely, that the separation process which is best for an early stage of separation is not necessarily best for a later stage. Factors such as those we have mentioned differ not only from stage to stage but from process to process. For example, recycling is far simpler in a diffusion plant than in an electromagnetic plant. A plant combining two or more processes may well be the best to accomplish the overall separation required. In the lower (larger) stages the size of the equipment and the power required for it may determine the choice of process. In the higher (smaller) stages these factors are outweighed by convenience of operation and hold-up time, which may point to a different process.

THE HEAVY WATER PLANTS; THE CENTRIFUGE PILOT PLANT

9.36. The next two chapters are devoted to descriptions of the three methods used for large-scale separation of the uranium isotopes. These are the only isotope-separation plants that have turned out to be of major importance to the project up to the present time. At an earlier stage it seemed likely that the centrifuge might be the best method for separating the uranium isotopes and that heavy water would be needed as a moderator. We shall describe briefly the centrifuge pilot plant and the heavy water production plants.

THE HEAVY WATER PLANTS

9.37. Two methods were used for the concentration of deuterium. These were the fractional distillation of water and the hydrogen-water exchange reaction method.

9.38. The first of these follows well established fractional distillation methods except that very extensive distillation is required because of the slight difference in boiling point of light and heavy water. Also, because of this same small difference, the amount of steam required is very large. The method is very expensive because of these factors, but plants could be constructed with a minimum of development work. Plants were started by du Pont in January 1943, and were put into operation about January 1944.

9.39. The second method for the preparation of heavy water depends upon the catalytic exchange of deuterium between hydrogen gas and water. When such an exchange is established by catalysts, the concentration of the deuterium in the water is greater than that in the gas by a factor of about three as we have already seen.

9.40. In this process water is fed into a tower and flows countercurrently to hydrogen and steam in an intricate manner. At the bottom of the tower the water is converted to hydrogen gas and oxygen gas in electrolytic cells and the hydrogen is fed back to the bottom of the tower mixed with steam. This steam and hydrogen mixture passes through beds of catalyst and bubbles through the downflowing water. Essentially, part of the deuterium originally in the hydrogen concentrates in the steam and then is transferred to the downflowing water. The actual plant consists of a cascade of towers with the largest towers at the feed end and the smallest towers at the production end. Such a cascade follows the same general principle as those discussed above in connection with separation problems in general. This process required the securing of very active catalysts for the exchange reactions. The most effective catalyst of this type was discovered by H. S. Taylor at Princeton University, while a second, less active catalyst was discovered by A. von Grosse. In the development of these catalysts R. H. Crist of Columbia University made the necessary determinations of physical constants and H. R. Arnold of du Pont did the development work on one of the catalysts.

9.41. This process was economical in operation. The plant was placed at the works of the Consolidated Mining & Smelting Co., at Trail, British Columbia, Canada, because of the necessity of using electrolytic hydrogen. The construction of the plant was under the direction of E. V. Murphree and F. T. Barr of the Standard Oil Development Co.

THE CENTRIFUGE PILOT PLANT

9.42. For a long time in the early days of the project the gaseous diffusion method and the centrifuge method were considered the two separation methods most likely to succeed with uranium. Both were going to be difficult to realize on a large scale. After the reorganization in December 1941 research and development on the centrifuge method continued at the University of Virginia and at the Standard Oil Development Company's laboratory at Bayway. To make large centrifuges capable of running at very high speeds was a major task undertaken by the Westinghouse Electric and Manufacturing Company of East Pittsburgh.

9.43. Because of the magnitude of the engineering problems involved, no large-scale production plant was ever authorized but a pilot plant was authorized and constructed at Bayway. It was operated successfully and gave approximately the degree of separation predicted by theory. This plant was later shut down and work on the centrifuge method was discontinued. For this reason no further discussion of the centrifuge method is given in this report.

ISOTOPE SEPARATION COMPARED WITH PLUTONIUM PRODUCTION

9.44. The most important methods of isotope separation that have been described were known in principle and had been reduced to practice before the separation of uranium isotopes became of paramount importance. They had not been applied to uranium except for the separation of a few micrograms, and they had not been applied to any substance on a scale comparable to that now required. But the fundamental questions were of costs, efficiency, and time, not of principle; in other words, the problem was fundamentally technical, not scientific. The plutonium production problem did not reach a similar stage until after the first self-sustaining chain-reacting pile had operated and the first microgram amounts of plutonium had been separated. Even after this stage many of the experiments done on the plutonium project were of vital interest for the military use either of U-235 or plutonium and for the future development of nuclear power. As a consequence, the plutonium project has continued to have a more general interest than the isotope separation projects. Many special problems arose in the separation projects which were extremely interesting and required a high order of scientific ability for their solution but which must still be kept secret. It is for such reasons that the present non-technical report has given first emphasis to the plutonium project and will give less space to the separation projects. This is not to say that the separation problem was any easier to solve or that its solution was any less important.

SUMMARY

9.45. Except in electromagnetic separators, isotope separation depends on small differences in the average behavior of molecules. Such effects are used in six "statistical" separation methods: (1) gaseous diffusion, (2) distillation, (3) centrifugation, (4) thermal diffusion, (5) exchange reactions, (6) electrolysis. Probably only (1), (3), and (4) are suitable for uranium; (2), (5), and (6) are preferred for the separation of deuterium from hydrogen. In all these "statistical" methods the separation factor is small so that many stages are required, but in the case of each method large amounts of material may be handled. All these methods had been tried with some success before 1940; however, none had been used on a large scale and none had been used for uranium. The scale of production by electromagnetic methods was even smaller but the separation factor was larger. There were apparent limitations of scale for the electromagnetic method. There were presumed to be advantages in combining two or more methods because of the differences in performance at different stages of separation. The problem of developing any or all of these separation methods was not a scientific one of principle but a technical one of scale and cost. These developments can therefore be reported more briefly than those of the plutonium project although they are no less important. A pilot plant was built using centrifuges and operated successfully. No large-scale plant was built. Plants were built for the production of heavy water by two different methods.

CHAPTER X. THE SEPARATION OF THE URANIUM ISOTOPES BY GASEOUS DIFFUSION

INTRODUCTION

10.1. It was in February 1940 that small amounts of concentrated fractions of the three uranium isotopes of masses 234, 235, and 238 were obtained by A. O. Nier using his mass spectrometer and were turned over to E. T. Booth, A. von Grosse, and J. R. Dunning for investigation with the Columbia University cyclotron. These men soon demonstrated that U-235 was the isotope susceptible to fission by thermal neutrons. It was natural, therefore, that this group, under the leadership of Dunning, became more interested than ever in the large-scale separation of the uranium isotopes.

10.2. The diffusion method was apparently first seriously reviewed by Dunning in a memorandum to G. B. Pegram, which was sent to L. J. Briggs in the fall of 1940. This memorandum summarized preliminary investigations that had been carried on by E. T. Booth, A. von Grosse and J. R. Dunning. Work was accelerated in 1941 with financial help provided by a contract that H. C. Urey had recived from the Navy for the study of isotope separation—principally by the centrifuge method. During this period F. G. Slack of Vanderbilt University and W. F. Libby of the University of California joined the group. An OSRD contract (OEMsr-106) calling specifically for diffusion studies went into effect on July 1, 1941, and ran for a year. The work continued on an expanding scale under a series of OSRD and Army contracts through the spring of 1945. Up until May 1943 Dunning was in immediate charge of this work; Urey was in charge of statistical methods in general. From that time until February 1945 Urey was in direct charge of the Columbia part of the diffusion work, with Dunning continuing as director of one of the principal divisions. On March 1, 1945, the laboratory was taken over from Columbia by Carbide and Carbon Chemicals Corporation. Early in 1942, at the suggestion of E. V. Murphree, the M. W. Kellogg Company was brought in to develop plans for large-scale production of diffusion-plant equipment and eventually to build a full-scale plant. To carry out this undertaking, a new subsidiary company was formed called the Kellex Corporation. In January 1943, Carbide and Carbon Chemicals Corporation was given the responsibility for operating the plant.

10.3. As stated in Chapter IV, by the end of 1941 the possibility of separating the uranium hexafluorides had been demonstrated in principle by means of a single-stage diffusion unit employing a porous barrier (for example, a barrier made by etching a thin sheet of silver-zinc alloy with hydrochloric acid). A considerable amount of work on barriers and pumps had also been done but no answer entirely satisfactory for large-scale operation had been found. Also, K. Cohen had begun a series of theoretical studies, to which reference has already been made, as to what might be the best way to use the diffusion process, i.e., as to how many stages would be required, what aggregate area of barrier would be needed, what volume of gas would have to be circulated, etc. Theoretical studies and process development by M. Benedict added much to knowledge in this field and served as the basis of design of the large plant.

10.4. Reports received from the British, and the visit by the British group in the winter of 1941–1942, clarified a number of points. At that time the British were planning a diffusion separation plant themselves so that the discussions with F. Simon, R. Peierls, and others were particularly valuable.

THE PRINCIPLES OF SEPARATION BY DIFFUSION

A Single Diffusion Stage

10.5. As was explained in the last chapter, the rate of diffusion of a gas through an ideal porous barrier is inversely proportional to the square root of its molecular weight. Thus if a gas consisting of two isotopes starts to diffuse through a barrier into an evacuated vessels, the lighter isotope (of molecular weight M_1) diffuses more rapidly than the heavier (of molecular weight M_2). The result, for a short period of time, at least, is that the relative concentration of the lighter isotope is greater on the far side of the barrier than on the near side. But if the process is allowed to continue indefinitely, equilibrium will become established and the concentrations will become identical on both sides of the barrier. Even if the diffusate gas (the gas which has passed through the barrier) is drawn away by a pump, the relative amount of the heavy isotope passing through the barrier will increase since the light isotope on the near side of the barrier has been depleted by the earlier part of the diffusion.

10.6. For a single diffusion operation, the increase in the relative concentration of the light isotope in the diffused gas compared to the feed gas can be expressed in terms of the separation factor r or the enrichment factor, r − 1, both defined in paragraph 9.8 of the last chapter. A rather simple equation can be derived which gives r − 1 in terms of the molecular weights and the fraction of the original gas which has diffused. If this fraction is very small, the equation reduces to $r = \alpha$, the "ideal separation factor" of paragraph 9.14. If the fraction diffused is appreciable, the equation shows the expected diminution in separation. For example, if half the gas diffuses, $r − 1 = .69(\alpha − 1)$, or for uranium hexafluoride $r = 1.003$ compared to the value of 1.0043 when a very small fraction of the original gas has diffused.

The Cascade

10.7. To separate the uranium isotopes, many successive diffusion stages (i.e., a cascade) must be used since $\alpha = 1.0043$ for $U^{235}F_6$ and $U^{238}F_6$, a possible gas for uranium separation. Studies by Cohen and others have shown that the best flow arrangement for the successive stages is that in which half the gas pumped into each stage diffuses through the barrier, the other (impoverished) half being returned to the feed of the next lower stage. For such an arrangement, as we have seen, the ideal separating effect between the feed and output of a single stage is $0.69(\alpha - 1)$. This is often called ϵ, the "overall enrichment per stage." For the uranium hexafluorides, $\epsilon = 0.003$, in theory; but it is somewhat less in practice as a result of "back diffusion," of imperfect mixing on the high pressure side, and of imperfections in the barrier. The first experimental separation of the uranium hexafluorides (by E. T. Booth, H. C. Paxton, and C. B. Slade) gave results corresponding to $\epsilon = 0.0014$. If one desires to produce 99 per cent pure $U^{235}F_6$, and if one uses a cascade in which each stage has a reasonable overall enrichment factor, then it turns out that roughly 4,000 stages are required.

GAS CIRCULATION IN THE CASCADE

10.8. Of the gas that passes through the barrier of any given stage, only half passes through the barrier of the next higher stage, the other half being returned to an earlier stage. Thus most of the material that eventually emerges from the cascade has been recycled many times. Calculation shows that for an actual uranium-separation plant it may be necessary to force through the barriers of the first stage 100,000 times the volume of gas that comes out the top of the cascade (i.e., as desired product $U^{235}F^6$). The corresponding figures for higher stages fall rapidly because of reduction in amount of unwanted material ($U^{238}F^6$) that is carried along.

THE PROBLEM OF LARGE-SCALE SEPARATION

INTRODUCTION

10.9. By the time of the general reorganization of the atomic-bomb project in December 1941, the theory of isotope separation by gaseous diffusion was well understood. Consequently it was possible to define the technical problems that would be encountered in building a large-scale separation plant. The decisions as to scale and location of such plant were not made until the winter of 1942–1943, that is, about the same time as the corresponding decisions were being made for the plutonium production plants.

THE OBJECTIVE

10.10. The general objective of the large-scale gaseous diffusion plant was the production each day of a specified number of grams of uranium containing of the order of ten times as much U-235 as is present in the same quantity of natural uranium. However, it was apparent that the plant would be rather flexible in operation, and that considerable variations might be made in the degree of enrichment and yield of the final product.

THE PROCESS GAS

10.11. Uranium hexafluoride has been mentioned as a gas that might be suitable for use in the plant as "process gas"; not the least of its advantages is that fluorine has only one isotope so that the UF_6 molecules of any given uranium isotope all have the same mass. This gas is highly reactive and is actually a solid at room temperature and atmospheric pressure. Therefore the study of other gaseous compounds of uranium was urgently undertaken. As insurance against failure in this search for alternative gases, it was necessary to continue work on uranium hexafluoride, as in devising methods for producing and circulating the gas.

THE NUMBER OF STAGES

10.12. The number of stages required in the main cascade of the plant depended only on the degree of enrichment desired and the value of overall enrichment per stage attainable with actual barriers. Estimates were made which called for several thousand stages. There was also to be a "stripping" cascade of several hundred stages, the exact number depending on how much unseparated U-235 could economically be allowed to go to waste.

BARRIER AREA

10.13. We have seen that the total value of gas that must diffuse through the barriers is very large compared to the volume of the final product. The rate at which the gas diffuses through unit area of barrier depends on the pressure difference on the two sides of the barrier and on the porosity of the barrier. Even assuming full atmospheric pressure on one side and zero pressure on the other side, and using an optimistic figure for the porosity, calculations showed that many acres of barrier would be needed in the large-scale plant.

BARRIER DESIGN

10.14. At atmospheric pressure the mean free path of a molecule is of the order of a ten-thousandth of a millimeter or one tenth of a micron. To insure true "diffusive" flow of the gas, the diameter of the myriad holes in the barrier must be less than one tenth the mean free path. Therefore the barrier material must have almost no holes which are appreciably larger than 0.01 micron (4×10^{-7} inch), but must have billions of holes of this size or smaller. These holes must not enlarge or plug up as the result of direct corrosion or dust coming from corrosion elsewhere in the system. The barrier must be able to withstand a pressure "head" of one atmosphere. It must be amenable to manufacture in large quantities and with uniform quality. By January 1942, a number of different barriers had been made on a small scale and tested for separation factor and porosity. Some were thought to be very promising, but none had been adequately tested for actual large-scale production and plant use.

PUMPING AND POWER REQUIREMENTS

10.15. In any given stage approximately half of the material entering the stage passes through the barrier and on to the next higher stage, while the other half passes back to the next lower stage. The diffused half is at low pressure and must be pumped to high pressure before feeding into the next stage. Even the undiffused portion emerges at somewhat lower pressure than it entered and cannot be fed back to the lower stage without pumping. Thus the total quantity of gas per stage (comprising twice the amount which flows through the barrier) has to be circulated by means of pumps.

10.16. Since the flow of gas through a stage varies greatly with the position of the stage in the cascade, the pumps also vary greatly in size or number from stage to stage. The type and capacity of the pump required for a given stage depends not only on the weight of gas to be moved but on the pressure rise required. Calculations made at this time assumed a fore pressure of one atmosphere and a back pressure (i.e., on the low pressure side of the barrier) of one tenth of an atmosphere. It was estimated that thousands of pumps would be needed and that thousands of kilowatts would be required for their operation. Since an unavoidable concomitant of pumping gas is heating it, it was evident that a large cooling system would have to be provided. By early 1942, a good deal of preliminary work had been done on pumps. Centrifugal pumps looked attractive in spite of the problem of sealing their shafts, but further experimental work was planned on completely sealed pumps of various types.

LEAKS AND CORROSION

10.17. It was clear that the whole circulating system comprising pumps, barriers, piping, and valves would have to be vacuum tight. If any lubricant or sealing medium is needed in the pumps, it should not react with the process gas. In fact none of the materials in the system should react with the process gas since such corrosion would lead not only to plugging of the barriers and various mechanical failures but also to absorption (i.e., virtual disappearance) of uranium which had already been partially enriched.

ACTUAL VS. IDEAL CASCADE

10.18. In an ideal cascade, the pumping requirements change from stage to stage. In practice it is not economical to provide a different type of pump for every stage. It is necessary to determine how great a departure from the ideal cascade (i.e., what minimum number of pump types) should be employed in the interest of economy of design, repair, etc. Similar compromises are used for other components of the cascade.

HOLD-UP AND START-UP TIME

10.19. When first started, the plant must be allowed to run undisturbed for some time, until enough separation has been effected so that each stage contains gas of appropriate enrichment. Only after such stabilization is attained is it desirable to draw off from the top stage any of the desired product. Both the amount of material involved (the hold-up) and the time required (the start-up time) are great enough to constitute major problems in their own right.

EFFICIENCY

10.20. It was apparent that there would be only three types of material loss in the plant contemplated, namely: loss by leakage, loss by corrosion (i.e., chemical combination and deposition), and loss in plant waste. It was expected that leakage could be kept very small and that—after an initial period of operation— loss from corrosion would be small. The percentage of material lost in plant waste would depend on the number of stripping stages.

DETAILED DESIGN

10.21. Questions as to how the barrier material was to be used (whether in tubes or sheets, in large units or small units), how mixing was to be effected, and what controls and instruments would be required were still to be decided. There was little reason to expect them to be unanswerable, but there was no doubt that they would require both theoretical and experimental study.

SUMMARY OF THE PROBLEM

10.22. By 1942 the theory of isotope separation by gaseous diffusion had been well worked out, and it became clear that a very large plant would be required. The major equipment items in this plant were diffusion barriers and pumps. Neither the barriers nor the pumps which were available at that time had been proved generally adequate. Therefore the further development of pumps and barriers was especially urgent. There were also other technical problems to be solved, these involving corrosion, vacuum seals, and instrumentation.

ORGANIZATION

10.23. As we mentioned at the beginning of this chapter, the diffusion work was initiated by J. R. Dunning. The work was carried on under OSRD auspices at Columbia University until May 1, 1943, when it was taken over by the Manhattan District. In the summer of 1943 the difficulties encountered in solving certain phases of the project led to a considerable expansion, particularly of the chemical group. H. C. Urey, then director of the work, appointed H. S. Taylor of Princeton associate director and added E. Mack, Jr. of Ohio State, G. M. Murphy of Yale, and P. H. Emmett of Johns Hopkins to the senior staff. Most of the work was moved out of the Columbia laboratories to a large building situated near by. The chemists at Princeton who had been engaged in heavy water studies were assigned some of the barrier research problems. Early in 1944, L. M. Currie of the National Carbon Company became another associate director to help Urey in his liaison and administrative work.

10.24. As has been mentioned, the M. W. Kellogg Company was chosen early in 1942 to plan the large scale plant. For this purpose Kellogg created a special subsidiary called The Kellex Corporation, with P. C. Keith as executive in charge and technical head and, responsible to him, A. L. Baker as Project Manager, and J. H. Arnold as Director of Research and Development. The new subsidiary carried on research and development in its Jersey City laboratories and in the laboratory building referred to in the paragraph above; developed the process and engineering designs; and procured materials for the large-scale plant and supervised its construction. The plant was constructed by the

J. A. Jones Construction Company, Incorporated, of Charlotte, North Carolina.

10.24-a. The Kellex Corporation, unlike conventional industrial firms, was a cooperative of scientists, engineers and administrators recruited from essentially all branches of industry and gathered for the express purpose of carrying forward this one job. Service was on a voluntary basis, individuals prominent in industry freely relinquishing their normal duties and responsibilities to devote full time to Kellex activities. As their respective tasks are being completed these men are returning to their former positions in industry.

10.25. In January 1943, Carbide and Carbon Chemicals Corporation were chosen to be the operators of the completed plant. Their engineers soon began to play a large role not only in the planning and construction but also in the research work.

RESEARCH, DEVELOPMENT, CONSTRUCTION, AND PRODUCTION, 1942 TO 1945

PRODUCTION OF BARRIERS

10.26. Even before 1942, barriers had been developed that were thought to be satisfactory. However, the barriers first developed by E. T. Booth, H. C. Paxton, and C. B. Slade were never used on a large scale because of low mechanical strength and poor corrosion resistance. In 1942, under the general supervision of Booth and F. G. Slack and with the cooperation of various scientists including F. C. Nix of the Bell Telephone Laboratories, barriers of a different type were produced. At one time, a barrier developed by E. O. Norris and E. Adler was thought sufficiently satisfactory to be specified for plant use. Other barriers were developed by combining the ideas of several men at the Columbia laboratories (by now christened the SAM Laboratories), Kellex, Bell Telephone Laboratories, Bakelite Corporation, Houdaille-Hershey Corporation, and others. The type of barrier selected for use in the plant was perfected under the general supervision of H. S. Taylor. One modification of this barrier developed by the SAM Laboratories represented a marked improvement in quality and is being used in a large number of stages of the plant. By 1945 the problem was no longer one of barely meeting minimum specifications, but of making improvements resulting in greater rate of output or greater economy of operation.

10.27. Altogether the history of barrier development reminds the writer of the history of the "canning" problem of the plutonium project. In each case the methods were largely cut and try, and satisfactory or nearly satisfactory solutions were repeatedly announced; but in each case a really satisfactory solution was not found until the last minute and then proved to be far better than had been hoped.

Pumps and Seals

10.28. The early work on pumps was largely under the supervision of H. A. Boorse of Columbia University. When Kellex came into the picture in 1942, its engineers, notably G. W. Watts, J. S. Swearingen and O. C. Brewster, took leading positions in the development of pumps and seals. It must be remembered that these pumps are to be operated under reduced pressure, must not leak, must not corrode, and must have as small a volume as possible. Many different types of centrifugal blower pumps and reciprocating pumps were tried. In one of the pumps for the larger stages, the impeller is driven through a coupling containing a very novel and ingenious type of seal. Another type of pump is completely enclosed, its centrifugal impeller and rotor being run from outside, by induction.

Miscellaneous Developments

10.29. As in the plutonium problem, so here also, there were many questions of corrosion, etc., to be investigated. New coolants and lubricants were developed by A. L. Henne and his associates, by G. H. Cady, by W. T. Miller and his co-workers, by E. T. McBee and his associates, and by scientists of various corporations including Hooker Electrochemical Co., the du Pont Co. and the Harshaw Chemical Co. The research and development and plant requirements for these materials and other special chemicals were coordinated by R. Rosen, first under OSRD and later for Kellex. Methods of pretreating surfaces against corrosion were worked out. Among the various instruments designed or adapted for project use, the mass spectrograph deserves special mention. The project was fortunate in having the assistance of A. O. Nier of the University of Minnesota and later of Kellex whose mass spectrograph methods of isotope analysis were sufficiently advanced to become of great value to the project, as in analyzing samples of enriched uranium. Mass spectrographs were also used in pretesting parts for vacuum leaks and for detecting impurities in the process gas in the plant.

Pilot Plants

10.30. Strictly speaking, there was no pilot plant. That is to say, there was no small-scale separation system set up using the identical types of blowers, barriers, barrier mountings, cooling, etc., that were put into the main plant. Such a system could not be set up because the various elements of the plant were not all available prior to the construction of the plant itself. To proceed with the construction of the full-scale plant under these circumstances required foresight and boldness.

10.31. There was, however, a whole series of so-called pilot plants which served to test various components or groups of components of the final plant. Pilot plant No. 1 was a 12-stage plant using a type of barrier rather like that used in the large-scale plant, but the barrier material was not fabricated in the form specified for the plant and the pumps used were sylphon-sealed reciprocating pumps, not centrifugal pumps. Work on this plant in 1943 tested not only the barriers and general system of separation but gave information about control valves, pressure gauges, piping, etc. Pilot plant No. 2, a larger edition of No. 1 but with only six stages, was used in late 1943 and early 1944, particularly as a testing unit for instruments. Pilot plant No. 3a, using centrifugal blowers and dummy diffusers, was also intended chiefly for testing instruments. Pilot plant No. 3b was a real pilot plant for one particular section of the large-scale plant. Pilot plants using full-scale equipment at the plant site demonstrated the vacuum tightness, corrosion resistance and general operability of the equipment.

PLANT AUTHORIZATION

10.32. In December 1942, the Kellogg Company was authorized to proceed with preliminary plant design and in January 1943 the construction of a plant was authorized.

THE SITE

10.33. As stated in an earlier chapter, a site in the Tennessee Valley had originally been chosen for all the Manhattan District plants, but the plutonium plant was actually constructed elsewhere. There remained the plutonium pilot plant already described, the gaseous diffusion plant, the electromagnetic separation plant (see Chapter XI), and later the thermal diffusion plant which were all built in the Tennessee Valley at the Clinton site, known officially as the Clinton Engineer Works.

10.34. This site was examined by Colonel Marshall, Colonel Nichols, and representatives of Stone and Webster Engineering Corporation in July 1942, and its acquisition was recommended. This recommendation was endorsed by the OSRD S-1 Executive Committee at a meeting in July 1942. Final approval was given by Major General L. R. Groves after personal inspection of the 70-square-mile site. In September 1942, the first steps were taken to acquire the tract, which is on the Clinch River about thirty miles from Knoxville, Tennessee, and eventually considerably exceeded 70 square miles. The plutonium pilot plant is located in one valley, the electromagnetic separation plant in an adjoining one, and the diffusion separation plant in a third.

10.35. Although the plant and site development at Hanford is very impressive, it is all under one company dealing with but one general operation so that it is in some respects less interesting than Clinton, which has a great multiplicity of activity. To describe the Clinton site, with its great array of new plants, its new residential districts, new theatres, new school system, seas of mud, clouds of dust, and general turmoil is outside the scope of this report.

DATES OF START OF CONSTRUCTION

10.36. Construction of the steam power plant for the diffusion plant began on June 1, 1943. It is one of the largest such power plants ever built. Construction of other major buildings and plants started between August 29, 1943 and September 10, 1943.

OPERATION

10.37. Unlike Hanford, the diffusion plant consists of so many more or less independent units that it was put into operation section by section, as permitted by progress in constructing and testing. Thus there was no dramatic start-up date nor any untoward incident to mark it. The plant was in successful operation before the summer of 1945.

10.38. For the men working on gaseous diffusion it was a long pull from 1940 to 1945, not lightened by such exciting half-way marks as the first chain-reacting pile at Chicago. Perhaps more than any other group in the project, those who have worked on gaseous diffusion deserve credit for courage and persistence as well as scientific and technical ability. For security reasons, we have not been able to tell how they solved their problems—even in many cases found several solutions, as insurance against failure in the plant. It has been a notable achievement. In these five years there have been periods of discouragement and pessimism. They are largely forgotten now that the plant is not only operating but operating consistently, reliably, and with a performance better than had been anticipated.

SUMMARY

10.39. Work at Columbia University on the separation of isotopes by gaseous diffusion began in 1940, and by the end of

1942 the problems of large-scale separation of uranium by this method had been well defined. Since the amount of separation that could be effected by a single stage was very small, several thousand successive stages were required. It was found that the best method of connecting the many stages required extensive recycling so that thousands of times as much material would pass through the barriers of the lower stages as would ultimately appear as product from the highest stage.

10.40. The principal problems were the development of satisfactory barriers and pumps. Acres of barrier and thousands of pumps were required. The obvious process gas was uranium hexafluoride for which the production and handling difficulties were so great that a search for an alternative was undertaken. Since much of the separation was to be carried out at low pressure, problems of vacuum technique arose, and on a previously unheard-of scale. Many problems of instrumentation and control were solved; extensive use was made of various forms of mass spectrograph.

10.41. The research was carried out principally at Columbia under Dunning and Urey. In 1942, the M. W. Kellogg Company was chosen to develop the process and equipment and to design the plant and set up the Kellex Corporation for the purpose. The plant was built by the J. A. Jones Construction Company. The Carbide and Carbon Chemicals Corporation was selected as operating company.

10.42. A very satisfactory barrier was developed although the final choice of barrier type was not made until the construction of the plant was well under way at Clinton Engineer Works in Tennessee. Two types of centrifugal blower were developed to the point where they could take care of the pumping requirements. The plant was put into successful operation before the summer of 1945.

CHAPTER XI. ELECTROMAGNETIC SEPARATION OF URANIUM ISOTOPES

INTRODUCTION

11.1. In Chapter IV we said that the possibility of large-scale separation of the uranium isotopes by electromagnetic means was suggested in the fall of 1941 by E. O. Lawrence of the University of California and H. D. Smyth of Princeton University. In Chapter IX we described the principles of one method of electromagnetic separation and listed the three limitations of that method: difficulty of producing ions, limited fraction of ions actually used, and space charge effects.

11.2. By the end of December 1941, when the reorganization of the whole uranium project was effected, Lawrence had already obtained some samples of separated isotopes of uranium and in the reorganization he was officially placed in charge of the preparation of further samples and the making of various associated physical measurements. However, just as the Metallurgical Laboratory very soon shifted its objective from the physics of the chain reaction to the large-scale production of plutonium, the objective of Lawrence's division immediately shifted to the effecting of large-scale separation of uranium isotopes by electromagnetic methods. This change was prompted by the success of the initial experiments at California and by the development at California and at Princeton of ideas on other possible methods. Of the many electromagnetic schemes suggested, three soon were recognized as being the most promising: the "calutron" mass separator, the magnetron-type separator later developed into the "ionic centrifuge," and the "isotron" method of "bunching" a beam of ions. The first two of these approaches were followed at California and the third at Princeton. After the first few months, by far the greatest effort was put on the calutron, but some work on the ionic centrifuge was continued at California during the summer of 1942 and was further continued by J. Slepian at the Westinghouse laboratories in Pittsburgh on a small scale through the winter of 1944–1945. Work on the isotron was continued at Princeton until February 1943, when most of the group was transferred to other work. Most of this chapter will be devoted to the calutron since that is the method that has resulted in large-scale production of U-235. A brief description will also be given of the thermal diffusion plant built to provide enriched feed material for the electromagnetic plant.

11.3. Security requirements make it impossible here—as for other parts of the project—to present many of the most interesting technical details. The importance of the development is considerably greater than is indicated by the amount of space which is given it here.

ELECTROMAGNETIC MASS SEPARATORS

PRELIMINARY WORK

11.4. A. O. Nier's mass spectrograph was set up primarily to measure relative abundances of isotopes, not to separate large samples. Using vapor from uranium bromide Nier had prepared several small samples of separated isotopes of uranium, but his rate of production was very low indeed, since his ion current amounted to less than one micro-ampere. (A mass spectrograph in which one micro-ampere of normal uranium ions passes through the separating fields to the collectors will collect about one microgram of U-235 per 16-hour day.) The great need of samples of enriched U-235 for nuclear study was recognized early by Lawrence, who decided to see what could be done with the help of the 37-inch (cyclotron) magnet at Berkeley. The initial stages of this work were assisted by a grant from the Research Corporation of New York, which was later repaid. Beginning January 1, 1942, the entire support came from the OSRD through the S-1 Committee. Later, as in other parts of the uranium project, the contracts were taken over by the Manhattan District.

11.5. At Berkeley, after some weeks of planning, the 37-inch cyclotron was dismantled on November 24, 1941, and its magnet was used to produce the magnetic field required in what came to be called a "calutron" (a name representing a contraction of "California University cyclotron"). An ion source consisting of an electron beam traversing the vapor of a uranium salt was set up corresponding to the ion source shown in the drawing in Chap. IX, p. 164. Ions were then accelerated to the slit s_2 through which they passed into the separating region where the magnetic field bent their paths into semicircles terminating at the collector slit. By December 1, 1941, molecular ion beams from the residual gas were obtained, and shortly thereafter the beam consisting of singly charged uranium ions (U+) was brought up to an appreciable strength. It was found that a considerable proportion of the ions leaving the source were U+ ions. For the purpose of testing the collection of separated samples, a collector with two pockets was installed, the two pockets being separated by a distance appropriate to the mass numbers 235 and 238. Two small collection runs using U+ beams of low strength were made in December, but subsequent analyses of the samples showed only a small separation factor. By the middle of January 1942, a run had been made with a reasonable beam strength and an aggregate flow or through-put of appreciable amount which showed a much improved separation factor. By early February 1942, beams of much greater strength were obtained, and Lawrence reported that good separation factors were obtainable with such beams. By early March 1942, the ion current had been raised still further. These results tended to bear out Lawrence's hopes that space charge could be neutralized by ionization of the residual gas in the magnet chamber.

INITIATION OF A LARGE PROGRAM

11.6. By this time it was clear that the calutron was potentially able to effect much larger scale separations than had ever before been approached by an electromagnetic method. It was evidently desirable to explore the whole field of electromagnetic separation. With this end in view, Lawrence mobilized his group at the Radiation Laboratory of the University of California at Berkeley and began to call in others to help. Among those initially at Berkeley were D. Cooksey, P. C. Aebersold, W. M. Brobeck, F. A. Jenkins, K. R. MacKenzie, W. B. Reynolds, D. H. Sloan, F. Oppenheimer, J. G. Backus, B. Peters, A. C. Helmholz, T. Finkelstein, and W. E. Parkins, Jr. Lawrence called back some of his former students, including R. L. Thornton, J. R. Richardson, and others. Among those working at Berkeley for various periods were L. P. Smith from Cornell, E. U. Condon and J. Slepian from Westinghouse, and I. Langmuir and K. H. Kingdon from General Electric. During this early period J. R. Oppenheimer was still at Berkeley and contributed some important ideas. In the fall of 1943 the group was further strengthened by the arrival of a number of English physicists under the leadership of M. L. Oliphant of the University of Birmingham.

11.7. Initially a large number of different methods were considered and many exploratory experiments were performed. The main effort, however, soon became directed towards the development of the calutron, the objective being a high separation factor and a large current in the positive ion beam.

IMMEDIATE OBJECTIVES

11.8. Of the three apparent limitations listed in the first paragraph—difficulty of producing ions, limited fraction of ions actually used, and space charge effects—only the last had yielded to the preliminary attack. Apparently space charge in the neighborhood of the positive ion beam could be nullified to a very great extent. There remained as the immediate objectives a more productive ion source and more complete utilization of the ions.

11.9. The factors that control the effectiveness of an ion source are many. Both the design of the source proper and the method of drawing ions from it are involved. The problems to be solved cannot be formulated simply and must be attacked by methods that are largely empirical. Even if security restrictions permitted an exposition of the innumerable forms of ion source and accelerating system that were tried, such exposition would be too technical to present here.

11.10. Turning to the problem of effecting more complete utilization of the ions, we must consider in some detail the principle of operation of the calutron. The calutron depends on the fact that singly charged ions moving in a uniform magnetic field perpendicular to their direction of _ption are bent into circular paths of radius proportional to their momenta. Considering now just a single isotope, it is apparent that the ions

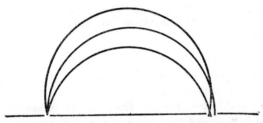

passing through the two slits (and thus passing into the large evacuated region in which the magnetic field is present) do not initially follow a single direction, but have many initial directions lying within a small angle, whose size depends on the width of the slits. Fortunately, however, since all the ions of the isotope in question follow curved paths of the *same* diameter, ions starting out in slightly different directions tend to meet again—or almost meet again—after completing a semicircle. It is, of course, at this position of reconvergence that the collector is placed. Naturally, the ions of another isotope (for example, ions of mass 238 instead of 235) behave similarly, except that they follow circles of slightly different diameter. Samples of the two isotopes are caught in collectors at the two different positions of reconvergence. Now the utilization of a greater fraction of the ions originally produced may be accomplished readily enough by widening the two slits referred to. But to widen the slits to any great extent without sacrificing sharpness of focus at the reconvergence positions is not easy. Indeed it can be accomplished only by use of carefully proportioned space variations in the magnetic field strength. Fortunately, such variations were worked out successfully.

11.11. Another problem, not so immediate but nevertheless recognized as important to any production plant, was that of more efficient use of the magnetic field. Since large electromagnets are expensive both to build and to operate, it was natural to consider using the same magnetic field for several ion beams. The experimental realization of such an economical scheme became a major task of the laboratory.

THE GIANT MAGNET

11.12. Although the scale of separation reached by March 1942 was much greater than anything that had previously been done with an electromagnetic mass separator, it was still very far from that required to produce amounts of material that would be of military significance. The problems that have been outlined not only had to be solved, but they had to be solved on a grand scale. The 37-inch cyclotron magnet that had been used was still capable of furnishing useful information, but larger equipment was desirable. Fortunately a very much larger magnet, intended for a giant cyclotron, had been under construction at Berkeley. This magnet, with a pole diameter of 184 inches and a pole gap of 72 inches, was to be the largest in existence. Work on it had been interrupted because of the war, but it was already sufficiently advanced so that it could be finished within a few months if adequate priorities were granted. Aside from the magnet itself, the associated building, laboratories, shops, etc., were almost ideal for the development of the calutron. Needless to say, work was resumed on the giant magnet and by the end of May 1942, it was ready for use.*

---

* The construction of the giant cyclotron had been undertaken with private funds largely supplied by the Rockefeller Foundation, augmented by donations from the Research Corporation, the John and Mary Markel Foundation, and the University of California. In order to push the construc-

DEVELOPMENT UP TO SEPTEMBER 1942

11.13. The first experiments using the 37-inch magnet have been described in a previous paragraph. Later developments proceeded principally along these two lines: construction and installation of a properly engineered separation unit for the 37-inch magnet, and design and construction of experimental separation units to go into the big magnet.

11.14. Besides the gradual increase in ion beam strength and separation factor that resulted from a series of developments in the ion source and in the accelerating system, the hoped-for improvement in utilization of ions was achieved during the summer of 1942, using the giant magnet. Further, it was possible to maintain more than one ion beam in the same magnetic separating region. Experiments on this latter problem did run into some difficulties, however, and it appeared that there might be limitations on the number of sources and receivers that could be put in a single unit as well as on the current that could be used in each beam without spoiling the separation.

11.15. It was evident that many separator units would be needed to get an amount of production of military significance. Therefore, consideration was given to various systems of combining groups of units in economical arrangements. A scheme was worked out which was later used in the production plants and which has proved satisfactory.

ADVANTAGES OF THE ELECTROMAGNETIC SYSTEM

11.16. In September 1942, both the gaseous diffusion and the centrifugal methods of uranium isotope separation had been under intensive study—and for a longer period than in the case of the electromagnetic method. Both of these methods—gaseous diffusion and centrifuge—looked feasible for large-scale production of U-235, but both would require hundreds of stages to achieve large-scale separation. Neither had actually produced

tion as fast as possible overtime work was required at additional expense. To cover these costs the Rockefeller Foundation made an extra appropriation.

any appreciable amounts of separated U-235. No large-scale plant for plutonium production was under way, and the self-sustaining chain reaction which was to produce plutonium had not yet been proved attainable. But in the case of the electromagnetic method, after the successful separation of milligram amounts, there was no question as to the scientific feasibility. If one unit could separate 10 mg a day, 100,000,000 units could separate one ton a day. The questions were of cost and time. Each unit was to be a complicated electromagnetic device requiring high vacuum, high voltages, and intense magnetic fields; and a great deal of research and development work would be required before complete, large-scale, units could be constructed. Many skilled operators would probably be needed. Altogether, at that time it looked very expensive, but it also looked certain and relatively quick. Moreover, the smallness of the units had the advantage that development could continue, modifications could be made in the course of construction or, within limits, after construction, and capacity could always be expanded by building new units.

POLICY QUESTION

11.17. On the basis of rather incomplete scientific and engineering information on all the methods and on the basis of equally dubious cost estimates, decisions had to be made on three issues: (1) whether to build an electromagnetic plant; (2) how big such a plant should be; (3) at what point of development the design should be frozen.

APPROVAL OF PLANT CONSTRUCTION

11.18. On the strength of the results reported on experiments at Berkeley in the summer of 1942, the S-1 Executive Committee, at a meeting at Berkeley on September 13–14, 1942, recommended that commitments be made by the Army for an electromagnetic separation plant to be built at the Tennessee Valley site (Clinton Engineer Works). It was recommended that it should be agreed that commitments for this plant might be cancelled on the basis of later information. It was recommended that a pilot plant should be erected at the Tennessee Valley site as soon as possible. (However, this recommendation was subsequently withdrawn and such a pilot plant was never built.) The construction of a production plant was authorized by General Groves on November 5, 1942, with the understanding that the design for the first units was to be frozen immediately.

ORGANIZATION FOR PLANNING AND CONSTRUCTION

11.19. In describing the production of plutonium, we discussed the division of responsibility between the Metallurgical Project and the du Pont Company. The electromagnetic separation plant was planned and built under a somewhat different scheme of organization. The responsibility was divided between six major groups. The Radiation Laboratory at the University of California was responsible for research and development; the Westinghouse Electric and Manufacturing Company for making the mechanical parts, i.e., sources, receivers, pumps, tanks, etc.; the General Electric Company for the electrical equipment and controls; the Allis-Chalmers Company for the magnets; the Stone and Webster Engineering Company for the construction and assembly; and the Tennessee Eastman Company for operation. All five industrial concerns kept groups of their engineers at Berkeley so that a system of frequent informal conference and cross-checking was achieved. Thus the major part of the planning was done cooperatively in a single group, even though the details might be left to the home offices of the various companies.

THE BASIS OF THE TECHNICAL DECISIONS

11.20. Strangely enough, although the theory of the self-sustaining chain-reacting pile is already well worked out, the theory of gaseous discharge, after fifty years of intensive study, is still inadequate for the prediction of the exact behavior of the ions in a calutron. The amount of U-235 collected per day, and the purity of the material collected, are affected by many factors, including: (1) the width, spacing, and shape of the collector,

(2) the pressure in the magnet space, (3) the strength and uniformity of the magnetic field, (4) the shape and spacing of the defining slits and accelerating system, (5) the accelerating voltage, (6) the size and shape of the slit in the arc source from which the ions come, (7) the current in the arc, (8) the position of the arc within the arc chamber, (9) the pressure of vapor in the arc chamber, (10) the chemical nature of the vapor. Evidently there was not time for a systematic study of all possible combinations of variables. The development had to be largely intuitive. A variety of conditions had to be studied and a number of partial interpretations had to be made. Then the accumulated experience of the group, the "feel" of the problem, had to be translated into specific plans and recommendations.

TECHNICAL DECISIONS REQUIRED

11.21. (a) *The Number of Stages.* As in all methods, a compromise must be made between yield and separation factor. In the electromagnetic system, the separation factor is much higher than in other systems so that the number of stages required is small. There was a possibility that a single stage might be sufficient. Early studies indicated that attempts to push the separation factor so high as to make single-stage operation feasible cut the yield to an impractically small figure.

11.22. (b) *Specifications.* The information and experience that had been acquired on the variables such as those mentioned above had to be translated into decisions on the following principal points before design could actually begin: (1) the size of a unit as determined by the radius of curvature of the ion path, the length of the source slit, and the arrangement of sources and receivers; (2) the maximum intensity of magnetic field required; (3) whether or not to use large divergence of ion beams; (4) the number of ion sources and receivers per unit; (5) whether the source should be at high potential or at ground potential; (6) the number of accelerating electrodes and the maximum potentials to be applied to them; (7) the power requirements for arcs, accelerating voltages, pumps, etc.; (8) pumping requirements; (9) number of units per pole gap; (10) number of units per building.

EXPERIMENTAL UNITS AT BERKELEY

11.23. Most of the design features for the first plant had to be frozen in the fall of 1942 on the basis of results obtained with runs made using the giant magnet at Berkeley. The plant design, however, called for units of a somewhat different type. While there was no reason to suppose that these changes would introduce any difference in performance, it was obviously desirable to build a prototype unit at Berkeley. The construction of this unit was approved at about the same time that the first plant units were ordered so that experience with it had no influence on fundamental design, but it was finished and operating by April 1943, that is, six months before the first plant unit. Consequently, it was invaluable for testing and training purposes. Later, a third magnet was built in the big magnet building at Berkeley. All told, there have been six separator units available simultaneously for experimental or pilot plant purposes at Berkeley. Much auxiliary work has also been done outside the complete units.

THE ISOTRON SEPARATOR

11.24. As we have already said, H. D. Smyth of Princeton became interested in electromagnetic methods of separation in the late summer and fall of 1941. He was particularly interested in devising some method of using an extended ion source and beam instead of one limited essentially to one dimension by a slit system as in the calutron mass separator. A method of actually achieving separation using an extended ion source was suggested by R. R. Wilson of Princeton. The device which resulted from Wilson's ideas was given the deliberately meaningless name "isotron."

11.25. The isotron is an electromagnetic mass separator using an extended source of ions, in contrast to the slit sources used in ordinary mass spectrographs. The ions from the extended source are first accelerated by a constant, high-intensity, electric field and are then further accelerated by a low-intensity electric field varying at radio frequency and in "saw tooth" manner. The effect of the constant electric field is to project a strong beam of ions down a tube with uniform kinetic energy and therefore with velocities inversely proportional to the square root of the masses of ions. The varying electric field, on the other hand, introduces small, periodic variations in ion velocity, and has the effect of causing the ions to "bunch" at a certain distance down the tube. (This same principle is used in the klystron high-frequency oscillator, where the electrons are "bunched" or "velocity-modulated.") The bunches of ions of different mass travel with different velocities and therefore become separated. At the position (actually on *area* perpendicular to the beam) where this occurs, an analyzer applies a transverse focussing electric field with a radio frequency component synchronized with the arrival of the bunches. The synchronization is such that the varying component of the transverse field strength is zero when the U-235 ion bunches come through and a maximum when the U-238 ion bunches come through. The U-235 beams are focussed on a collector, but the U-238 bunches are deflected. Thus the separation is accomplished.

11.26. This scheme was described at the December 18, 1941 meeting of the Uranium Committee and immediately thereafter was discussed more fully with Lawrence, who paid a visit to Princeton. The promise of the method seemed sufficient to justify experimental work, which was begun immediately under an OSRD contract and continued until February 1943. Since the idea involved was a novel one, there were two outstanding issues: (1) whether the method would work at all; (2) whether it could be developed for large-scale production promptly enough to compete with the more orthodox methods already under development.

11.27. An experimental isotron was constructed and put into operation by the end of January 1942. Preliminary experiments at that time indicated that the isotopes of lithium could be separated by the method. The first successful collection of partially separated uranium isotopes was made in the spring of 1942.

11.28. Unfortunately, progress during the summer and fall of 1942 was not as rapid as had been hoped. Consequently, it was decided to close down the Princeton project in order to permit sending the personnel to the site where the atomic-bomb laboratory was about to get under way. Before the group left Princeton a small experimental isotron collected several samples of partly separated uranium. Thus, the method worked; but its large-scale applicability was not fully investigated.

The Magnetron and the Ionic Centrifuge

11.29. In December 1941, when the whole subject of isotope separation was under discussion at Berkeley, the magnetron was suggested as a possible mass separator. In the meantime, Smyth of Princeton had been in contact with L. P. Smith of Cornell and had discovered that Smith and his students had done a considerable amount of work—and with evidence of success—on the separation of the isotopes of lithium by just such a method. This was reported to Lawrence in Washington at one of the December, 1941, meetings of the Uranium Committee. Lawrence immediately got in touch with Smith, with the result that Smith worked on the method at Berkeley from February 1942 to June 1942. J. Slepian of the Westinghouse Research Laboratory in East Pittsburgh came to Berkeley in the winter of 1941–1942 at Lawrence's invitation and became interested in a modification of the magnetron which he called an ionic centrifuge. Slepian stayed at Berkeley most of the time until the fall of 1942, after which he returned to East Pittsburgh where he continued the work.

11.30. No separation of uranium was actually attempted in the magnetron. Experiments with lithium with low ion currents showed some separation, but no consistent results were obtained with high ion currents. In the case of the ionic centrifuge, uranium samples have been collected showing appreciable separation, but the results have not been clear-cut or consistent.

THE SITUATION AS OF EARLY 1943

11.31. With the virtual elimination of the isotron and the ionic centrifuge from the development program, the calutron separator became the only electromagnetic method worked on intensively. Construction of initial units of a plant had been authorized and designs had been frozen for such units, but the whole electromagnetic program had been in existence for only a little more than a year and it was obvious that available designs were based on shrewd guesses rather than on adequate research. A similar situation might have occurred with the chain-reacting pile if unlimited amounts of uranium and graphite had been available before the theory had been worked out or before the nuclear constants had been well determined. Fortunately the nature of the two projects was very different, making it a less speculative venture to build an electromagnetic plant unit hastily than would have been the case for the pile. Further research and development could proceed advantageously even while initial units of the plant were being built and operated.

CONSTRUCTION AND OPERATION; MARCH 1943 TO JUNE 1945

COMPARISON WITH DIFFUSION AND PLUTONIUM PLANTS

11.32. The preceding chapters show that the end of 1942 was a time of decision throughout the uranium project. For it was at that time that a self-sustaining chain reaction was first produced, that construction was authorized for the Hanford plutonium plant, the diffusion plant at Clinton, and the electromagnetic plant at Clinton. The diffusion plant was more flexible than the plutonium plant, since the diffusion plant could be broken down into sections and stages, built in whole or in part, to produce varying amounts of U-235 of varying degrees of enrichment. The electromagnetic plant was even more flexible, since each separator unit was practically independent of the other units. The separation process consisted of loading a charge into a unit, running the unit for a while, then stopping it and removing the product. To be sure, the units were built in groups, but most of the controls were separate for each unit. This feature made it possible to build the plant in steps and to start operating the first part even before the second was begun. It was also possible to change the design of subsequent units as construction proceeded; within limits it was possible even to replace obsolescent units in the early groups with new improved units.

NATURE AND ORGANIZATION OF DEVELOPMENT WORK

11.33. Construction of the first series of electromagnetic units at Clinton began in March of 1943 and this part of the plant was ready for operation in November 1943. The group at Berkeley continued to improve the ion sources, the receivers, and the auxiliary equipment, aiming always at greater ion currents. In fact, Berkeley reports describe no less than seventy-one different types of source and one hundred and fifteen different types of receiver, all of which reached the design stage and most of which were constructed and tested. As soon as the value of a given design change was proved, every effort was made to incorporate it in the designs of new units.

11.34. Such developments as these required constant interchange of information among laboratory, engineering, construction, and operating groups. Fortunately the liaison was excellent. The companies stationed representatives at Berkeley, and members of the research group at Berkeley paid frequent and prolonged visits to the plant at Clinton. In fact, some of the research men were transferred to the payroll of the Tennessee Eastman Company operating the plant at Clinton, and a group of over one hundred physicists and research engineers still kept on the Berkeley payroll were assigned to Clinton. Particularly in the early stages of operation the Berkeley men stationed at Clinton were invaluable as "trouble shooters" and in instructing operators. A section of the plant continued to be maintained as a pilot unit for testing modified equipment and revised operating procedures, and was run jointly by the Berkeley group and by

Tennessee Eastman. In addition to the British group under Oliphant already mentioned, there was a British group of chemists at Clinton under J. W. Baxter.

CHEMICAL PROBLEMS

11.35. Originally, the uranium salts used as sources of vapor for the ion-producing arcs had not been investigated with any very great thoroughness at Berkeley, but as the process developed, a good deal of work was done on these salts, and a search was made for a uranium compound that would be better than that originally used. Some valuable studies were also made on methods of producing the compound chosen.

11.36. By far the most important chemical problem was the recovery of the processed uranium compounds from the separation units. This recovery problem had two phases. In units of the first stage it was essential to recover the separated uranium from the receivers with maximum efficiency; whereas recovery of the scattered unseparated uranium from other parts of the unit was less important. But if higher stage units are used even the starting material contains a high concentration of U-235, and it is essential to recover all the material in the unit at the end of each run, i.e., material remaining in the ion source and material deposited on the accelerating electrodes, on the walls of the magnet chamber, and on the receiver walls.

THE THERMAL DIFFUSION PLANT

11.37. For nearly a year the electromagnetic plant was the only one in operation. Therefore the urge to increase its production rate was tremendous. It was realized that any method of enriching—even slightly enriching—the material to be fed into the plant would increase the production rate appreciably. For example, an electromagnetic unit that could produce a gram a day of 40 per cent pure U-235 from natural uranium could produce two grams a day of 80 per cent U-235 if the concentration of U-235 in the feed material was twice the natural concentration (1.4 per cent instead of 0.7 per cent).

11.38. We have already referred to the work done by P. H. Abelson of the Naval Research Laboratory on the separation of the uranium isotopes by thermal diffusion in a liquid compound of uranium. By the spring of 1943 Abelson had set up a pilot plant that accomplished appreciable separation of a considerable quantity of uranium compound. It was therefore proposed that a large-scale thermal diffusion plant should be constructed. Such a plant would be cheaper than any of the other large-scale plants, and it could be built more quickly. Its principal drawback was its enormous consumption of steam, which made it appear impracticable for the whole job of separation.

11.39. Not only was a pilot plant already in operation at the Naval Research Laboratory, but a second, somewhat larger plant was under construction at the Philadelphia Navy Yard. Through the cooperation of the Navy both the services of Abelson and the plans for a large-scale plant were made available to the Manhattan District. It was decided to erect the large-scale thermal diffusion plant at Clinton (using steam from the power plant constructed for the gaseous diffusion plant) and to use the thermal-diffusion-plant product as feed material for the electromagnetic plant.

11.40. This new thermal diffusion plant was erected in amazingly short time during the late summer of 1944. In spite of some disappointments, operation of this plant has succeeded in its purpose of considerably increasing the production rate of the electromagnetic plant. It has also stimulated work on the uranium recovery problem. The future of this plant is uncertain. Operation of the gaseous-diffusion plant makes it difficult to get enough steam to operate the thermal diffusion plant, but also furnishes another user for its product.

Miscellaneous Problems

11.41. Although the scientific and technical problems which confronted the Berkeley groups were probably not as varied or numerous as the problems encountered at Chicago and Columbia, they were nevertheless numerous. Thus many problems arose in the designing of the electric power and control circuits, magnetic fields, insulators, vacuum pumps, tanks, collectors, and sources. Many equipment items had to be designed from scratch and then mass-produced under high priority.

PRESENT STATUS

11.42. The electromagnetic separation plant was in large-scale operation during the winter of 1944–1945, and produced U-235 of sufficient purity for use in atomic bombs. Its operating efficiency is being continually improved. Research work is continuing although on a reduced scale.

SUMMARY

11.43. In the early days of the uranium project, electromagnetic methods of isotope separation were rejected primarily because of the expected effects of space-charge. In the fall of 1941 the question was reopened; experiments at Berkeley showed that space-charge effects could be largely overcome. Consequently a large-scale program for the development of electromagnetic methods was undertaken.

11.44. Of the various types of electromagnetic methods proposed, the calutron (developed at Berkeley) received principal attention. Two other novel methods were studied, one at Berkeley and one at Princeton. The calutron mass separator consists of an ion source from which a beam of uranium ions is drawn by an electric field, an accelerating system in which the ions are accelerated to high velocities, a magnetic field in which the ions travel in semicircles of radius depending on ion mass, and a receiving system. The principal problems of this method involved the ion source, accelerating system, divergence of the ion beam, space charge, and utilization of the magnetic field. The chief advantages of the calutron were large separation factor, small hold-up, short start-up time, and flexibility of operation. By the fall of 1942 sufficient progress had been made to justify authorization of plant construction, and a year later the first plant units were ready for trial at the Clinton Engineer Works in Tennessee.

11.45. Research and development work on the calutron were carried out principally at the Radiation Laboratory of the University of California, under the direction of Lawrence. Westinghouse, General Electric, and Allis Chalmers constructed a majority of the parts; Stone and Webster built the plant, and Tennessee Eastman operated it.

11.46. Since the calutron separation method was one of batch operations in a large number of largely independent units, it was possible to introduce important improvements even after plant operation had begun.

11.47. In the summer of 1944 a thermal-diffusion separation plant was built at the Clinton Engineer Works to furnish enriched feed material for the electromagnetic plant and thereby increase the production rate of this latter plant. The design of the thermal-diffusion plant was based on the results of research carried out at the Naval Research Laboratory and on the pilot plant built by the Navy Department at the Philadelphia Navy Yard.

11.48. Although research work on the calutron was started later than on the centrifuge and diffusion systems, the calutron plant was the first to produce large amounts of the separated isotopes of uranium.

CHAPTER XII. THE WORK ON THE ATOMIC BOMB

THE OBJECTIVE

12.1. The entire purpose of the work described in the preceding chapters was to explore the possibility of creating atomic bombs and to produce the concentrated fissionable materials which would be required in such bombs. In the present chapter, the last stage of the work will be described—the development at Los Alamos of the atomic bomb itself. As in other parts of the project, there are two phases to be considered: the organization, and the scientific and technical work itself. The organization will be described briefly; the remainder of the chapter will be devoted to the scientific and technical problems. Security considerations prevent a discussion of many of the most important phases of this work.

HISTORY AND ORGANIZATION

12.2. The project reorganization that occurred at the beginning of 1942, and the subsequent gradual transfer of the work from OSRD auspices to the Manhattan District have been described in Chapter V. It will be recalled that the responsibilities of the Metallurgical Laboratory at Chicago originally included a preliminary study of the physics of the atomic bomb. Some such studies were made in 1941; and early in 1942 G. Breit got various laboratories (see Chapter VI, paragraph 6.38) started on the experimental study of problems that had to be solved before progress could be made on bomb design. As has been mentioned in Chapter VI, J. R. Oppenheimer of the University of California gathered a group together in the summer of 1942 for further theoretical investigation and also undertook to coordinate this experimental work. This group was officially under the Metallurgical Laboratory but the theoretical group did most of its work at the University of California. By the end of the summer of 1942, when General L. R. Groves took charge of the entire project, it was decided to expand the work considerably, and, at the earliest possible time, to set up a separate laboratory.

12.3. In the choice of a site for this atomic-bomb laboratory, the all-important considerations were secrecy and safety. It was therefore decided to establish the laboratory in an isolated location and to sever unnecessary connection with the outside world.

12.4. By November 1942 a site had been chosen—at Los Alamos, New Mexico. It was located on a mesa about 30 miles from Santa Fe. One asset of this site was the availability of considerable area for proving grounds, but initially the only structures on the site consisted of a handful of buildings which once constituted a small boarding school. There was no laboratory, no library, no shop, no adequate power plant. The sole means of approach was a winding mountain road. That the handicaps of the site were overcome to a considerable degree is a tribute to the unstinting efforts of the scientific and military personnel.

12.5. J. R. Oppenheimer has been director of the laboratory from the start. He arrived at the site in March 1943, and was soon joined by groups and individuals from Princeton University, University of Chicago, University of California, University of Wisconsin, University of Minnesota, and elsewhere. With the vigorous support of General L. R. Groves, J. B. Conant, and others, Oppenheimer continued to gather around him scientists of recognized ability, so that the end of 1944 found an extraordinary galaxy of scientific stars gathered on this New Mexican mesa. The recruiting of junior scientific personnel and technicians was more difficult, since for such persons the disadvantages of the site were not always counterbalanced by an appreciation of the magnitude of the goal; the use of Special Engineer Detachment personnel improved the situation considerably.

12.6. Naturally, the task of assembling the necessary apparatus, machines, and equipment was an enormous one. Three carloads of apparatus from the Princeton project filled some of the most urgent requirements. A cyclotron from Harvard, two Van de Graaff generators from Wisconsin, and a Cockcroft-Walton high-voltage device from Illinois soon arrived. As an illustration of the speed with which the laboratory was set up, we may record that the bottom pole piece of the cyclotron magnet was not laid until April 14, 1943, yet the first experiment was performed in early July. Other apparatus was acquired in quantity; subsidiary laboratories were built. Today this is probably the best-equipped physics research laboratory in the world.

12.7. The laboratory was financed under a contract between the Manhattan District and the University of California.

STATE OF KNOWLEDGE IN APRIL 1943

GENERAL DISCUSSION OF THE PROBLEM

12.8. In Chapter II we stated the general conditions required to produce a self-sustaining chain reaction. It was pointed out that there are four processes competing for neutrons: (1) the capture of neutrons by uranium which results in fission; (2) non-fission capture by uranium; (3) non-fission capture by impurities; and (4) escape of neutrons from the system. Therefore the condition for obtaining such a chain reaction is that process (1) shall produce as many new neutrons as are consumed or lost in all four of the processes. It was pointed out that (2) may be reduced by removal of U-238 or by the use of a lattice and moderator, that (3) may be reduced by achieving a high degree of chemical purity, and that (4) may be reduced (relatively) by increasing the size of the system. In our earlier discussions of chain reactions it was always taken for granted that the chain-reacting system must not blow up. Now we want to consider how to make it blow up.

12.9. By definition, an explosion is a sudden and violent release of a large amount of energy in a small region. To produce an efficient explosion in an atomic bomb, the parts of the bomb must not become appreciably separated before a substantial fraction of the available nuclear energy has been released, since expansion leads to increased escape of neutrons from the system and thus to premature termination of the chain reaction. Stated differently, the efficiency of the atomic bomb will depend on the ratio of (a) the speed with which neutrons generated by the first fissions get into other nuclei and produce further fission, and (b) the speed with which the bomb flies apart. Using known principles of energy generation, temperature and pressure rise, and expansion of solids and vapors, it was possible to estimate the order of magnitude of the time interval between the beginning and end of the nuclear chain reaction. Almost all the technical difficulties of the project come from the extraordinary brevity of this time interval.

12.10. In earlier chapters we stated that no self-sustaining chain reaction could be produced in a block of pure uranium metal, no matter how large, because of parasitic capture of the neutrons by U-238. This conclusion has been borne out by various theoretical calculations and also by direct experiment. For purposes of producing a non-explosive pile, the trick of using a lattice and a moderator suffices—by reducing parasitic capture sufficiently. For purposes of producing an explosive unit, however, it turns out that this process is unsatisfactory on two counts. First, the thermal neutrons take so long (so many micro-seconds) to act that only a feeble explosion would result. Second, a pile is ordinarily far too big to be transported. It is therefore necessary to cut down parasitic capture by removing the greater part of the U-238—or to use plutonium.

12.11. Naturally, these general principles—and others—had been well established before the Los Alamos project was set up.

CRITICAL SIZE

12.12. The calculation of the critical size of a chain-reacting unit is a problem that has already been discussed in connection with piles. Although the calculation is simpler for a homogeneous metal unit than for a lattice, inaccuracies remained in the course of the early work, both because of lack of accurate knowledge of constants and because of mathematical difficulties. For example, the scattering, fission, and absorption cross sections of the nuclei involved all vary with neutron velocity. The details of such variation were not known experimentally and were difficult to take into account in making calculations. By the spring of 1943 several estimates of critical size had been made using various methods of calculation and using the best available nuclear constants, but the limits of error remained large.

The Reflector or Tamper

12.13. In a uranium-graphite chain-reacting pile the critical size may be considerably reduced by surrounding the pile with a layer of graphite, since such an envelope "reflects" many neutrons back into the pile. A similar envelope can be used to reduce the critical size of the bomb, but here the envelope has an additional role: its very inertia delays the expansion of the reacting material. For this reason such an envelope is often called a tamper. Use of a tamper clearly makes for a longer lasting, more energetic, and more efficient explosion. The most effective tamper is the one having the highest density; high tensile strength turns out to be unimportant. It is a fortunate coincidence that materials of high density are also excellent as reflectors of neutrons.

Efficiency

12.14. As has already been remarked, the bomb tends to fly to bits as the reaction proceeds and this tends to stop the reaction. To calculate how much the bomb has to expand before the reaction stops is relatively simple. The calculation of how long this expansion takes and how far the reaction goes in that time is much more difficult.

12.15. While the effect of a tamper is to increase the efficiency both by reflecting neutrons and by delaying the expansion of the bomb, the effect on the efficiency is not as great as on the critical mass. The reason for this is that the process of reflection is relatively time-consuming and may not occur extensively before the chain reaction is terminated.

Detonation and Assembly

12.16. As stated in Chapter II, it is impossible to prevent a chain reaction from occurring when the size exceeds the critical size. For there are always enough neutrons (from cosmic rays, from spontaneous fission reactions, or from alpha-particle-induced reactions in impurities) to initiate the chain. Thus until detonation is desired, the bomb must consist of a number of separate pieces each one of which is below the critical size either by reason of small size or unfavorable shape. To produce detonation, the parts of the bomb must be brought together rapidly. In the course of this assembly process the chain reaction is likely to start—because of the presence of stray neutrons—*before* the bomb has reached its most compact (most reactive) form. Thereupon the explosion tends to prevent the bomb from reaching that most compact form. Thus it may turn out that the explosion is so inefficient as to be relatively useless. The problem, therefore, is two-fold: (1) to reduce the time of assembly to a minimum; and (2) to reduce the number of stray (predetonation) neutrons to a minimum.

12.17. Some consideration was given to the danger of producing a "dud" or a detonation so inefficient that even the bomb itself would not be completely destroyed. This would, of course, present the enemy with a supply of highly valuable material.

Effectiveness

12.18. In Chapters II and IV it was pointed out that the amount of energy released was not the sole criterion of the value of a bomb. There was no assurance that one uranium bomb releasing energy equal to the energy released by 20,000 tons of TNT would be as effective in producing military destruction as, say, 10,000 two-ton bombs. In fact, there were good reasons to believe that the destructive effect per calorie released decreases as the total amount of energy released increases. On the other hand, in atomic bombs the total amount of energy released per kilogram of fissionable material (i.e., the efficiency of energy release) *increases* with the size of the bomb. Thus the optimum size of the atomic bomb was not easily determined. A tactical aspect that complicates the matter further is the advantage of simultaneous destruction of a large area of enemy territory. In a complete appraisal of the effectiveness of an atomic bomb, attention must also be given to effects on morale.* The bomb is detonated in combat at such a height above the ground as to give the maximum blast effect against structures, and to disseminate the radioactive products as a cloud. On account of the height of the explosion practically all the radioactive products are carried upward in the ascending column of hot air and dispersed harmlessly over a wide area. Even in the New Mexico test, where the height of explosion was necessarily low, only a very small fraction of the radioactivity was deposited immediately below the bomb.

Method of Assembly

12.19. Since estimates had been made of the speed that would bring together subcritical masses of U-235 rapidly enough to avoid predetonation, a good deal of thought had been given to practical methods of doing this. The obvious method of very rapidly assembling an atomic bomb was to shoot one part as a projectile in a gun against a second part as a target. The projectile mass, projectile speed, and gun caliber required were not far from the range of standard ordnance practice, but novel problems were introduced by the importance of achieving sudden and perfect contact between projectile and target, by the use of tampers, and by the requirement of portability. None of these technical problems had been studied to any appreciable extent prior to the establishment of the Los Alamos laboratory.

12.20. It had also been realized that schemes probably might be devised whereby neutron absorbers could be incorporated in the bomb in such a way that they would be rendered less effective by the initial stages of the chain reactions. Thus the tendency for

---

* The rest of this paragraph is from a War Department release subsequent to the first use of atomic bombs against Japan.

the bomb to detonate prematurely and inefficiently would be minimized. Such devices for increasing the efficiency of the bomb are called auto-catalytic.

12.21. In April 1943 the available information of interest in connection with the design of atomic bombs was preliminary and inaccurate. Further and extensive theoretical work on critical size, efficiency, effect of tamper, method of detonation, and effectiveness was urgently needed. Measurements of the nuclear constants of U-235, plutonium, and tamper material had to be extended and improved. In the cases of U-235 and plutonium, tentative measurements had to be made using only minute quantities until larger quantities became available.

12.22. Besides these problems in theoretical and experimental physics, there was a host of chemical, metallurgical, and technical problems that had hardly been touched. Examples were the purification and fabrication of U-235 and plutonium, and the fabrication of the tamper. Finally, there were problems of instantaneous assembly of the bomb that were staggering in their complexity.

THE WORK OF THE LABORATORY

INTRODUCTION

12.23. For administrative purposes the scientific staff at Los Alamos was arranged in seven divisions, which have been rearranged at various times. During the spring of 1945 the divisions were: Theoretical Physics Division under H. Bethe, Experimental Nuclear Physics Division under R. R. Wilson, Chemistry and Metallurgy Division under J. W. Kennedy and C. S. Smith, Ordnance Division under Capt. W. S. Parsons (USN), Explosives Division under G. B. Kistiakowsky, Bomb Physics Division under R. F. Bacher, and an Advanced Development Division under E. Fermi. All the divisions reported to J. R. Oppenheimer, Director of the Los Alamos Laboratory who has been assisted in coordinating the research by S. K. Allison since December 1944. J. Chadwick of England and N. Bohr of Denmark spent a great deal of time at Los Alamos and gave invaluable advice. Chadwick was the head of a British delegation which contributed materially to the success of the laboratory. For security reasons, most of the work of the laboratory can be described only in part.

THEORETICAL PHYSICS DIVISION

12.24. There were two considerations that gave unusual importance to the work of the Theoretical Physics Division under H. Bethe. The first of these was the necessity for effecting simultaneous development of everything from the fundamental materials to the method of putting them to use—all despite the virtual unavailability of the principal materials (U-235 and plutonium) and the complete novelty of the processes. The second consideration was the impossibility of producing (as for experimental purposes) a "small-scale" atomic explosion by making use of only a small amount of fissionable material. (No explosion occurs at all unless the mass of the fissionable material exceeds the critical mass.) Thus it was necessary to proceed from data obtained in experiments on infinitesimal quantities of materials and to combine it with the available theories as accurately as possible in order to make estimates as to what would happen in the bomb. Only in this way was it possible to make sensible plans for the other parts of the project, and to make decisions on design and construction without waiting for elaborate experiments on large quantities of material. To take a few examples, theoretical work was required in making rough determinations of the dimensions of the gun, in guiding the metallurgists in the choice of tamper materials, and in determining the influence of the purity of the fissionable material on the efficiency of the bomb.

12.25. The determination of the critical size of the bomb was one of the main problems of the Theoretical Physics Division. In the course of time, several improvements were made in the theoretical approach whereby it was possible to take account of practically all the complex phenomena involved. It was at first considered that the diffusion of neutrons was similar to the diffusion of heat, but this naive analogy had to be forsaken. In the early theoretical work the assumptions were made that the neutrons all had the same velocity and all were scattered isotropically. A method was thus developed which permitted calculation of the critical size for various shapes of the fissionable material provided that the mean free path of the neutrons was the same in the tamper material as in the fissionable material. This method was later improved first by taking account of the angular dependence of the scattering and secondly by allowing for difference in mean free path in core and tamper materials. Still later, means were found of taking into account the effects of the distribution in velocity of the neutrons, the variations of cross sections with velocity, and inelastic scattering in the core and tamper materials. Thus it became possible to compute critical sizes assuming almost any kind of tamper material.

12.26. The rate at which the neutron density decreases in bomb models which are smaller than the critical size can be calculated, and all the variables mentioned above can be taken into account. The rate of approach to the critical condition as the projectile part of the bomb moves toward the target part of the bomb has been studied by theoretical methods. Furthermore, the best distribution of fissionable material in projectile and target was determined by theoretical studies.

12.27. Techniques were developed for dealing with set-ups in which the number of neutrons is so small that a careful statistical analysis must be made of the effects of the neutrons. The most important problem in this connection was the determination of the probability that, when a bomb is larger than critical size, a stray neutron will start a continuing chain reaction. A related problem was the determination of the magnitude of the fluctuations in neutron density in a bomb whose size is close to the critical size. By the summer of 1945 many such calculations had been checked by experiments.

12.28. A great deal of theoretical work was done on the equation of state of matter at the high temperatures and pressures to be expected in the exploding atomic bombs. The expansion of the various constituent parts of the bomb during and after the moment of chain reaction has been calculated. The effects of radiation have been investigated in considerable detail.

12.29. Having calculated the energy that is released in the explosion of an atomic bomb, one naturally wants to estimate the military damage that will be produced. This involves analysis of the shock waves in air and in earth, the determination of the effectiveness of a detonation beneath the surface of the ocean, etc.

12.30. In addition to all the work mentioned above, a considerable amount of work was done in evaluating preliminary experiments. Thus an analysis was made of the back-scattering of neutrons by the various tamper materials proposed. An analysis was also made of the results of experiments on the multiplication of neutrons in subcritical amounts of fissionable material.

EXPERIMENTAL NUCLEAR PHYSICS DIVISION

12.31. The experiments performed by the Experimental Nuclear Physics group at Los Alamos were of two kinds: "differential" experiments as for determining the cross section for fission of a specific isotope by neutrons of a specific velocity, and "integral" experiments as for determining the average scattering of fission neutrons from an actual tamper.

12.32. Many nuclear constants had already been determined at the University of Chicago Metallurgical Laboratory and elsewhere, but a number of important constants were still undetermined—especially those involving high neutron velocities. Some of the outstanding questions were the following:

1. What are the fission cross sections of U-234, U-235, U-238, Pu-239, etc.? How do they vary with neutron velocity?

2. What are the elastic scattering cross sections for the same nuclei (also for nuclei of tamper materials)? How do they vary with neutron velocity?

3. What are the inelastic cross sections for the nuclei referred to above?

4. What are the absorption cross sections for processes other than fission?

5. How many neutrons are emitted per fission in the case of each of the nuclei referred to above?

6. What is the full explanation of the fact that the number of neutrons emitted per fission is not a whole number?

7. What is the initial energy of the neutrons produced by fission?

8. Does the number or energy of such neutrons vary with the speed of the incident neutrons?

9. Are fission neutrons emitted immediately?

10. What is the probability of spontaneous fission of the various fissionable nuclei?

12.33. In addition to attempting to find the answers to these questions the Los Alamos Experimental Nuclear Physics Division investigated many problems of great scientific interest which were expected to play a role in their final device. Whether or not this turned out to be the case, the store of knowledge thus accumulated by the Division forms an integral and invaluable part of all thinking on nuclear problems.

12.34. *Experimental Methods.* The earlier chapters contain little or no discussion of experimental techniques except those for the observing of fast (charged) particles (See Appendix 1.). To obtain answers to the ten questions posed above, we should like to be able to:

(1) determine the number of neutrons of any given energy;
(2) produce neutrons of any desired energy;
(3) determine the angles of deflection of scattered neutrons;
(4) determine the number of fissions occurring;
(5) detect other consequences of neutron absorption, e.g., artificial radioactivity.

We shall indicate briefly how such observations are made.

12.35. *Detection of Neutrons.* There are three ways in which neutrons can be detected: by the ionization produced by light atomic nuclei driven forward at high speeds by elastic collisions with neutrons, by the radioactive disintegration of unstable nuclei formed by the absorption of neutrons, and by fission resulting from neutron absorption. All three processes lead to the production of ions and the resulting ionization may be detected using electroscopes, ionization chambers, Geiger-Müller counters, Wilson cloud chambers, tracks in photographic emulsion, etc.

12.36. While the mere detection of neutrons is not difficult, the measurement of the neutron velocities is decidedly more so. The Wilson cloud chamber method and the photographic emulsion method give the most direct results but are tedious to apply. More often various combinations of selective absorbers are used. Thus, for example, if a foil known to absorb neutrons of only one particular range of energies is inserted in the path of the neutrons and is then removed, its degree of radioactivity is presumably proportional to the number of neutrons in the particular energy range concerned. Another scheme is to study the induced radioactivity known to be produced only by neutrons whose energy lies above a certain threshold.

12.37. One elegant scheme for studying the effects of neutrons of a single, arbitrarily-selected velocity is the "time of flight" method. In this method a neutron source is modulated, i.e., the source is made to emit neutrons in short "bursts" or "pulses." In each pulse there are a great many neutrons—of a very wide range of velocities. The target material and the detector are situated a considerable distance from the source (several feet or yards from it). The detector is "modulated" also, and with the same periodicity. The timing or phasing is made such that the detector is responsive only for a short interval beginning a certain time after the pulse of neutrons leaves the source. Thus any effects recorded by the detector (e.g., fissions in a layer of uranium deposited on an inner surface of an ionization chamber) are the result only of neutrons that arrive just at the moment of responsivity and therefore have travelled from the source in a certain time interval. In other words, the measured effects are due only to the neutrons having the appropriate velocity.

12.38. *Production of Neutrons.* All neutrons are produced as the result of nuclear reactions, and their initial speed depends on the energy balance of the particular reaction. If the reaction is endothermic, that is, if the total mass of the resultant particles is greater than that of the initial particles, the reaction does not occur unless the bombarding particle has more than the "threshold" kinetic energy. At higher bombarding energies the kinetic energy of the resulting particles, specifically of the neutrons, goes up with the increase of kinetic energy of the bombarding particle above the threshold value. Thus the $Li^7(p, n)Be^7$ reaction absorbs 1.6 Mev energy since the product particles are heavier than the initial particles. Any further energy of the incident protons goes into kinetic energy of the products so that the maximum speed of the neutrons produced goes up with the speed of the incident protons. However, to get neutrons of a narrow range of speed, a thin target must be used, the neutrons must all come off at the same angle, and the protons must all strike the target with the same speed.

12.39. Although the same energy and momentum conservation laws apply to exothermic nuclear reactions, the energy release is usually large compared to the kinetic energy of the bombarding particles and therefore essentially determines the neutron speed. Often there are several ranges of speed from the same reaction. There are some reactions that produce very high energy neutrons (nearly 15 Mev).

12.40. Since there is a limited number of nuclear reactions usable for neutron sources, there are only certain ranges of neutron speeds that can be produced originally. There is no difficulty about slowing down neutrons, but it is impossible to slow them down uniformly, that is, without spreading out the velocity distribution. The most effective slowing-down scheme is the use of a moderator, as in the graphite pile; in fact, the pile itself is an excellent source of thermal (i.e., very low speed) or nearly thermal neutrons.

12.41. *Determination of Angles of Deflection.* The difficulties in measuring the angles of deflection of neutrons are largely of intensity and interpretation. The number of neutrons scattered in a particular direction may be relatively small, and the "scattered" neutrons nearly always include many strays not coming from the intended target.

12.42. *Determination of Number of Fissions.* The determination of the number of fissions which are produced by neutrons or occur spontaneously is relatively simple. Ionization chambers, counter tubes, and many other types of detectors can be used.

12.43. *Detection of Products of Capture of Neutrons.* Often it is desirable to find in detail what has happened to neutrons that are absorbed but have not produced fission, e.g., resonance or "radiative" capture of neutrons by U-238 to form U-239 which leads to the production of plutonium. Such studies usually involve a combination of microchemical separations and radioactivity analyses.

12.44. *Some Experiments on Nuclear Constants.* By the time that the Los Alamos laboratory had been established, a large amount of work had been done on the effects of slow neutrons on the materials then available. For example, the thermal-neutron fission cross section of natural uranium had been evaluated, and similarly for the separated isotopes of uranium and for plutonium. Some data on high-speed-neutron fission cross sections had been published, and additional information was available in project laboratories. To extend and improve such data, Los Alamos perfected the use of the Van de Graaff generator for the $Li^7(p, n)Be^7$ reaction, so as to produce neutrons of any desired energy lying in the range from 3,000 electron volts to two million electron volts. Success was also achieved in modulating the cyclotron beam and developing the neutron time-of-flight method to produce effects of many speed intervals at once. Special methods were devised for filling in the gaps in neutron energy range. Particularly important was the refinement of measurement made possible as greater quantities of U-235, U-238 and plutonium began to be received. On the whole, the value of the cross section for fission as a function of neutron energy from practically zero electron volts to three million electron volts is now fairly well known for these materials.

12.45. *Some Integral Experiments.* Two "integral experiments" (experiments on assembled or integrated systems comprising fissionable material, reflector, and perhaps moderator also) may be described. In the first of these integral experiments a chain-reacting system was constructed which included a relatively large amount of U-235 in liquid solution. It was designed to operate at a very low power level, and it had no cooling system. Its purpose was to provide verification of the effects predicted for reacting systems containing enriched U-235. The results were very nearly as expected.

12.46. The second integral experiment was carried out on a pile containing a mixture of uranium and a hydrogenous moderator. In this first form, the pile was thus a slow-neutron chain-reacting pile. The pile was then rebuilt using less hydrogen. In this version of the pile, fast-neutron fission became important. The pile was rebuilt several more times, less hydrogen being used each time. By such a series of reconstructions, the reaction character was successively altered, so that thermal neutron fission became less and less important while fast neutron fission became more and more important—approaching the conditions to be found in the bomb.

12.47. *Summary of Results on Nuclear Physics.* The nuclear constants of U-235, U-238, and plutonium have been measured with a reasonable degree of accuracy over the range of neutron energies from thermal to three million electron volts. In other words, questions 1, 2, 3, 4, and 5 of the ten questions posed at the beginning of this section have been answered. The fission spectrum (question 7) for U-235 and Pu-239 is reasonably well known. Spontaneous fission (question 10) has been studied for several types of nuclei. Preliminary results on questions 6, 8, and 9, involving details of the fission process, have been obtained.

CHEMISTRY AND METALLURGY DIVISION

12.48. The Chemistry and Metallurgy Division of the Los Alamos Laboratory was under the joint direction of J. W. Kennedy and C. S. Smith. It was responsible for final purification of the enriched fissionable materials, for fabrication of the bomb core, tamper, etc., and for various other matters. In all this division's work on enriched fissionable materials especial care had to be taken not to lose any appreciable amounts of the materials which are worth much more than gold. Thus the procedures already well-established at Chicago and elsewhere for purifying and fabricating natural uranium were often *not* satisfactory for handling highly-enriched samples of U-235.

ORDNANCE, EXPLOSIVES, AND BOMB PHYSICS DIVISIONS

12.49. The above account of the work of the Theoretical Physics, Experimental Nuclear Physics, and Chemistry and Metallurgy Divisions is very incomplete because important aspects of this work cannot be discussed for reasons of security. For the same reasons none of the work of the Ordnance, Explosives, and Bomb Physics Divisions can be discussed at all.

SUMMARY

12.50. In the spring of 1943 an entirely new laboratory was established at Los Alamos, New Mexico, under J. R. Oppenheimer for the purpose of investigating the design and construction of the atomic bomb, from the stage of receipt of U-235 or plutonium to the stage of use of the bomb. The new laboratory improved the theoretical treatment of design and performance problems, refined and extended the measurements of the nuclear constants involved, developed methods of purifying the materials to be used, and, finally, designed and constructed operable atomic bombs.

CHAPTER XIII. GENERAL SUMMARY

PRESENT OVERALL STATUS

13.1. As the result of the labors of the Manhattan District organization in Washington and in Tennessee, of the scientific groups at Berkeley, Chicago, Columbia, Los Alamos, and elsewhere, of the industrial groups at Clinton, Hanford, and many other places, the end of June 1945 finds us expecting from day to day to hear of the explosion of the first atomic bomb devised by man. All the problems are believed to have been solved at least well enough to make a bomb practicable. A sustained neutron chain reaction resulting from nuclear fission has been demonstrated; the conditions necessary to cause such a reaction to occur explosively have been established and can be achieved; production plants of several different types are in operation, building up a stock pile of the explosive material. Although we do not know when the first explosion will occur nor how effective it will be, announcement of its occurrence will precede the publication of this report. Even if the first attempt is relatively ineffective, there is little doubt that later efforts will be highly effective; the devastation from a single bomb is expected to be comparable to that of a major air raid by usual methods.

13.2. A weapon has been developed that is potentially destructive beyond the wildest nightmares of the imagination; a weapon so ideally suited to sudden unannounced attack that a country's major cities might be destroyed overnight by an ostensibly friendly power. This weapon has been created not by the devilish inspiration of some warped genius but by the arduous labor of thousands of normal men and women working for the safety of their country. Many of the principles that have been used were well known to the international scientific world in 1940. To develop the necessary industrial processes from these principles

223

has been costly in time, effort, and money, but the processes which we selected for serious effort have worked and several that we have not chosen could probably be made to work. We have an initial advantage in time because, so far as we know, other countries have not been able to carry out parallel developments during the war period. We also have a general advantage in scientific and particularly in industrial strength, but such an advantage can easily be thrown away.

13.3. Before the surrender of Germany there was always a chance that German scientists and engineers might be developing atomic bombs which would be sufficiently effective to alter the course of the war. There was therefore no choice but to work on them in this country. Initially many scientists could and did hope that some principle would emerge which would prove that atomic bombs were inherently impossible. This hope has faded gradually; fortunately in the same period the magnitude of the necessary industrial effort has been demonstrated so that the fear of German success weakened even before the end came. By the same token, most of us are certain that the Japanese cannot develop and use this weapon effectively.

PROGNOSTICATION

13.4. As to the future, one may guess that technical developments will take place along two lines. From the military point of view it is reasonably certain that there will be improvements both in the processes of producing fissionable material and in its use. It is conceivable that totally different methods may be discovered for converting matter into energy since it is to be remembered that the energy released in uranium fission corresponds to the utilization of only about one-tenth of one per cent of its mass. Should a scheme be devised for converting to energy even as much as a few per cent of the matter of some common material, civilization would have the means to commit suicide at will.

13.5. The possible uses of nuclear energy are not all destructive, and the second direction in which technical development can be expected is along the paths of peace. In the fall of 1944 General

Groves appointed a committee to look into these possibilities as well as those of military significance. This committee (Dr. R. C. Tolman, chairman; Rear Admiral E. W. Mills (USN) with Captain T. A. Solberg (USN) as deputy, Dr. W. K. Lewis, and Dr. H. D. Smyth) received a multitude of suggestions from men on the various projects, principally along the lines of the use of nuclear energy for power and the use of radioactive by-products for scientific, medical, and industrial purposes. While there was general agreement that a great industry might eventually arise, comparable, perhaps, with the electronics industry, there was disagreement as to how rapidly such an industry would grow; the consensus was that the growth would be slow over a period of many years. At least there is no immediate prospect of running cars with nuclear power or lighting houses with radioactive lamps although there is a good probability that nuclear power for special purposes could be developed within ten years and that plentiful supplies of radioactive materials can have a profound effect on scientific research and perhaps on the treatment of certain diseases in a similar period.

PLANNING FOR THE FUTURE

13.6. During the war the effort has been to achieve the maximum military results. It has been apparent for some time that some sort of government control and support in the field of nuclear energy must continue after the war. Many of the men associated with the project have recognized this fact and have come forward with various proposals, some of which were considered by the Tolman Committee, although it was only a temporary advisory committee reporting to General Groves. An interim committee at a high level is now engaged in formulating plans for a continuing organization. This committee is also discussing matters of general policy about which many of the more thoughtful men on the project have been deeply concerned since the work was begun and especially since success became more and more probable.

THE QUESTIONS BEFORE THE PEOPLE

13.7. We find ourselves with an explosive which is far from completely perfected. Yet the future possibilities of such explosives are appalling, and their effects on future wars and international affairs are of fundamental importance. Here is a new tool for mankind, a tool of unimaginable destructive power. Its development raises many questions that must be answered in the near future.

13.8. Because of the restrictions of military security there has been no chance for the Congress or the people to debate such questions. They have been seriously considered by all concerned and vigorously debated among the scientists, and the conclusions reached have been passed along to the highest authorities. These questions are not technical questions; they are political and social questions, and the answers given to them may affect all mankind for generations. In thinking about them the men on the project have been thinking as citizens of the United States vitally interested in the welfare of the human race. It has been their duty and that of the responsible high government officials who were informed to look beyond the limits of the present war and its weapons to the ultimate implications of these discoveries. This was a heavy responsibility. In a free country like ours, such questions should be debated by the people and decisions must be made by the people through their representatives. This is one reason for the release of this report. It is a semi-technical report which it is hoped men of science in this country can use to help their fellow citizens in reaching wise decisions. The people of the country must be informed if they are to discharge their responsibilities wisely.

APPENDIX 1. METHODS OF OBSERVING FAST PARTICLES FROM NUCLEAR REACTIONS

In Chapter I we pointed out the importance of ionization in the study of radioactivity and mentioned the electroscope. In this appendix we shall mention one method of historical importance comparable with the electroscope but no longer used, and then we shall review the various methods now in use for observing alpha particles, beta particles (or positrons), gamma rays, and neutrons, or their effects.

SCINTILLATIONS

The closest approach that can be made to "seeing" an atom is to see the bright flash of light that an alpha particle or high-speed proton makes when it strikes a fluorescent screen. All that is required is a piece of glass covered with zinc sulphide, a low-power microscope, a dark room, a well-rested eye, and a source of alpha particles. Most of Rutherford's famous experiments, including that mentioned in paragraph 1.17, involved "counting" scintillations but the method is tedious and, as far as the author knows, has been entirely superseded by electrical methods.

THE PROCESS OF IONIZATION

When a high-speed charged particle like an alpha particle or a high-speed electron passes through matter, it disrupts the molecules that it strikes by reason of the electrical forces between the charged particle and the electrons in the molecule. If the material is gaseous, the resultant fragments or ions may move apart and, if there is an electric field present, the electrons knocked out of the molecules move in one direction and the residual positive ions in another direction. A beta particle with a million electron volts energy will produce some 18,000 ionized atoms before it is stopped completely since on the average it uses up about 60 volts energy in each ionizing collision. Since each ionization process gives both a positive and a negative ion, there is a total of 36,000 charges set free by one high-speed electron, but since each charge is only 1.6×10^{-19} coulomb, the total is only about 6×10^{-15} coulomb and is still very minute. The best galvanometer can be made to measure a charge of about 10^{-10} coulomb. It is posssible to push the sensitivity of an electrometer to about 10^{-16} coulomb, but the electrometer is a very inconvenient instrument to use.

An alpha particle produces amounts of ionization comparable with the beta particle. It is stopped more rapidly, but it produces more ions per unit of path. A gamma ray is much less efficient as an ionizer since the process is quite different. It does occasionally set free an electron from a molecule by Compton scattering or the photoelectric effect, and this secondary electron has enough energy to produce ionization. A neutron, as we have already mentioned in the text, produces ionization only indirectly by giving high velocity to a nucleus by elastic collision, or by disrupting a nucleus with resultant ionization by the fragments.

If we are to detect the ionizing effects of these particles, we must evidently use the resultant effect of a great many particles or have very sensitive means of measuring electric currents.

THE ELECTROSCOPE

Essentially the electroscope determines to what degree the air immediately around it has become conducting as the result of the ions produced in it.

The simplest form of electroscope is a strip of gold leaf a few centimeters long, suspended by a hinge from a vertical insulated rod. If the rod is charged, the gold leaf also takes up the same charge and stands out at an angle as a result of the repulsion of like charges. As the charge leaks away, the leaf gradually swings down against the rod, and the rate at which it moves is a measure of the conductivity of the air surrounding it.

A more rugged form of electroscope was devised by C. C. Lauritsen, who substituted a quartz fiber for the gold leaf and used the elasticity of the fiber as the restoring force instead of gravity. The fiber is made conducting by a thin coating of metal. Again the instrument is charged, and the fiber, after initial deflection, gradually comes back to its uncharged position. The position of the fiber is read in a low-power microscope. These instruments can be made portable and rugged and fairly sensitive. They are the standard field instrument for testing the level of gamma radiation, particularly as a safeguard against dangerous exposure.

IONIZATION CHAMBERS

An ionization chamber measures the total number of ions produced directly in it. It usually consists of two plane electrodes between which there is a strong enough electric field to draw all the ions to the electrodes before they recombine but not strong enough to produce secondary ions as in the instruments we shall describe presently.

By careful design and the use of sensitive amplifiers an ionization chamber can measure a number of ions as low as that produced by a single alpha particle, or it can be used much like an electroscope to measure the total amount of ionizing radiation present instantaneously, or it can be arranged to give the total amount of ionization that has occurred over a period of time.

PROPORTIONAL COUNTERS

While ionization chambers can be made which will respond to single alpha particles, it is far more convenient to use a self-amplifying device, that is, to make the ions originally produced make other ions in the same region so that the amplifier circuits need not be so sensitive.

In a proportional counter one of the electrodes is a fine wire along the axis of the second electrode, which is a hollow cylinder. The effect of the wire is to give strong electric field strengths close to it even for relatively small potential differences between it and the other electrode. This strong field quickly accelerates the primary ions formed by the alpha or beta particle or photon, and these accelerated primary ions (particularly the electrons) in turn form secondary ions in the gas with which the counter is filled so that the total pulse of current is much increased.

It is possible to design and operate such counters in such a way that the total number of ions formed is proportional to the number of primary ions formed. Thus after amplification a current pulse can be seen on an oscilloscope, the height of which will indicate how effective an ionizer the initial particle was. It is quite easy to distinguish in this way between alpha particles and beta particles and photons, and the circuits can be arranged to count only the pulses of greater than a chosen magnitude. Thus a proportional counter can count alpha particles against a background of betas or can even count only the alpha particles having more than a certain energy.

Geiger-Müller Counters

If the voltage on a proportional counter is raised, there comes a point when the primary ions from a single alpha particle, beta particle, or photon will set off a discharge through the whole counter, not merely multiply the number of primary ions in the region where they are produced. This is a trigger action and the current is independent of the number of ions produced; furthermore, the current would continue indefinitely if no steps were taken to quench it. Quenching can be achieved entirely by arranging the external circuits so that the voltage drops as soon as current passes or by using a mixture of gases in the counter which "poison" the electrode surface as soon as the discharge passes and temporarily prevent the further emission of electrons, or by combining both methods.

The Geiger-Müller counter was developed before the proportional counter and remains the most sensitive instrument for detecting ionizing radiation, but all it does is "count" any ionizing radiation that passes through it whether it be an alpha particle, proton, electron, or photon.

THE ART OF COUNTER MEASUREMENTS

It is one thing to describe the principles of various ionization chambers, counters, and the like; quite another to construct and operate them successfully.

First of all, the walls of the counter chamber must allow the particles to enter the counter. For gamma rays this is a minor problem, but for relatively low-speed electrons or positrons or for alpha particles the walls of the counter must be very thin or there must be thin windows.

Then there are great variations in the details of the counter itself, spacing and size of electrodes, nature of the gas filling the chamber, its pressure, and so on.

Finally, the interpretation of the resultant data is a tricky business. The absorption of the counter walls and of any external absorbers must be taken into account; the geometry of the counter with relation to the source must be estimated to translate observed counts into actual number of nuclear events; last but not always least, statistical fluctuations must be considered since all nuclear reactions are governed by probability laws.

THE WILSON CLOUD CHAMBER

There is one method of observing nuclear particles that depends directly on ionization but is not an electrical method. It uses the fact that supersaturated vapor will condense more readily on ions than on neutral molecules. If air saturated with water vapor is cooled by expansion just after an alpha particle has passed through it, tiny drops of water condense on the ions formed by the alpha particle and will reflect a bright light strongly enough to be seen or photographed so that the actual path of the alpha particle is recorded.

This method developed by C. T. R. Wilson in Cambridge, England, about 1912 has been enormously useful in studying the behavior of individual particles, alphas, protons, electrons, positrons, mesotrons, photons, and the fast atoms caused by collisions with alphas, protons, or neutrons. Unlike the scintillation method, its companion tool for many years, it has not been superseded and is still used extensively, particularly to study details of collisions between nuclear particles and atoms.

THE PHOTOGRAPHIC METHOD

The tracks of individual particles passing through matter can also be observed in photographic emulsions, but the lengths of path are so small that they must be observed under a microscope, where they appear as a series of developed grains marking the passage of the particle. This method of observation requires practically no equipment but is tedious and of limited usefulness. It is possible, however, to use the general blackening of a photographic film as a measure of total exposure to radiation, a procedure that has been used to supplement or to replace electroscopes for safety control in many parts of the project.

THE OBSERVATION AND MEASUREMENT OF NEUTRONS

None of the methods we have described is directly applicable to neutrons, but all of them are indirectly applicable since neutrons produce ions indirectly. This happens in two ways—by elastic collision and by nuclear reaction. As we have already described, a fast neutron in passing through matter occasionally approaches an atomic nucleus so closely as to impart to it a large amount of momentum and energy according to the laws of elastic collision. The nucleus thereby becomes a high-speed charged particle which will produce ionization in an ionization chamber, counter, or cloud chamber. But if the neutron has low speed, e.g., thermal, the struck nucleus will not get enough energy to cause ionization. If, on the other hand, the neutron is absorbed and the resultant nucleus breaks up with the release of energy, ionization will be produced. Thus, for the detection of high-speed neutrons one has a choice between elastic collisions and nuclear reaction, but for thermal speeds only nuclear reaction will serve.

The reaction most commonly used is the $_5B^{10}(n, \alpha)_3Li^7$ reaction which releases about 2.5 Mev energy shared between the resultant alpha particle and $_3Li^7$ nucleus. This is ample to produce ionization. This reaction is used by filling an ionization chamber or proportional counter with boron trifluoride gas so that the reaction occurs in the region where ionization is wanted; as an alternative the interior of the chamber or counter is lined with boron. The ionization chamber then serves as an instrument to measure overall neutron flux while the proportional counter records numbers of individual neutrons.

One of the most valuable methods of measuring neutron densities by nuclear reactions depends on the production of artificial radioactive nuclei. A foil known to be made radioactive by neutron bombardment is inserted at a point where the neutron intensity is wanted. After a given time it is removed and its activity measured by an electroscope or counter. The degree of activity that has been built up is then a measure of the number of neutrons that have been absorbed. This method has the obvious disadvantage that it does not give an instantaneous response as do the ionization chamber and counter.

One of the most interesting methods developed on the project is to use the fission of uranium as the nuclear reaction for neutron detection. Furthermore, by separating the isotopes, fast and slow neutrons can be differentiated.

Since the probability of a neutron reaction occurring is different for every reaction and for every neutron speed, difficulties of translating counts or current measurements into numbers and speeds of neutrons present are even greater than for other nuclear particles. No one need be surprised if two able investigators give different numbers for supposedly the same nuclear consant. It is only by an intricate series of interlocking experiments carefully compared and interpreted that the fundamental facts can be untangled from experimental and instrumental variables.

APPENDIX 2. THE UNITS OF MASS, CHARGE AND ENERGY

MASS

Since the proton and the neutron are the fundamental particles out of which all nuclei are built, it would seem natural to use the mass of one or the other of them as a unit of mass. The choice would probably be the proton, which is the nucleus of a hydrogen atom. There are good reasons, historical and otherwise, why neither the proton nor the neutron was chosen. Instead, the mass unit used in atomic and nuclear physics is one sixteenth of the mass of the predominant oxygen isotope, O^{16}, and is equal to 1.6603×10^{-24} gram. Expressed in terms of this unit, the mass of the proton is 1.00758 and the mass of the neutron is 1.00893. (Chemists usually use a very slightly different unit of mass.)

CHARGE

The unit of electric charge used in nuclear science is the positive charge of the proton. It is equal in magnitude but opposite in sign to the charge on the electron and is therefore often called the electronic charge. One electronic charge is 1.60×10^{-19} coulomb. It may be recalled that a current of one ampere flowing for one second conveys a charge of one coulomb; i.e., one electronic charge equals 1.60×10^{-19} ampere second.

ENERGY

The energy unit used in nuclear physics is the electron volt, which is defined as equal to the kinetic energy which a particle carrying one electronic charge acquires in falling freely through a potential drop of one volt. It is often convenient to use the million-times greater unit: million electron volt (Mev).

The relationships among the electron volt and other common units of energy are in the following table:

CONVERSION TABLE FOR ENERGY UNITS

MULTIPLY	BY	TO OBTAIN
Mev	1.07×10^{-3}	mass units
	1.60×10^{-6}	ergs
	3.83×10^{-14}	g. cal.
	4.45×10^{-20}	kw. hrs.
mass units	9.31×10^{2}	Mev
	1.49×10^{-3}	ergs
	3.56×10^{-11}	g. cal.
	4.15×10^{-17}	kw. hrs.
ergs	6.71×10^{2}	mass units
	6.24×10^{5}	Mev
	2.39×10^{-8}	g. cal.
	2.78×10^{-14}	kw. hrs.
g. cal.	2.81×10^{10}	mass units
	2.62×10^{13}	Mev
	4.18×10^{7}	ergs
	1.16×10^{-6}	kw. hrs.
kw. hrs.	2.41×10^{16}	mass units
	2.25×10^{19}	Mev
	3.60×10^{13}	ergs
	8.60×10^{5}	g. cal.

APPENDIX 3. DELAYED NEUTRONS FROM URANIUM FISSION

As was pointed out in Chapter VI, the control of a chain-reacting pile is greatly facilitated by the fact that some of the neutrons resulting from uranium fission are not emitted until more than a second after fission occurs. It was therefore important to study this effect experimentally. Such experiments were described by Snell, Nedzel and Ibser in a report dated May 15, 1942 from which we quote as follows:

"The present experiment consists of two interrelated parts—one concerned with the decay curve, and one concerned with the intensity of the delayed neutrons measured in terms of that of the 'instantaneous' fission neutrons.

THE DECAY CURVE OF THE DELAYED NEUTRONS

"The neutron source was the beryllium target of the University of Chicago cyclotron struck by a beam of up to 20 μA of 8 Mev deuterons. Near the target was placed a hollow shell made of tinned iron and containing 106 lbs. of U_3O_8. This was surrounded by about 2'' of paraffin. The interior of the shell was filled with paraffin, except for an axial hole which accommodated a BF_3-filled proportional counter. The counter was connected through an amplifier to a scaling circuit ('scale of 64') equipped with interpolating lights and a Cenco impulse counter. A tenth-second timer, driven by a synchronous motor, and hundredth-second stop watch were mounted on the panel of the scaler, close to the interpolating lights and impulse counter. This group of dials and lights was photographed at an appropriately varying rate by a Sept camera which was actuated by hand. The result was a record on movie film of times and counts, from which the decay curves were plotted.

"The actual procedure was as follows: During bombardment the stop watch was started and the timer was running continuously; the counter and amplifier were on, but the pulses leaving the amplifier were grounded. The scaler was set at zero. After a warning signal the cyclotron was shut off by one operator, while another operator switched the output of the amplifier from ground into the scaler, and started taking photographs. It was easy to take the first photograph within half a second of turning off the cyclotron. Sixty to a hundred photographs were taken during a typical run. The necessity of using both a stop watch and a timer arose from the fact that the hundredth-second precision of the stop watch was needed for the small time intervals between photographs during the initial part of the run, but the watch ran down and stopped before the counting was complete. The timer then gave sufficient precision for the later time intervals.

"Some forty runs were taken under varying experimental conditions. Short activations of one or two seconds were given for best resolution of the short periods. Long, intense bombardments lasting 15–20 minutes, as close as possible to the target, were made to make the long period activities show up with a maximum intensity. Some 5-minute bombardments were made, keeping the cyclotron beam as steady as possible, to study the relative saturation intensities of the various activities; in these activations the cyclotron beam was reduced to 1 or 2 μA to prevent the initial counting rate from becoming too high for a counter (300 per sec. was taken as a reasonable upper limit for reliable counting). Two BF_3 counters were available, one having a thermal neutron cross section of 2.66 sq. cm., and the other 0.43 sq. cm. After a strong activation, we could follow the decay of the delayed neutrons for some 13 minutes. Background counts (presumably chiefly due to spontaneous fission neutrons) were taken and were subtracted from the readings. They amounted to about 0.4 counts per sec. for the large counter.

"A study of all the decay curves gives the following as a general picture of the neutron-emitting activities present:

TABLE 1

HALF-LIFE	RELATIVE INITIAL INTENSITY ACTIVATED TO SATURATION
57 ± 3 sec.	0.135
24 ± 2 sec.	1.0
7 sec.	1.2
2.5 sec.	1.2

"Any activity of period longer than 57 sec. failed to appear even after the most intense bombardment we could give, lasting 20 minutes. The relative initial intensities given are the average values obtained from three curves.

"These results give the following equation for the decay curve, of the delayed neutrons after activation to saturation:

$$\text{Activity} = \text{constant} \ (1.2e^{-0.28t} + 1.2e^{-0.099t} + 1.0e^{-0.029t} + 0.135e^{-0.012t})$$

where t is in seconds."

The second part of the experiment measured the total number of neutrons emitted in the time interval 0.01 sec. to 2.0 min. after the cyclotron was turned off. Assuming that all the delayed neutrons observed were in the four groups measured in the first part of the experiment, this second result indicated that 1.0 ± 0.2 per cent of the neutrons emitted in uranium fission are delayed by at least 0.01 sec. and that about 0.07 per cent are delayed by as much as a minute. By designing the effective value of k, the multiplication factor, for a typical operating pile to be only 1.01 with all the controls removed and the total variation in k from one control rod to be 0.002, the number of delayed neutrons is sufficient to allow easy control.

APPENDIX 4. THE FIRST SELF-SUSTAINING CHAIN REACTING PILE

In Chapter VI the construction and operation of the first self-sustaining chain-reacting pile were described briefly. Though details must still be withheld for security reasons, the following paragraphs give a somewhat fuller description based on a report by Fermi. This pile was erected by Fermi and his collaborators in the fall of 1942.

DESCRIPTION OF THE PILE

The original plan called for an approximately spherical pile with the best materials near the center. Actually control measurements showed that the critical size had been reached before the sphere was complete, and the construction was modified accordingly. The final structure may be roughly described as an oblate spheroid flattened at the top, i.e., like a door knob. It was desired to have the uranium or uranium oxide lumps spaced in a cubic lattice imbedded in graphite. Consequently, the graphite was cut in bricks and built up in layers, alternate ones of which contained lumps of uranium at the corners of squares. The critical size was reached when the pile had been built to a height only three quarters of that needed according to the most cautious estimates. Consequently only one more layer was added. The graphite used was chiefly from the National Carbon Company and the Speer Carbon Company. The pile contained 12,400 lbs. of metal, part of which was supplied by Westinghouse, part by Metal Hydrides, and part by Ames. Since there were many more lattice points than lumps of metal, the remaining ones were filled with pressed oxide lumps.

For purposes of control and experiment there were ten slots passing completely through the pile. Three of those near the center were used for control and safety rods. Further to facilitate experiment, particularly the removal of samples, one row of graphite bricks carrying uranium and passing near the center of the pile was arranged so that it could be pushed completely out of the pile.

This whole graphite sphere was supported by a timber framework resting on the floor of a squash court under the West Stands of Stagg Field.

PREDICTED PERFORMANCE OF THE PILE

The metal lattice at the center of the pile and the two other major lattices making up the bulk of the rest of the pile had each been studied separately in exponential experiments #18, #27, and #29. These had given a multiplication factor of 1.07 for the metal lattice and 1.04 and 1.03 for the oxide lattices, the difference in the last two resulting from difference in the grade of graphite used. It is to be remembered that these figures are multiplication factors for lattices of infinite size. Therefore a prediction of the actual effective multiplication factor k_{eff} for the pile as constructed depended on the validity of the deduction of k from the exponential experiments, on a proper averaging for the different lattices, and on a proper deduction of k_{eff} from the average k for infinite size. Although the original design of the pile had been deliberately generous, its success when only partly completed indicated that the values of the multiplication factors as calculated from exponential experiments had been too low. The observed effective multiplication factor of the part of the planned structure actually built was about 1.0006 when all neutron absorbers were removed.

MEASUREMENTS PERFORMED DURING CONSTRUCTION

A series of measurements was made while the pile was being assembled in order to be sure that the critical dimensions were not reached inadvertently. These measurements served also to check the neutron multiplication properties of the structure during assembly, making possible a prediction of where the critical point would be reached.

In general, any detector of neutrons or gamma radiation can be used for measuring the intensity of the reaction. Neutron detectors are somewhat preferable since they give response more

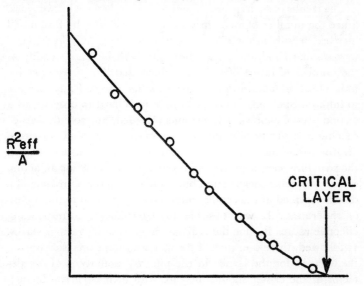

$$\frac{R^2 eff}{A}$$

CRITICAL LAYER

NUMBER OF COMPLETED LAYERS

FIGURE 1

quickly and are not affected by fission-product radiations after shut down. Actually both neutron detectors (boron trifluoride counters) and gamma-ray ionization chambers were distributed in and around the pile. Certain of the ionization chambers were used to operate recording instruments and automatic safety controls.

In the pile itself measurements were made with two types of detector. A boron trifluoride counter was inserted in a slot about

43" from the ground and its readings taken at frequent intervals. In addition, an indium foil was irradiated every night in a position as close as possible to the effective center of the pile, and its induced activity was measured the following morning and compared with the readings of the boron trifluoride counter.

The results of such measurements can be expressed in two ways. Since the number of secondary neutrons produced by fission will increase steadily as the pile is constructed, the activity A induced in a standard indium foil at the center will increase steadily as the number of layers of the pile is increased. Once the effective multiplication factor is above one, A would theoretically increase to infinity. Such an approach to infinity is hard to observe, so a second way of expressing the results was used. Suppose the lattice spacing and purity of materials of a graphite-uranium structure are such that the multiplication factor would be exactly one if the structure were a sphere of infinite radius. Then, for an actual sphere of similar construction but finite radius, the activation of a detector placed at the center would be proportional to the square of the radius. It was possible to determine a corresponding effective radius R_{eff} for the real pile in each of its various stages. It followed, therefore, that, if the factor k_∞ were precisely one on the average for the lattice in the pile, the activity A of the detector at the center should increase with increasing R_{eff} in such a way that R^2_{eff}/A remained constant, but, if k_∞ for the lattice were greater than one, then as the pile size approached the critical value, that is, as k_{eff} approached one, A should approach infinity and therefore R^2_{eff}/A approach zero. Therefore by extrapolating a curve of R^2_{eff}/A vs. size of the pile i.e., number of layers, to where it cut the axis, it was possible to predict at what layer k_{eff} would become one. Such a curve, shown in Fig. 1, indicated at what layer the critical size would be reached. The less useful but more direct and dramatic way of recording the results is shown in Fig. 2, which shows the growth of the neutron activity of the pile as layers were added.

During the construction, appreciably before reaching this critical layer, some cadmium strips were inserted in suitable slots.

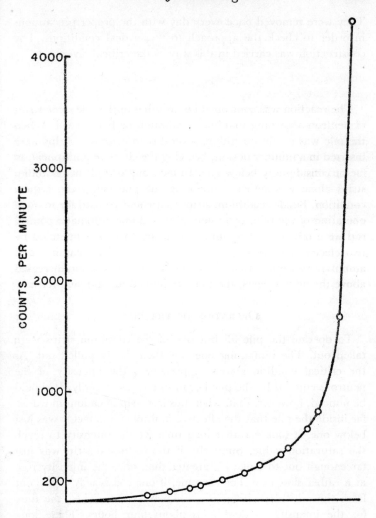

NUMBER OF COMPLETED LAYERS

FIGURE 2

They were removed once every day with the proper precautions in order to check the approach to the critical conditions. The construction was carried in this way to the critical layer.

CONTROL

The reaction was controlled by inserting in the pile some strips of neutron-absorbing material—cadmium or boron steel. When the pile was not in operation, several such cadmium strips were inserted in a number of slots, bringing the effective multiplication factor considerably below one. In fact, any one of the cadmium strips alone was sufficient to bring the pile below the critical condition. Besides cadmium strips that could be used for manual operation of the pile, two safety rods and one automatic control rod were provided. The automatic control rod was operated by two electric motors responding to an ionization chamber and amplifying system so that, if the intensity of the reaction increased above the desired level, the rod was pushed in, and vice versa.

OPERATION OF THE PILE

To operate the pile all but one of the cadmium strips were taken out. The remaining one was then slowly pulled out. As the critical conditions were approached, the intensity of the neutrons emitted by the pile began to increase rapidly. It should be noticed, however, that, when this last strip of cadmium was so far inside the pile that the effective multiplication factor was just below one, it took a rather long time for the intensity to reach the saturation value. Similarly, if the cadmium strip was just far enough out to make k_{eff} greater than one, the intensity rose at a rather slow rate. For example, if one rod is only 1 cm. out from the critical position, the "relaxation time," i.e., the time for the intensity to double, is about four hours. These long "relaxation times" were the result of the small percentage of delayed neutrons which have been discussed in Appendix 3, and make it relatively easy to keep the pile operating at a constant level of intensity.

The pile was first operated on December 2, 1942 to a maximum energy production of about $\frac{1}{2}$ watt. On December 12th the intensity was run up to about 200 watts, but it was not felt safe to go higher because of the danger of the radiation to personnel in and around the building. During this high intensity run, measurements were made of radiation intensity beside the pile, in the building, and on the sidewalk outside.

APPENDIX 5. SAMPLE LIST OF REPORTS

Presented below is a list of titles of representative reports prepared in the Metallurgical Laboratory of the University of Chicago in 1942.

A Table for Calculating the Percentage Loss Due to the Presence of Impurities in Alloy

Concerning the Radium-Beryllium Neutron Sources

Preliminary Estimates of the Radiations from Fission Products

Background of Natural Neutrons in Multiplying Pile

Absorption Cross Sections for Rn plus Be Fast Neutrons

On Mechanical Stresses Produced by Temperature Gradients in Rods and Spheres

Effect of Geometry on Resonance Absorption of Neutrons by Uranium

Protection against Radiations

Planning Experiments on Liquid Cooling

Report on the Possibility of Purifying Uranium by Carbonyl Formation and Decomposition

On the Radioactivity of Cooling Helium

Estimation of Stability of Ether under Various Conditions of Irradiation

Uranium Poisoning

Transuranic and Fission Product Activities

Chemical Effects of Radiation on Air Surrounding the Pile

An Estimate of the Chemical Effects of Radiation on the Cooling Water in the Pile

The Extraction Method of Purification of Uranyl Nitrate

The Diffusion of Fission Products from Cast Metal at 600°C and 1000°C

APPENDIX 6. WAR DEPARTMENT RELEASE ON NEW MEXICO TEST, JULY 16, 1945

"Mankind's successful transition to a new age, the Atomic Age, was ushered in July 16, 1945, before the eyes of a tense group of renowned scientists and military men gathered in the desertlands of New Mexico to witness the first end results of their $2,000,000,000 effort. Here in a remote section of the Alamogordo Air Base 120 miles southeast of Albuquerque the first man-made atomic explosion, the outstanding achievement of nuclear science, was achieved at 5:30 a.m. of that day. Darkening heavens, pouring forth rain and lightning immediately up to the zero hour, heightened the drama.

"Mounted on a steel tower, a revolutionary weapon destined to change war as we know it, or which may even be the instrumentality to end all wars, was set off with an impact which signalized man's entrance into a new physical world. Success was greater than the most ambitious estimates. A small amount of matter, the product of a chain of huge specially constructed industrial plants, was made to release the energy of the universe locked up within the atom from the beginning of time. A fabulous achievement had been reached. Speculative theory, barely established in pre-war laboratories, had been projected into practicality.

"This phase of the Atomic Bomb Project, which is headed by Major General Leslie R. Groves, was under the direction of Dr. J. R. Oppenheimer, theoretical physicist of the University of California. He is to be credited with achieving the implementation of atomic energy for military purposes.

"Tension before the actual detonation was at a tremendous pitch. Failure was an ever-present possibility. Too great a success, envisioned by some of those present, might have meant an uncontrollable, unusable weapon.

"Final assembly of the atomic bomb began on the night of

247

July 12 in an old ranch house. As various component assemblies arrived from distant points, tension among the scientists rose to an increasing pitch. Coolest of all was the man charged with the actual assembly of the vital core, Dr. R. F. Bacher, in normal times a professor at Cornell University.

"The entire cost of the project, representing the erection of whole cities and radically new plants spread over many miles of countryside, plus unprecedented experimentation, was represented in the pilot bomb and its parts. Here was the focal point of the venture. No other country in the world had been capable of such an outlay in brains and technical effort.

"The full significance of these closing moments before the final factual test was *not* lost on these men of science. They fully knew their position as pioneers into another age. They also knew that one false move would blast them and their entire effort into eternity. Before the assembly started a receipt for the vital matter was signed by Brigadier General Thomas F. Farrell, General Groves' deputy. This signalized the formal transfer of the irreplaceable material from the scientists to the Army.

"During final preliminary assembly, a bad few minutes developed when the assembly of an important section of the bomb was delayed. The entire unit was machine-tooled to the finest measurement. The insertion was partially completed when it apparently wedged tightly and would go no farther. Dr. Bacher, however, was undismayed and reassured the group that time would solve the problem. In three minutes' time, Dr. Bacher's statement was verified and basic assembly was completed without further incident.

"Specialty teams, comprised of the top men on specific phases of science, all of which were bound up in the whole, took over their specialized parts of the assembly. In each group was centralized months and even years of channelized endeavor.

"On Saturday, July 14, the unit which was to determine the success or failure of the entire project was elevated to the top of the steel tower. All that day and the next, the job of preparation went on. In addition to the apparatus necessary to cause the detonation, complete instrumentation to determine the pulse beat and all reactions of the bomb was rigged on the tower.

"The ominous weather which had dogged the assembly of the bomb had a very sobering affect on the assembled experts whose work was accomplished amid lightning flashes and peals of thunder. The weather, unusual and upsetting, blocked out aerial observation of the test. It even held up the actual explosion scheduled at 4:00 a.m. for an hour and a half. For many months the approximate date and time had been set and had been one of the high-level secrets of the best kept secret of the entire war.

"Nearest observation point was set up 10,000 yards south of the tower where in a timber and earth shelter the controls for the test were located. At a point 17,000 yards from the tower at a point which would give the best observation the key figures in the atomic bomb project took their posts. These included General Groves, Dr. Vannevar Bush, head of the Office of Scientific Research and Development and Dr. James B. Conant, president of Harvard University.

"Actual detonation was in charge of Dr. K. T. Bainbridge of Massachusetts Institute of Technology. He and Lieutenant Bush, in charge of the Military Police Detachment, were the last men to inspect the tower with its cosmic bomb.

"At three o'clock in the morning the party moved forward to the control station. General Groves and Dr. Oppenheimer consulted with the weathermen. The decision was made to go ahead with the test despite the lack of assurance of favorable weather. The time was set for 5:30 a.m.

"General Groves rejoined Dr. Conant and Dr. Bush, and just before the test time they joined the many scientists gathered at the Base Camp. Here all present were ordered to lie on the ground, face downward, heads away from the blast direction.

"Tension reached a tremendous pitch in the control room as the deadline approached. The several observation points in the area were tied in to the control room by radio and with twenty minutes to go, Dr. S. K. Allison of Chicago University took over the radio net and made periodic time announcements.

"The time signals, 'minus 20 minutes, minus fifteen minutes,' and on and on increased the tension to the breaking point as the group in the control room which included Dr. Oppenheimer and General Farrell held their breaths, all praying with the intensity of the moment which will live forever with each man who was there. At 'minus 45 seconds,' robot mechanism took over and from that point on the whole great complicated mass of intricate mechanism was in operation without human control. Stationed at a reserve switch, however, was a soldier scientist ready to attempt to stop the explosion should the order be issued. The order never came.

"At the appointed time there was a blinding flash lighting up the whole area brighter than the brightest daylight. A mountain range three miles from the observation point stood out in bold relief. Then came a tremendous sustained roar and a heavy pressure wave which knocked down two men outside the control center. Immediately thereafter, a huge multi-colored surging cloud boiled to an altitude of over 40,000 feet. Clouds in its path disappeared. Soon the shifting substratosphere winds dispersed the now grey mass.

"The test was over, the project a success.

"The steel tower had been entirely vaporized. Where the tower had stood, there was a huge sloping crater. Dazed but relieved at the success of their tests, the scientists promptly marshalled their forces to estimate the strength of America's new weapon. To examine the nature of the crater, specially equipped tanks were wheeled into the area, one of which carried Dr. Enrico Fermi, noted nuclear scientist. Answer to their findings rests in the destruction effected in Japan today in the first military use of the atomic bomb.

"Had it not been for the desolated area where the test was held and for the cooperation of the press in the area, it is certain that the test itself would have attracted far-reaching attention. As it was, many people in that area are still discussing the effect of the smash. A significant aspect, recorded by the press, was the experience of a blind girl near Albuquerque many miles from the scene, who, when the flash of the test lighted the sky before the explosion could be heard, exclaimed, 'What was that?'

"Interviews of General Groves and General Farrell give the following on-the-scene versions of the test. General Groves said: 'My impressions of the night's high points follow: After about an hour's sleep I got up at 0100 and from that time on until about five I was with Dr. Oppenheimer constantly. Naturally he was tense, although his mind was working at its usual extraordinary efficiency. I attempted to shield him from the evident concern shown by many of his assistants who were disturbed by the uncertain weather conditions. By 0330 we decided that we could probably fire at 0530. By 0400 the rain had stopped but the sky was heavily overcast. Our decision became firmer as time went on.

" 'During most of these hours the two of us journeyed from the control house out into the darkness to look at the stars and to assure each other that the one or two visible stars were becoming brighter. At 0510 I left Dr. Oppenheimer and returned to the main observation point which was 17,000 yards from the point of explosion. In accordance with our orders I found all personnel not otherwise occupied massed on a bit of high ground.

" 'Two minutes before the scheduled firing time, all persons lay face down with their feet pointing towards the explosion. As the remaining time was called from the loud speaker from the 10,000-yard control station there was complete awesome silence. Dr. Conant said he had never imagined seconds could be so long. Most of the individuals in accordance with orders shielded their eyes in one way or another.

" 'First came the burst of light of a brilliance beyond any comparison. We all rolled over and looked through dark glasses at the ball of fire. About forty seconds later came the shock wave followed by the sound, neither of which seemed startling after our complete astonishment at the extraordinary lighting intensity.

" 'A massive cloud was formed which surged and billowed upward with tremendous power, reaching the substratosphere in about five minutes.

" 'Two supplementary explosions of minor effect other than the lighting occurred in the cloud shortly after the main explosion.

" 'The cloud traveled to a great height first in the form of a ball, then mushroomed, then changed into a long trailing chimney-shaped column and finally was sent in several directions by the variable winds at the different elevations.

" 'Dr. Conant reached over and we shook hands in mutual congratulations. Dr. Bush, who was on the other side of me, did likewise. The feeling of the entire assembly, even the uninitiated, was of profound awe. Drs. Conant and Bush and myself were struck by an even stronger feeling that the faith of those who had been responsible for the initiation and the carrying on of this Herculean project had been justified.''

General Farrell's impressions are: "The scene inside the shelter was dramatic beyond words. In and around the shelter were some twenty odd people concerned with last-minute arrangements. Included were Dr. Oppenheimer, the Director who had borne the great scientific burden of developing the weapon from the raw materials made in Tennessee and Washington, and a dozen of his key assistants, Dr. Kistiakowsky, Dr. Bainbridge, who supervised all the detailed arrangements for the test; the weather expert, and several others. Besides those, there were a handful of soldiers, two or three Army officers and one Naval Officer. The shelter was filled with a great variety of instruments and radios.

" 'For some hectic two hours preceding the blast, General Groves stayed with the Director. Twenty minutes before the zero hour, General Groves left for his station at the base camp, first because it provided a better observation point and second, because of our rule that he and I must not be together in situations where there is an element of danger which existed at both points.

" 'Just after General Groves left, announcements began to be broadcast of the interval remaining before the blast to the other groups participating in and observing the test. As the time interval grew smaller and changed from minutes to seconds, the tension increased by leaps and bounds. Everyone in that room knew the awful potentialities of the thing that they thought was about to happen. The scientists felt that their figuring must be right and that the bomb had to go off but there was in everyone's mind a strong measure of doubt.

" 'We were reaching into the unknown and we did not know what might come of it. It can safely be said that most of those present were praying—and praying harder than they had ever prayed before. If the shot were successful, it was a justification of the several years of intensive effort of tens of thousands of people—statesmen, scientists, engineers, manufacturers, soldiers, and many others in every walk of life.

" 'In that brief instant in the remote New Mexico desert, the tremendous effort of the brains and brawn of all these people came suddenly and startlingly to the fullest fruition. Dr. Oppenheimer, on whom had rested a very heavy burden, grew tenser as the last seconds ticked off. He scarcely breathed. He held on to a post to steady himself. For the last few seconds, he stared directly ahead and then when the announcer shouted "Now!" and there came this tremendous burst of light followed shortly thereafter by the deep growling roar of the explosion, his face relaxed into an expression of tremendous relief. Several of the observers standing back of the shelter to watch the lighting effects were knocked flat by the blast.

" 'The tension in the room let up and all started congratulating each other. Everyone sensed 'This is it!'. No matter what might happen now all knew that the impossible scientific job had been done. Atomic fission would no longer be hidden in the cloisters of the theoretical physicists' dreams. It was almost full grown at birth. It was a great new force to be used for good or for evil. There was a feeling in that shelter that those concerned with its nativity should dedicate their lives to the mission that it would always be used for good and never for evil.

" 'Dr. Kistiakowsky threw his arms around Dr. Oppenheimer and embraced him with shouts of glee. Others were equally enthusiastic. All the pent-up emotions were released in those few minutes and all seemed to sense immediately that the explosion had far exceeded the most optimistic expectations and wildest hopes of the scientists. All seemed to feel that they had been present at the birth of a new age—The Age of Atomic Energy—and felt their profound responsibility to help in guiding into right channels the tremendous forces which had been unlocked for the first time in history.

" 'As to the present war, there was a feeling that no matter what else might happen, we now had the means to insure its speedy conclusion and save thousands of American lives. As to the future, there had been brought into being something big and something new that would prove to be immeasurably more important than the discovery of electricity or any of the other great discoveries which have so affected our existence.

" 'The effects could well be called unprecedented, magnificent, beautiful, stupendous and terrifying. No man-made phenomenon of such tremendous power had ever occurred before. The lighting effects beggared description. The whole country was lighted by a searing light with the intensity many times that of the midday sun. It was golden, purple, violet, gray and blue. It lighted every peak, crevasse and ridge of the nearby mountain range with a clarity and beauty that cannot be described but must be seen to be imagined. It was that beauty the great poets dream about but describe most poorly and inadequately. Thirty seconds after, the explosion came first, the air blast pressing hard against the people and things, to be followed almost immediately by the strong, sustained, awesome roar which warned of doomsday and made us feel that we puny things were blasphemous to dare tamper with the forces heretofore reserved to the Almighty. Words are inadequate tools for the job of acquainting those not present with the physical, mental and psychological effects. It had to be witnessed to be realized.' "

APPENDIX 7. BRITISH INFORMATION SERVICE STATEMENT, "BRITAIN AND THE ATOMIC BOMB," AUGUST 12, 1945

INTRODUCTION

The Prime Minister has issued a statement describing the events leading up to the production, in the United States, of atomic bombs and the dropping, by the United States Army Air Force, of the first of these on Japan.

Statements have also been made by President Truman and Mr. Howe, the Canadian Minister of Munitions and Supply. Further statements have been issued by the U.S. and Canadian Governments giving an account of the work carried out in their respective countries which led up to or was associated with this remarkable achievement. These supplementary statements also give an outline of the scientific background without which it is impossible to appreciate the great advance which has been made.

The following official statement has been prepared to fulfil a similar purpose for the Government of the United Kingdom.

The statement begins with a very brief account of the outstanding discoveries in that branch of physics, known as "nuclear" physics, which by the year 1939 had led scientists to the belief that it should be possible to find a way of releasing atomic energy on a significant scale and under controlled conditions.

It will be seen that scientists of many countries shared in this development and that the contribution of British laboratories was outstanding.

There follows an account of the examination of the problem in this country from the beginning of 1940 to the middle of 1941 when a scientific committee reported that there was a good chance that "atomic bombs" could be produced in time for use in the war.

The next section of the statement deals with the organization of the work in the U.K. and with the scope of the research programs undertaken.

Reference is made to the interchange of information with the corresponding U.S. organization and to the decision, already referred to in the Prime Minister's statement, that full-scale plants for the production of atomic bombs should be built not in the U.K. but in the U.S.A.

There is a short reference to the decision to transfer to Canada one section of the work. This was at first a joint Anglo-Canadian project but became later, with the cooperation of the American Government, a tripartite enterprise.

In the Prime Minister's statement there is a reference to the setting up in Washington, after discussions between President Roosevelt and Mr. Churchill, of a Combined Policy Committee.

This committee accepted certain recommendations from its scientific advisers for a closer integration of the scientific work, which involved the transfer to the U.S.A. and Canada of many of the scientists working on this project in the U.K.

The present statement ends with a note on the effect of this on the British programs.

This statement is intended to be read in conjunction with the American and Canadian statements. It is, therefore, confined as far as possible to work in the U.K. and to the share taken by British scientists in the American and Canadian projects.

Consequently no reference is made to the gigantic scale of the American scientific and technical effort the successful outcome of which constitutes, as the Prime Minister has already said, one of the greatest triumphs of human genius of which there is record.

HISTORICAL SURVEY

The discovery of the fission of uranium and its application in the atomic bomb is no isolated event but follows a series of discoveries which, since the end of the last century, have been the basis of the modern science of physics. This work has been done in many countries and is the result of full and free collaboration between scientists, among whom those working in Britain have played a most important part.

Classical ideas on the nature and properties of matter culminated in the atomic theory of the nineteenth century. It was accepted that all matter was made up of discrete, indestructible particles or atoms which were classified into 92 different species or elements. From the atoms of one or more of these elements all the different chemical compounds that exist in nature are built up. But it was regarded as a cardinal point that the atoms of any one element could in no way be changed or converted into those of another.

RADIOACTIVITY

The fundamental break with this theory occurred when the French physicist H. Becquerel, in 1896, discovered that one of the elements—uranium—was continuously emitting radiation of an unknown type which could penetrate matter and affect a photographic plate. Further study of this new-found property of uranium led to the isolation of another element—radium—from the uranium mineral deposits in Joachimstal by Pierre and Marie Curie in 1898. Radium showed, to a much greater degree, this same property of emitting radiation and it was clear that the phenomenon of "radio-activity," as it was called, was altogether different from those associated with normal chemical reactions between atoms. In 1902 Rutherford and Soddy, who were then working at McGill University, Montreal, suggested that it could only be explained by the assumption that the atoms of uranium, radium, and of other radioactive elements which had by then been discovered were unstable and were continuously breaking up at rates which were characteristic for each element.

This suggestion was conclusively proved by detailed experimental work in the course of which the nature and properties of the radiation from radioactive elements were discovered. Part of this radiation, the so-called "alpha rays," consists of helium atoms, carrying a positive charge of electricity, and these were found to be of the greatest value as a tool for further exploration of the structure of atoms.

It was, in fact, research on the penetration of matter by alpha rays which led Rutherford, at Manchester University in 1911, to the fundamental discovery that the whole mass of each atom was concentrated in a minute central nucleus which carried a positive electric charge. Round this nucleus, but at relatively very great distances, revolved elementary negative electric charges—the electrons—in numbers sufficient to neutralize exactly the positive charge of the nucleus. The mass of these electrons was negligible compared with that of the nucleus. In terms of classical electromagnetic theory, however, such a system would be unstable and the energy of the revolving electrons would, in a very short time, be lost as radiation. Niels Bohr, of Copenhagen, put forward a theory in 1913 which combined Rutherford's model of the "nuclear atom" with the quantum theory of energy which had been enunciated by Planck to explain limitations of the classical electromagnetic theory.

The resulting Rutherford-Bohr model of the atom proved to be of the greatest value in explaining the results of experimental work in every branch of physics and, in particular, the relationship between the different elements as regards their ordinary physical and chemical properties. These are determined entirely by the electrons revolving round the nucleus and are therefore practically independent of the mass of the nucleus. It was, therefore, immediately understood that any element, with a given charge on the nucleus, could exist in more than one modification with different atomic masses but almost identical physical and chemical properties.

The existence of such modifications of any element, which were known as "isotopes," had first been suggested by Soddy in 1910 as a result of studies of the decay products of the natural radioactive elements.

Aston, at Cambridge, followed up work which had been started by J. J. Thomson and developed the so-called "mass-spectrograph," which subjected a stream of electrically charged atoms—or ions—to a crossed electric and magnetic field and brought those of different mass to a focus at different points. It was proved, with the help of this instrument, that the great majority of elements consisted of a mixture of two or more isotopes and that the relative weight of the atom of any given isotope of any element was very nearly a simple multiple of the weight of a hydrogen nucleus, or proton.

Because the isotopes of an element have almost identical chemical properties it is in general extremely difficult to separate them or even to change appreciably their relative concentration. We must take recourse to processes which depend on the nuclear mass of the atoms, making use of the difference in mass between isotopes. This difference is usually only a small fraction of the total mass. Moreover, while some of these methods, such as that used in the mass-spectrograph, are not difficult to apply, they can ordinarily deal only with very small quantities of material, too small to be of much practical use.

In 1932 Urey and Brickwedde of Columbia University, New York, showed that hydrogen itself is not a simple element but contains a small amount (about $\frac{1}{5000}$) of an isotope known as "heavy hydrogen" or deuterium which has almost double the mass of a proton. Because, in this case, the ratio of the masses of the isotopes is as two to one the physical and chemical properties of hydrogen and deuterium are sensibly different and it was found possible to separate them, in a pure state, in large amounts by normal technical methods.

The atoms of nearly all the elements are stable and there are only a few heavy elements which are radioactive and disintegrate spontaneously. It was one of the more obvious facts of radioactivity that the disintegration is accompanied by a release of energy. The amount of energy released in a single event, that is in the disintegration of a single radioactive nucleus, is incomparably greater than the amount obtained from a single event in a chemical reaction, say the burning of one atom of carbon. On the other hand, the amount of energy which can be obtained from radioactive elements is of no practical use, because the number of disintegrating atoms is small, only a minute fraction of the atoms present, and because the rate of disintegration cannot be influenced in any way. The phenomena of radioactivity thus indicated that there was an enormous reserve of energy in the atomic nuclei but gave no clue to methods of influencing its release. It was obvious that any hope of understanding the conditions under which the energy could be released would depend on an understanding of the structure of the atomic nucleus.

ARTIFICIAL DISINTEGRATION OF ATOMS

The first decisive step in the solution of this problem was taken by Rutherford who, in 1919, showed experimentally that the charged alpha particles from radium-C could, in rare instances, collide with the nucleus of an atom of the common element nitrogen in such a way that it broke up, forming a nucleus of an oxygen atom and a hydrogen nucleus or proton.

While the discovery of radioactivity had shown that some of the elements could, spontaneously, break up to form other elements, Rutherford had now shown that the particles emitted in this process could be used to break up, or transmute, the atoms of other elements which were normally stable.

This development was pursued in the following years by Rutherford and Chadwick, who found that many other light elements could be transmuted in a similar way. In each case a proton was ejected, and generally the process of transmutation was accompanied by the release of a considerable amount of energy. It thus appeared that the proton was a common constituent of atomic nuclei and one of the fundamental particles of which matter is built up. Moreover, the release of energy in these processes was a further indication of the store of energy resident in atomic nuclei.

In parallel with this development, Rutherford with Chadwick and other colleagues and students of the Cavendish Laboratory attacked many other questions concerning the properties of atomic nuclei and their structure, laying the experimental foundations of a whole new branch of physics, now known as nuclear physics, arising from Rutherford's discoveries, first of the nature of the phenomenon of natural radioactivity, secondly, of the existence of the atomic nucleus, and thirdly, that some nuclei could be transmuted by bombardment with alpha particles.

A further very important step was taken in U.K. in 1932 when Cockcroft and Walton carried out an experiment in which hydrogen nuclei, produced artificially in an electric discharge and accelerated to a high velocity by means of an applied voltage, were used to bombard another stable element, lithium. The atoms of this element were found to disintegrate, and transmutation, the dream of the alchemists, had been achieved in a completely controlled laboratory experiment.

In this transmutation, and in others which followed this new discovery, the release of energy was enormous for such a minute event as a reaction involving a single nucleus. Nevertheless, the number of nuclear reactions was so small that the amount of energy generated by the reaction was extremely small compared with the total input of energy used to produce the bombarding particles. The practical value of these nuclear reactions as a source of energy was still completely negligible.

The reason is not far to seek; not only are the nuclear reactions very rare events, but the reactions are not self-propagating. This is quite different from the chemical reactions with which we are familiar in our daily life, such as the combustion of coal or oil. Once started, these propagate themselves and the reactions develop and spread, involving the whole bulk of material; thus the lighting of a fire releases enough heat to ignite the neighboring fuel, which in turn releases more heat to ignite more fuel, and so on. This is not the case for the nuclear reactions which have so far been mentioned; the particles which are formed in them are insufficient to affect neighboring nuclei so as to maintain the reaction and propagate it. It is clear that if we wish to tap the hidden reserves of energy in atomic nuclei and put them to practical use we must find a reaction which can propagate itself; for example, a reaction in which particles are emitted of the same kind that initiated it and in sufficient numbers to affect neighboring nuclei, which in their turn emit new particles to react with other nuclei, so beginning a chain-reaction which spreads through the whole mass.

It is convenient at this point to consider the form of this reserve of energy in atomic nuclei. As long ago as 1905 Einstein showed that, according to the theory of relativity, there is no essential difference between mass and energy, but that energy has mass and mass represents energy. For many years the proof that energy and mass were equivalent depended on indirect, although conclusive, evidence. The reason for this lack of immediate evidence is the extreme size of the ratio between mass and energy. A very small mass corresponds to a very large amount of energy. For example, a mass of one ounce transformed entirely into heat energy would be sufficient to convert nearly a million tons of water into steam. The fantastic size of the figure for conversion of mass to energy explains why a loss of mass has never been observed in ordinary chemical processes; the heat given off in combustion has, we believe, mass associated with it, but its amount is so small that it cannot be detected by the most sensitive balance.

Very striking and direct evidence for the equivalence of mass and energy was furnished by the experiments on the artificial transmutation of atoms. It was shown that in these nuclear reactions a release of energy was always accompanied by a decrease of mass and that the equivalence between mass and energy was exactly as predicted by Einstein. It thus appears that in these nuclear reactions matter is being partially converted into energy and that the reserve of energy of the atomic nucleus is hidden in the most obvious place, its own mass. There is therefore a store of energy resident in matter which is enormously greater than that available to us from any known chemical process. It is clear that since no such extraordinary sources are known on this earth there can be no appreciable conversion of matter into energy. On the other hand, it is now generally accepted that it is this store of energy in matter itself which maintains the heat of the sun and of other stars, through a cycle of nuclear changes in which matter is converted into energy.

DISCOVERY OF THE NEUTRON

In 1932 Chadwick, working in the Cavendish Laboratory, made a discovery of fundamental importance. Some years earlier Bothe and Becker in Germany made the observation that the element beryllium, when bombarded with the alpha particles emitted by polonium, emitted a very penetrating radiation. Joliot and his wife Irene Curie-Joliot, in Paris, found that this radiation exhibited some quite extraordinary properties. From a close study of these properties and by detailed measurements Chadwick was able to prove that this radiation consisted of fundamental particles which had a mass almost the same as that of a proton, but had no electric charge. These new-found particles were called "neutrons" and it was at once realized that they, together with protons, were likely to be the ultimate constituents of the nuclei of atoms of all elements. The nucleus of any atom could be built up from the number of protons required to give the observed positive electric charge together with the additional number of neutrons to bring the nuclear mass up to the observed value.

The discovery of the neutron was, however, of even greater practical importance in that its lack of electric charge made it an ideal projectile for carrying out nuclear transformations.

The use of neutrons as a means of exploring the structure and reactions of atomic nuclei was taken up vigorously in physics laboratories throughout the world. Neutron sources could be made either by mixing radium or polonium with beryllium so as to take advantage of the nuclear reaction already mentioned or by the use of an instrument, known as the "cyclotron," which had been developed by E. O. Lawrence of the University of California, Berkeley. This instrument has been of great value in the production of high-energy beams of charged atoms or nuclei and many nuclear reactions, which could be carried out with such beams, were found to produce neutrons.

In the meantime an important contribution to the rapid advance in the new science of nuclear physics was made by Joliot and Mme. Irene Curie-Joliot who, in 1933, showed that certain elements, which are normally stable, undergo nuclear reactions when bombarded by alpha rays and yield new atomic nuclei which are isotopes of known elements but which are not stable and decay in the way characteristic of the natural radioactive elements.

In 1934 E. Fermi, and the school of physicists then working with him at Rome, began an intensive study of the reactions produced when the nuclei of all atomic species were subjected to neutron bombardment. In the course of this work the heaviest known elements were examined and, in particular, uranium— with the atomic number 92—was subjected to neutron bombardment. The results of this work showed that new isotopes were formed which were unstable and were subject to radioactive decay.

It therefore seemed that, by bombardment of the heaviest known atom with neutrons, it was possible to produce in the laboratory atoms of higher atomic number, 93 and upwards, than were found in nature.

Further experimental work, however, led to certain difficulties in this explanation and it was found to be impossible to account for the existence, in the normal arrangement of atomic species, of the very large number of so-called "transuranic" elements that were discovered. At this time it was generally accepted that these new elements were all, in fact of higher atomic number than uranium, and elaborate chemical tests had proved that they certainly could not be identified with any of the elements immediately below uranium in atomic number or weight.

Discovery of Fission

Professor O. Hahn and Dr. Strassmann in Berlin became interested in this problem at the end of 1938 and, from the particular point of view of their chemical nature, carefully reexamined the new elements.

In January 1939 they published a most important paper in which they reported positive chemical evidence to show that one, at least, of the new isotopes which were believed to be of higher atomic number and mass than uranium was, in fact, an isotope of the element barium which has an atomic number and mass not very different from half that of uranium.

Immediately afterwards Dr. O. Frisch and Professor Lise Meitner pointed out that this discovery could only mean that, when uranium was bombarded by neutrons, a nuclear reaction took place of a kind utterly different from any so far studied and that the uranium nucleus split into two parts of roughly equal mass. This phenomenon, for which they proposed the name "nuclear fission," could be explained in terms of the theory of nuclear reactions which had been developed by Professor Bohr in the preceding years. They also pointed out that the fragments of the uranium nucleus would fly apart with great energy and this prediction was given a direct proof by experiments carried out by Dr. Frisch in Copenhagen.

Confirmation of the reality of the fission process with uranium, and of the greatest energy release which accompanied it, was obtained by Professor Joliot in Paris independently (and at nearly the same time) and by other physicists throughout the world as soon as the original work was known to them.

Very shortly afterwards, in the spring of 1939, Professor Joliot and his collaborators Drs. Halban and Kowarski gave an experimental proof of the additional fact, which was expected on theoretical grounds, that when the fission of uranium takes place a number of free neutrons is also produced. Their first experiments showed this number to be about 3.

Experiments of the same type were carried out by Drs. Anderson, Fermi, Hanstein, Szilard and Zinn in the U.S.A. and independent confirmation was obtained of the fact that more than one free neutron is produced for each fission of a uranium nucleus. It was immediately recognized that this discovery was of the very greatest significance and that, for the first time, there was an experimental basis for the hope that the useful realization of the enormous store of atomic energy in matter could be achieved.

This hope depended on the facts that the fission process was initiated by a neutron and that more than one neutron appeared to be released during the process. The later fact opened up the possibility of a chain reaction. If one atom in a block of uranium were to undergo fission, the neutrons emitted in this fission would be available to initiate fission in neighboring atoms of uranium; these fissions in turn provide further neutrons to affect more atoms of uranium, and so on. Thus conditions might be found in which whole chains of fissions would be produced, each fission being caused by a neutron released in a previous fission. In this way the process might become self-propagating and self-increasing, so that what started as an action affecting only one or two atoms might, in a short time, affect a large proportion of the atoms in the uranium block. In other words, a chain reaction would be set up. If these conditions could be realized, the energy released in the fission process could be made available on a large scale and the store of energy resident in matter put to practical use.

It was therefore only natural that there should be an outburst of activity in most of the physics laboratories of the world with a spate of publications in the scientific press. This continued until the outbreak of war, when an increasing sense of the great potential value of this work imposed restrictions.

Certain important facts emerged from the work that was published during this period and theoretical conclusions and expectations were announced but it is hardly possible to give any strictly chronological account of them. The work was done in so many laboratories and the results, sometimes in a very preliminary form were communicated to so many journals and published at such varying intervals after communication that details of priority cannot be clearly settled.

But reference should be made to the visit which Professor Bohr paid to the U.S.A. from January to May 1939. He was able to report directly to American physicists the experiments carried out by Hahn, Frisch and Meitner and their suggested interpretation of the results. In addition, while in the U.S.A. Bohr developed and published, in collaboration with Professor J. A. Wheeler of Princeton University, New Jersey, a theory of the fission process.

One important prediction which was made from this theory related to the different behavior of the various isotopes of uranium. This element consists, for much the greater part (99.3 per cent) of atoms of mass number 238, but there is also an isotope (0.7 per cent) of mass 235 and a very small proportion (0.008 per cent) of an isotope U-238 and U-235 respectively, are the most important in connection with the uranium fission project. Bohr predicted in February 1939 that the common isotope, U-238, would be expected to undergo fission only when the bombarding neutrons had a high energy, but that the rarer U-235 isotope would behave differently in that it would not only show this reaction with high energy neutrons but in addition would be particularly liable to undergo fission when the energy, and therefore the velocity, of the bombarding neutrons was very low.

This prediction was, in fact, confirmed in March 1940 by experiments carried out by Nier of Minnesota and Booth, Dunning and Grosse of Columbia University, New York. They used a sample of uranium in which the content of U-235 had been increased above the normal value by means of Nier's mass-spectrograph.

It is relevant, at this point, to refer to a different phenomenon shown by the U-238 isotope when bombarded by neutrons of one rather narrowly defined energy value which is intermediate between the very high energy required to cause fission of this isotope and the very low energy which is most effective in causing fission of U-235.

Neutrons which have this so-called "resonance" energy are very strongly absorbed by the U-238 nucleus but fission does not follow. Instead the new nucleus, which now has a mass number 239, emits two electrons in successive steps and is thereby converted first to an isotope of an element with atomic number 93 (for which the name "neptunium" has been suggested) and then to one of an element with atomic number 94. This latter has, provisionally, been named "plutonium" and the isotope formed from U-238 after resonance capture of a neutron may be represented by the symbol Pu-239. Neptunium and plutonium are true "transuranic" elements, of the type suggested by Fermi, and are not found in nature.

Of the two, Pu-239 is of particular interest in connection with the general problem of fission and the release of atomic energy because it could be expected, from the Bohr-Wheeler theory, to show the same sort of properties as U-235 and to be capable of undergoing fission with the greatest ease when bombarded by neutrons of very low energy.

Reference must also be made to the fact that the three nuclear species U-235, U-238 and Pu-239 are not the only ones that can undergo fission. The two elements next below uranium in the atomic series were also shown to have this same property. Thorium, with atomic number 90 and consisting of one isotope only of atomic mass 232, behaves in the same way as U-238, and fission can only be brought about when the bombarding neutrons have very high energy. The very rare radioactive element protoactinium, with atomic number 91 and atomic mass 231, behaves, as regards fission, in a manner intermediate between U-235 and U-238. These facts, again, are all explicable in terms of the Bohr-Wheeler theory which enumerates certain general rules covering the behavior to be expected with regard to fission of any heavy nucleus, known or unknown.

CHAIN REACTION AND THE ATOMIC BOMB

The foregoing survey of the development of atomic and nuclear physics, though necessarily brief and incomplete, has traced the growth of the idea that there are enormous reserves of energy in all matter; that these are of a nature quite different from those involved in chemical processes, such as the burning of coal or oil or the detonation of TNT or other explosives, and that the nuclear reactions by which they are released are more comparable to those occurring in the sun or stars or in the natural radioactive elements found on the earth.

While this idea has been formed and steadily strengthened since the discovery of the phenomenon of radioactivity at the end of the last century it is only since the discovery, reported at the beginning of 1939, of the special phenomenon of fission that a way has been clearly seen by which this atomic or nuclear energy in matter would be released, controlled and put to use by man.

In recent years the enormous effort expended on the solution of this problem, practically all of which has been borne by the U.S.A., has been concentrated on the development of an atomic bomb. Considerations of security make it impossible to disclose many of the details of this work but, in what follows, some indication is given of the share in it which has been carried out in Britain. Before doing this, however, it may be worth summarizing the nature of the problems relating to the use of fission, either to produce a violent explosion to liberate atomic energy under controlled conditions, as they appeared when the work was organized, with a new sense of its urgency and importance, at the beginning of the war.

It was generally accepted that a chain reaction might be obtained in uranium which would yield enormous amounts of energy. This, on a basis of equal weights, would be millions of times greater than that produced by the combustion of coal or oil. But it was realized that, if this chain reaction was to be divergent and self-sustaining, certain critical conditions must be satisfied. In the first place the system as a whole must be of such a size that there was not too great a probability that neutrons, produced in the fission process, would escape from the system and so be unable to take any further part in the chain process.

Secondly, the system must not contain more than a limited amount of material that would absorb neutrons and, in this way again, remove their chance of contributing to the divergent fission chain reaction.

Thirdly, the fact was appreciated that, if the reaction was not to "run away," it was essential to make use of neutrons of very low energy in the individual steps of the chain process. Only then would it be possible to introduce methods which would allow the rate of development of the process to be controlled. The neutrons produced when fission occurs have very high energies but this is dissipated as a result of elastic collisions with the nuclei of other atoms that may be present.

Professor Joliot and his co-workers in Paris, Professor Fermi and other physicists in the U.S.A., and Professor Sir George Thomson and his colleagues in London, were giving thought to the possibility of using a mixture of uranium and some suitable "slowing-down" medium arranged in such a way that the fast neutrons produced by fission would lose their energy by elastic collisions before initiating further fission in the uranium. A suitable "slowing-down" medium must, above all, not have any large probability of capturing a neutron and its atoms should be of as small mass as possible in order to get the maximum rate of loss of energy in the neutrons through elastic collisions. The most suitable materials to fulfill both these conditions were "heavy hydrogen" or its compound "heavy water," helium, beryllium and carbon.

At the beginning of 1940 Dr. Frisch and Professor Peierls, of Birmingham University, and Professor Sir James Chadwick, of Liverpool University, independently called attention to the possibility of producing a military weapon of unprecedented power. They pointed out that the slow neutron chain reaction would not produce explosive effects much greater than those obtained with ordinary explosives but that if a chain reaction with fast neutrons could be realized the explosive effects might be enormous. It was realized that ordinary uranium would not be suitable, for even if a fast chain reaction could be realized with it a very large quantity of metal would be required. On the other hand, the isotope U-235, if it could be separated, offered great possibilities. It seemed that the amount required to make a bomb would not be very large, certainly between one and one hundred kilograms, and rough calculations of the energy released showed that the explosion of such a bomb might be equivalent to many thousands of tons of TNT.

The explosion of an atomic bomb is very different in its mechanism from the ordinary chemical explosion for it can occur only if the quantity of U-235 is greater than a certain critical amount. This is because the reaction depends on the conservation of the neutrons produced in the fissions. In a block of pure, or nearly pure, U-235 the neutrons will either be absorbed in the mass of metal, producing new fissions, or they will escape into the outer air, thus being wasted and useless for propagating the reaction. The proportion of neutrons which escape can be reduced by increasing the size of the block of metal, since the production of neutrons is a volume effect and will therefore increase more rapidly with size than the loss by escape, which is a surface effect. It follows that if the explosion is possible it will require a certain minimum amount of material, which is called the critical size. The chain reaction will develop so fully that an explosion occurs only if the quantity of U-235 is greater than this critical amount. Quantities less than this are quite stable and perfectly safe. On the other hand, if the amount of material exceeds the critical size it is unstable and a reaction will develop and multiply itself with enormous rapidity, resulting in an explosion of unprecedented violence. Thus all that is necessary to detonate a bomb of U-235 is to bring together two pieces each less than the critical size but which when in contact form an amount exceeding it.

If an appreciable fraction of the atoms in a mass of U-235 undergo fission within a very short time the amount of energy liberated will be so great that the mass will attain a temperature of many million degrees and a pressure of many millions of atmospheres. It will consequently expand with very great rapidity. As the density of the mass decreases the neutrons can escape more easily from it, and the chain reaction will come to an end. In order to release an appreciable fraction of the available energy, it is therefore necessary that the reaction should develop so rapidly that a substantial part of the material can react before the system has time to fly apart. The neutrons produced in the fission process are fast enough to fulfill this condition (but not if they are slowed down by artificial means as mentioned in the paragraphs above). The interval of time between the beginning and end of the nuclear reaction is exceedingly brief. In this interval the mass will have expanded so much that the nuclear reaction breaks off, owing to the escape of neutrons. During this interval a substantial part of the mass of U-235 should undergo fission, releasing a large amount of energy. If only one pound of U-235 is affected this release of energy will be as much as from 8,000 tons of TNT.

THE REALIZATION OF THE ATOMIC BOMB. BRITISH ACTIVITIES AND ORGANIZATION

PROFESSOR SIR GEORGE THOMSON'S COMMITTEE

A committee of scientists, with Professor Sir George Thomson as chairman, was set up in April 1940 originally under the Air Ministry and later under the Ministry of Aircraft Production. This committee was instructed to examine the whole problem, to coordinate work in progress and to report, as soon as possible; whether the possibilities of producing atomic bombs during this war, and their military effect, were sufficient to justify the necessary diversion of effort for this purpose.

The first step to be taken was to establish the nuclear data on which depended the possibility of an atomic bomb and which determined its size. This work had already begun at Liverpool early in 1940 under Professor Sir James Chadwick and it was now pushed on more rapidly with Drs. Frisch and Rotblat as his senior collaborators. As the work developed and further problems appeared, it was extended to the Cavendish Laboratory, Cambridge, under Drs. Feather and Bretscher. This also had the advantage of providing an insurance against possible interruption from the effects of enemy bombing, to which the Liverpool laboratory was somewhat exposed.

The many theoretical aspects of the problem were investigated by Professor Peierls, assisted by Dr. Fuchs and others in Birmingham University, and also by Dr. M. H. L. Pryce, in Liverpool. They used the experimental data provided by Liverpool and Cambridge to calculate the critical size of the bomb, they examined the mechanics of the reaction, and calculated the amount of energy likely to be released in an atomic explosion, studying the conditions for increasing the amount. Professor Sir Geoffrey Taylor, of Cambridge, examined certain points in connection with the effect to be expected from the explosion of an atomic bomb.

This was clearly only one side of the problem for it would not have been of immediate practical use to show that an atomic bomb was feasible provided that a certain quantity of U-235 were available, unless it could also be shown that there was a reasonable possibility of separating such a quantity of U-235 from ordinary uranium and in a reasonable time.

This aspect of the problem was also considered by the committee. It has already been mentioned that isotopes of an element have practically identical chemical properties and that consequently separation processes must depend on their difference in mass. In the case of the uranium isotopes, the relative difference in mass is very small and an already difficult problem becomes a formidable one. In the early stage of the work not much actual experiment could be done owing to the scarcity of men and of facilities, but one method of separation was examined at Liverpool and shown to be unpromising. There are of course several methods available for separating isotopes on a laboratory scale. These were examined very carefully by the committee, having in mind that it was essential to select and concentrate on what was likely to be the most economical method, owing to the fact that the manpower and industrial resources of Britain were already wholly engaged on production for immediate war needs. The committee came to the conclusion that the gaseous diffusion method was by far the most promising for large scale production. It is based on physical principles which have long been fully understood and which are easily amenable to calculation, and it seemed likely to make fewer demands for highly-skilled precision work.

Research on this method of separation was taken up by a team of workers under the direction of Dr. F. E. Simon in the Clarendon Laboratory, Oxford. They were aided on the theoretical aspects by Professor Peierls and his group, and on the chemical side by

Professor W. N. Haworth and a group of men under his direction in the Chemistry Department, Birmingham University. The Metropolitan-Vickers Electrical Company and Imperial Chemical Industries Ltd. were consulted on the many technical questions which were involved. Some experimental work on the diffusion method was also started at Imperial College, London University.

By the early summer of 1941, the committee decided that the feasibility of a military weapon based on atomic energy was definitely established and that this weapon had unprecedented powers of destruction, that a method of producing the amounts of material required was in view, and that a fair estimate of the industrial effort needed to accomplish the project could be given. Accordingly, the committee drew up a report dated July 15, 1941, which summarized its findings and which made recommendations for the prosecution of the project on a large scale.

By agreement between the Minister of Aircraft Production and the Lord President of the Council this report was referred to the Scientific Advisory Committee of the War Cabinet of which Lord Hankey was at that time chairman.

It is proper at this point to consider in general terms what had been done and what remained to be done.

The experiments of the nuclear properties of uranium had confirmed that ordinary uranium itself would be useless for the purpose of an atomic bomb and that it would be necessary to use the isotope U-235 which is present in ordinary uranium only to the extent of 0.7 per cent. They had further shown that if pure or nearly pure 235 were available in sufficient bulk a chain reaction could develop which would result in an explosion of extreme violence. The data which had been obtained were sufficient to give an estimate of the amount of U-235 required, but this estimate was very rough and the critical size was known only to a factor of three.

The theoretical work had confirmed the early result that the amount of energy released in an atomic explosion would be very large compared with the effect of ordinary bombs. Calculations had been made on the effect of "tampers" and on the best size of bomb. The method of assembly of the material for use as a weapon and the method of fusing had been considered, but no experiments had been made.

On the problem of production of the material U-235, it had been decided to concentrate on the gaseous diffusion method, and research and development on some aspects had shown considerable promise. A scheme had been put forward by Dr. Simon and Professor Peierls which had proceeded to the first stage of design. Leading experts of industrial firms had been consulted who had agreed that it should be possible to build a satisfactory plant, although difficulties were to be anticipated. Estimates were given for the cost of a plant to provide adequate quantities of U-235 and for the time required to build it.

In short, the committee was completely convinced that an atomic bomb depending on the fission of U-235 was feasible and that its effect would be comparable with that of some thousands of tons of TNT, and that a method of separation of U-235 from ordinary uranium could be realized on a large scale, so that sufficient quantities of the material could be obtained.

Admittedly, a great deal of work remained to be done on all aspects of the project. More precise nuclear data were required so that, for example, the critical size could be estimated with better precision; some points needed confirmation; methods of assembly and of fusing of the material had to be thoroughly examined. The main problem, however, was the design and construction of a plant for the separation of U-235 on a large scale. As the committee pointed out, an outstanding difficulty of the atomic bomb scheme is that the bomb cannot be tested on a small scale; it is all or nothing. The firmness of the committee's conviction that it was indeed all and not nothing can be judged by their daring in putting forward a project of this magnitude, when some most essential parts of the scheme were still in the early stages.

A different but important aspect of the application of the fission of uranium was also reviewed by the committee. This was the possibility, mentioned in a previous section of this statement, of finding conditions under which a mixture of uranium and some suitable "slowing-down" medium might give a neutron chain reaction in which the release of energy was obtained in a controlled way. This work was being carried out at Cambridge by Drs. Halban and Kowarski.

These two French physicists had been sent by Professor Joliot to Britain at the time of the fall of France in June 1940.

They brought with them the 165 liters of "heavy water"—practically the whole world stock of this material—which the French Government had brought from the Norsk Hydro Company just before the invasion of Norway. Drs. Halban and Kowarski were instructed by Professor Joliot to make every effort to get in England the necessary facilities to enable them to carry out, with the cooperation of the British Government, and in the joint interest of the Allies, a crucial experiment which had been planned in Paris and for which the "heavy water" had been acquired.

Facilities were provided at the Cavendish Laboratory, Cambridge, and, by December 1940, they produced strong evidence that, in a system composed of uranium oxide (as actually used) or uranium metal with "heavy water" as the slowing-down medium, a divergent slow neutron fission chain reaction would be realized if the system were of sufficient size.

It seemed likely that, if uranium metal were used, this critical size would involve not more than a few tons of "heavy water."

The committee concluded that this work had great potential interest for power production but that this particular application was not likely to be developed in time for use in the war.

It was, however, recognized that the slow neutron work had a bearing on the military project, for the plutonium which would be produced in such a system could be extracted chemically and might be capable of use in an atomic bomb instead of U-235. The difficulties in the way of building a slow neutron system seemed to be prohibitive at that time. In order to produce the quantities of plutonium which it was guessed, from analogy with U-235, might be required for a bomb, many tons of uranium and many tons of "heavy water" would have been necessary. The latter particularly would have demanded a major industrial effort.

During this period April 1940–July 1941 similar problems were occupying the minds of American scientists. Contact was maintained partly by the transmission of reports through the normal scientific liaison machine and partly by visits in both directions by scientists on general scientific missions.

Professor Bainbridge of the National Defense Research Committee of America (NDRC) was in England in April 1941, and Professor Lauritsen (NDRC) was in England in July of the same year on general scientific matters. Both were invited to attend meetings of Sir George Thomson's committee.

DIRECTORATE OF TUBE ALLOYS D.S.I.R.

The Scientific Advisory Committee of the War Cabinet, of which Lord Hankey was the chairman, endorsed the view of Sir George Thomson's committee on the importance of the atomic bomb, with the result that Mr. Churchill, who had been kept informed on the developments by Lord Cherwell, asked Sir John Anderson, in September 1941, to undertake personal responsibility for the supervision of this project as one of great urgency and secrecy. To advise him he set up, under his chairmanship, a consultative council of which the members were the chairman of the Scientific Advisory Committee of the War Cabinet (Lord Hankey and later Mr. R. A. Butler), the president of the Royal Society (Sir Henry Dale), the secretary of the Department of Scientific and Industrial Research (Sir Edward Appleton) and Lord Cherwell. To ensure continuity the Minister of Aircraft Production, Lord Brabazon of Tara, served on this council at the beginning.

The direction of the work was entrusted to a new division of the Department of Scientific and Industrial Research and thus fell under the general administrative charge of Sir Edward Appleton as secretary of the Department. It was known, for reasons of security, as the Directorate of Tube Alloys. Mr. W. A. Akers was at Sir John Anderson's request, released by the Board of Imperial Chemical Industries Ltd. to act as director, with direct access to the Minister on all questions of policy.

Mr. Akers had, as his deputy and principal assistant, Mr. M. W. Perrin, who was also lent by I.C.I. Akers was advised by a technical committee, under this chairmanship, composed of the scientists who were directing the different sections of the work and some others. The original members were Professor Sir James Chadwick, Professor Peierls and Drs. Halban, Simon and Slade, with Mr. Perrin as secretary. Later it was joined by Sir Charles Darwin and Professors Cockcroft, Oliphant and Feather.

VISIT OF U.S. MISSION TO BRITAIN NOVEMBER 1941

In November 1941, at the time when the new T.A. (Tube Alloys) organization was set up, an American Mission composed of Professors Pegram and Urey, of Columbia University, came to Britain to study the experimental and theoretical work which had been done on the T.A. project, to learn our ideas for future work and to agree on arrangements for complete and rapid interchange of information.

They visited all the establishments where T.A. work was in progress and took part in a meeting of the new T.A. Technical Committee at which progress was reviewed and new programs discussed.

VISIT OF BRITISH T.A. MISSION TO U.S.A., FEBRUARY–APRIL 1942

Under the new organization a great extension of the scale of work both in university and industrial laboratories was started; in the U.S.A. also a greatly intensified T.A. effort had followed the return of Professors Pegram and Urey from England. A mission composed of Mr. Akers, Dr. Halban, Professor Peierls and Dr. Simon visited America at the beginning of 1942 to ensure that the programs planned for the U.K. were coordinated as efficiently as possible with the American work.

Every section of the American program was examined in detail and it was already clear that the new American T.A. organization intended to make the fullest use of the enormous resources available in the universities and in industry.

British T.A. Program

It was clear in 1942 that, even though granted very high priority, the scale upon which T.A. research and development could be undertaken in the U.K. must be far smaller than in America. A large portion of the qualified physicists was occupied in other urgent war work and the industrial resources of Britain were engaged, at that time, in War Production to a much greater extent than was the case in the U.S.A. Consequently it was necessary to limit the field of T.A. investigation.

Broadly the programs chosen were: Determination of essential nuclear physical data; theoretical investigations into chain reaction in an atomic bomb, the dimensions and design of a bomb and its blast effect; the gaseous diffusion U-235 separation process. This included theoretical and experimental research on the process, the design and production of prototype machines, the manufacture of materials needed, studies on materials of construction, etc.; investigation of slow neutron divergent systems, especially with "heavy water" as the slowing-down medium; the manufacture of uranium metal for the slow neutron systems of "piles"; the manufacture of "heavy water."

Location of Work

Experimental Determination of Nuclear Physical Data. The research teams at Liverpool and Cambridge Universities were considerably strengthened and small programs were started at Bristol and Manchester Universities. Professor Sir James Chadwick exercised general supervision over all this work.

Slow Neutron System. This work continued at Cambridge under Drs. Halban and Kowarski with the collaboration of Dr. Bretscher.

Theoretical Investigations into Chain Reaction, etc. Professor Peierls and his team continued their studies at Birmingham, with collaboration, on special problems, with Professor Dirac of Cambridge. Later, when Professor Peierls moved to U.S.A., Dr. A. H. Wilson led this group.

THE GASEOUS DIFFUSION PROCESS

University Research. The experimental work was under the general direction of Dr. Simon. His extended team at the Clarendon Laboratory had, as leaders, Mr. Arms and Drs. Kurti and Kuhn. The theoretical study of the process remained in the hands of Professor Peierls and his group at Birmingham. Also at Birmingham University Professor Haworth, who had been very active in T.A. from the days of the Thomson Committee, has a group working on a number of chemical problems connected with the diffusion project.

RESEARCH AND DEVELOPMENT IN INDUSTRIAL ESTABLISHMENTS

The Metropolitan-Vickers Electrical Co. Ltd. accepted a contract for the design and construction of certain prototype machines embodying the principles worked out by Dr. Simon and Professor Peierls. The successful construction of these machines was a considerable technical achievement in view of the novel features contained in them. They were later abandoned in favor of a simpler design which offered certain advantages in operation.

Imperial Chemical Industries Ltd. (I.C.I.) were entrusted with the contract for the development of the diffusion plant as a whole, and the work was carried out by the Billingham Division of that company. This program was a very extensive one as it covered everything involved in the design of a complete plant, including the working-out of flow-sheets, research on materials of construction and the development of new types of valves, instruments, etc. to meet novel conditions.

In this work they were assisted by the Metals Division of I.C.I. which studied various manufacturing processes. I.C.I. Metals Ltd. had as sub-contractors, Percy Lund Humphries and Co. Ltd. and the Sun Engraving Co. Ltd., coordinated by Dr. Banks whose services were made available by the Printing and Allied Trades

Research Association. Metallisation Ltd. also made a valuable contribution to this section of the work.

Processes for the manufacture of the many special chemicals required were worked out by the general Chemicals Division of I.C.I. assisted by the Dyestuffs Division.

The Mond Nickel Co. Ltd., under a separate contract, made a very successful investigation of certain metallurgical problems.

Although some of these research programs will be carried on a little longer, largely in order to establish optimum conditions, I.C.I. Billingham Division has been able to close down the main program after producing flow-sheets and designs for diffusion plants operating over a fairly wide range of conditions.

In broad outline the plant is, of course, similar to the American diffusion plant now in operation, but it embodies certain novel features.

The Manufacture of Uranium Metal

I.C.I. (General Chemicals) Ltd. undertook the manufacture of uranium metal, and succeeded in developing a satisfactory method.

The conversion of metal into rods, as required for a "pile," was tackled by I.C.I. metals division.

It soon became apparent that many problems required study in connection with the physical, metallurgical and chemical properties of the metal. Research on these points was undertaken by the National Physical Laboratory, Dr. Simon at Oxford with a sub-group at Birmingham, the British non-ferrous metals research association, Dr. Crowan at Cambridge and the Alkali Division of I.C.I.

Heavy Water

I.C.I. Billingham Division, which had some experience in the separation of "heavy water" on a laboratory scale, was asked to prepare a scheme for the production of this material on a large scale.

After examining various methods they reported that the most suitable process to adopt in Britain if speed of construction and certainty of operation were paramount, was the electrolytic process incorporating the vapor phase catalytic exchange principle introduced by Professor Taylor of Princeton University, U.S.A.

Flow-sheets and designs were prepared for a plant in which the exchange system was of a novel design believed to be simpler and more efficient than any of those hitherto used or suggested.

ELECTROMAGNETIC METHOD

Through the interchange of information we were aware of the remarkable development work which was being carried on at the University of California under Professor E. O. Lawrence, with the object of converting the mass-spectrograph, used for the separation of isotopes in minute quantities, into a large-scale production apparatus.

But it was decided not to start any corresponding research in Britain as the physicist most suitable for this work, Professor Oliphant of Birmingham, was engaged in other urgent war work.

In July 1943 it was possible to release him from that work so that it was decided to start a research program at Birmingham on this method. Before work had really started Professor Oliphant visited America in connection with discussions on a closer integration of British and American T.A. effort, in which it was agreed, as described below, that the most efficient course to follow, in the joint interest, was for Professor Oliphant and most of his team to move to the U.S.A.

The British Electro-Magnetic program was therefore abandoned.

After Professor Oliphant's return to the U.K. in March 1945, it was decided to arrange for research to be started on some of the electrical engineering problems involved in this type of plant. With this object research contracts have been placed with the British Thomson-Houston Company, the General Electric Company and Metropolitan-Vickers Electrical Company. In addition the first and last of these companies had already given considerable assistance by lending to the British T.A. organization the services of Dr. V. J. R. Wilkinson, Dr. T. E. Allibone and other physicists and engineers.

COORDINATION OF PROGRAMS

It will be seen, from the account of the diffusion plant research project, that many university and industrial teams were concerned, so that proper coordination of the work became an important matter.

The same applied to the work on the production of uranium metal and its metallurgy.

It was also evident that some of the chemical research carried out for one project would be of interest in connection with another.

To ensure satisfactory coordination of the work certain committees and panels were set up.

The diffusion work was dealt with by the diffusion project committee reporting to the T.A. Technical Committee.

The members of this diffusion committee were: Mr. W. A. Akers, director T.A. (D.S.I.R.), chairman; Major K. Gordon (later Dr. G. I. Higson), I.C.I. Billingham Division, deputy chairman; Dr. F. E. Simon and Mr. H. S. Arms, Oxford University; Professor R. Peierls (later Dr. A. H. Wilson), Birmingham University; Mr. J. D. Brown, Dr. J. B. Harding, Mr. C. F. Kearton, Mr. S. Labrow and Mr. J. R. Park, I.C.I. Billingham Division; Mr. N. Elce and Mr. H. Smethurst, Metropolitan-Vickers Electrical Company; Mr. M. J. S. Clapham and Mr. S. S. Smith, I.C.I. Metals Division; Mr. M. W. Perrin, T.A. Directorate (D.S.I.R.), secretary.

The chemical research was coordinated by a panel reporting to the T.A. Technical Committee. The constitution of this panel was: Professor W. N. Haworth, Birmingham University, chairman; Dr. R. E. Slade, I.C.I., vice-chairman; Dr. F. E. Simon,

Oxford University; Dr. J. P. Baxter, I.C.I. General Chemicals Division; Dr. J. Ferguson, I.C.I. Alkali Division; Mr. J. R. Park, I.C.I. Billingham Division; Mr. M. W. Perrin, T.A. Directorate (D.S.I.R.), secretary.

Uranium metal production and metallurgical matters were handled by a metal panel, whose members were: Mr. E. Colbeck, I.C.I. Alkali Division, chairman; Dr. W. O. Alexander, I.C.I. Metals Division; Dr. N. P. Allen, National Physical Laboratory; Mr. G. L. Bailey, British Non-Ferrous Metals Research Association; Dr. A. M. Roberts, I.C.I. General Chemicals Division; Mr. D. C. G. Gattiker, T.A. Directorate (D.S.I.R.), secretary.

RESEARCH CONTRACTS. PATENTS

The contracts under which research is carried on in university laboratories contain clauses reserving exclusively to the government all discoveries, inventions and other results arising from the work.

In the case of researches carried on by industrial firms all results, inventions and developments in detail applicable within the T.A. field become exclusively the property of the government.

Where an invention is also usable outside the T.A. field provision has been made whereby its use outside the field can be made available to industry.

It is within the discretion of the government to decide whether or not a particular use is within or without the field.

Questions relating to inventions and patents are dealt with by a small patents committee composed of: Mr. A. Block, D.S.I.R., chairman; Mr. W. A. Akers, Directorate T.A. (D.S.I.R.); Mr. M. W. Perrin, Directorate T.A. (D.S.I.R.).

JOINT BRITISH-CANADIAN-AMERICAN SLOW-NEUTRON PROJECT IN CANADA

During the spring of 1942 it was decided that the slow-neutron research in progress at Cambridge would proceed more quickly and efficiently if it were transferred to a place geographically nearer to Chicago where the corresponding American work was being carried on.

A proposal was made to the Canadian Government that a joint British-Canadian research establishment should be set up in Canada to work in close touch with the American group.

The Canadian Government welcomed the suggestion, with the result that, at the beginning of 1943, a large research establishment was set up in Montreal under the general direction of the National Research Council of Canada.

Practically the whole of the Cambridge Group, under Dr. Halban, was moved to Montreal, where the research staff was rapidly augumented by many Canadian scientists several new recruits from the United Kingdom and a certain number from the United States.

The laboratory was at first directed by Dr. Halban. He resigned this position early in 1944 and Professor J. D. Cockcroft was appointed to succeed him.

During the spring of 1944 the Americans joined actively in that project which now became a Joint British-Canadian-American enterprise. Its scope was enlarged and in 1944 a site was selected on the Ottawa River, near Petawawa, Ontario, for the construction of a pilot scale "pile" using "heavy water" (supplied by the U.S. Government) as the slowing-down medium.

This joint enterprise in Canada has been described more fully in statements issued by the Canadian Government. It represents a great contribution, both in men and money, by that government to the development of this new branch of science and its application.

Transfer of British T.A. Research Groups to U.S.A.

In August 1943 Sir John Anderson visited America and discussed with the U.S. authorities the means by which the cooperation between the two countries might best be placed upon a more formal basis. Further discussions took place subsequently between

President Roosevelt and Mr. Churchill which led to the setting up of the Combined Policy Committee in Washington.

Professor Sir James Chadwick who was appointed scientific adviser to the British members of this committee examined, with those responsible for the scientific and technical direction of the American project, the question whether there were any further steps which could be taken, in the pooling of scientific and technical effort, which would accelerate the production of atomic bombs in the United States.

As a result of these discussions it was decided to move to America a large number of the scientists working in England on T.A. in order that they might work in the appropriate American groups.

At this time Professor Bohr escaped from Denmark and the British Government appointed him as an adviser on scientific matters. This scientific advice on the T.A. project has been available both in the U.K. and in the U.S. to the two Governments.

Professor Oliphant and his team from Birmingham University were moved to Berkeley to work with Professor Lawrence's group engaged in research on the electromagnetic isotope separation project. They were joined by other physicists from Britian including Professor Massey of University College, London, Dr. H. W. B. Skinner of Bristol University, Dr. Allibone and Dr. Wilkinson who worked partly at Berkeley and partly at the Electro-Magnetic Separation Plant itself.

Dr. Emeleus of Imperial College, London, Dr. J. P. Baxter and others were transferred to the Electro-Magnetic Plant.

Dr. Frisch from the Liverpool nuclear physics group and Dr. Bretscher from the corresponding Cambridge section, together with some members of their teams, were moved into the great American T.A. Research establishment at Los Alamos, which is described in American statements on the project.

They were joined, at that time or later, by a number of other British scientists including Professor Peierls and Dr. Penny, of Imperial College, London University. Professor Sir Geoffrey Taylor paid several visits to the establishment.

The effect of these transfers and others which were made to the Montreal project was to close down entirely all work in the U.K. on the electromagnetic process and to reduce almost to nothing the nuclear physical research.

Nevertheless there is no doubt that this was the proper course to follow in the light of the decision which had been taken to give the highest priority to the production, in the shortest possible time, of an atomic bomb for use in this war.

APPENDIX 8. CANADIAN INFORMATION SERVICE STATEMENT AUGUST 13, 1945

"Enquiries received from all parts of the world indicate the widespread interest in the work carried on in Canada in making possible the production of the atomic bomb," said the Hon. C. D. Howe, Minister of Munitions and Supply and Reconstruction, here (Ottawa) today.

"The dropping of the first atomic bombs is, however, the culmination of the work of scientists from many nations, the pooling of the scientific and natural resources of the United States, Britain and Canada and the expenditure of hundreds of millions of dollars in the United States and smaller, but substantial, sums in Canada on plant and equipment in the most extensive scientific effort ever directed towards the attainment of a new weapon.

"Having ample supplies of basic materials, good water supplies, and isolated sites well suited to the work, Canada, with foresight and enterprise and the organization of the National Research Council, has been able to enter as a pioneer into an important new field of technology. The future will disclose the full peacetime potentialities of this remarkable new source of energy.

"Interest in the scientific aspects of the achievement is such that after consultation with Dr. C. J. Mackenzie, President of the National Research Council, it has been decided to make public the following details."

LARGE LABORATORY ESTABLISHED IN MONTREAL

Canada has been associated with scientific development in this field since the time when Rutherford began his investigations on radioactivity in McGill University in 1899. Investigations were, however, confined to university laboratories until the outbreak of war in 1939. From that time, the interests of scientists working on this subject in Britain, the United States, Canada and France were directed to the possibility of a practical application. On the fall of France, French scientists working on the problem were sent by Professor Joliot to join the British scientists. In October 1940 information on this and other war research was interchanged between Britain, the United States and Canada. Towards the end of 1942, the British proposed that an important section of the work should be carried on in Canada as a joint enterprise. Accordingly a joint laboratory of United Kingdom and Canadian staff was established in Montreal under the administration of the National Research Council. This laboratory has now grown to a staff of over 340, by far the largest organization ever created in this country to carry out a single research project.

Plant at Petawawa

As a result of agreements reached between the three partner governments, the work of this laboratory was closely coordinated with the tremendous research activity in this field in the United States. Its work led to the design of a pilot plant for the production of atomic bomb materials, now under construction at Petawawa, Ontario, by Defence Industries Limited, as a part of the combined United Kingdom-United States-Canadian program. A branch of the National Research Council will be established there in close association with the pilot plant to carry out research on the application of atomic energy in war and in industry, and on the use of its products in research and medicine.

The primary material required for the operation of this pilot plant and for its production of materials for atomic bombs is uranium. One of the world's two most important deposits of this substance was discovered by Gilbert Labine near Great Bear Lake in Canada. To preserve this important asset for the people of Canada and to protect the supply for the United Nations, the Dominion Government took over the ownership of the mines and the extraction plant.

Bursting the Uranium Atom

The possibilities of the release of atomic energy have been known to physicists for some time. The first indications came shortly after the discovery of radium, when Curie found that it generates heat and maintains itself at a temperature some degrees above its surroundings. The source of this heat energy was investigated by Rutherford during his researches at McGill University in the early years of this century when he showed that new kinds of rays were emitted from radium and a few other similar materials. These rays come from the innermost part of the radium atom which is called its nucleus.

In 1919, Rutherford went further and showed that the nucleus of an atom could be made to emit rays by artificial means, releasing energy in the process. In this process, the atomic nucleus expels a small part of itself as a projectile of very high velocity. This is called the artificial transmutation of an atom, because the loss of the small part changes its nature.

During succeeding years, many new methods of disrupting the nucleus were discovered. Among the most powerful was the use of neutrons, a projectile discovered by Chadwick in 1932. A neutron is actually a part of the nucleus of an atom which may be ejected when the atom is transmuted. A neutron expelled from one atom eventually collides with and enters the nucleus of another atom, often producing a transmutation of the second atom.

In these early experiments, the atomic energy was released from single atoms at a time and required special and delicate apparatus for its detection. It was not until 1939 that the discovery of "fission," or bursting of uranium atoms, gave the first hope that it might be possible to release atomic energy on a large scale capable of military and industrial applications. Physicists and chemists in various laboratories throughout the world had been trying to understand the behavior of the heavy element uranium when it is exposed to neutron rays. Gradually, bit by bit, with careful experimenting they found the explanation. They discovered that the rays caused the uranium atom to split in two. They found that this bursting, or "fission" as it is called, of a uranium atom was over ten million times more violent than the bursting of a molecule of a modern high explosive.

The bursting of a molecule of high explosive is a chemical process—one of the many chemical processes that are familiar to us, like the rusting of iron and the burning of coal. These processes are brought about by the forces *between atoms* which are called chemical forces. The bursting of the uranium atom, on the other hand, is caused by forces *inside the atomic nucleus*, forces enormously stronger than the chemical forces between atoms.

NEUTRON PROVIDES "TRIGGER"

The fission of uranium differs from ordinary atomic transmutation processes. Transmutation involves the ejection of a relatively small part of the atomic nucleus, such as a neutron or an electron. The loss of this part alters the properties of the atom, including its chemical behavior. In the case of fission, however, the uranium atom splits into two large parts which become two new atoms of chemically different elements, a discovery so surprising that the scientists feared that no one would believe it. In addition, the fission of a uranium atom is accompanied by the expulsion of neutrons. The number of neutrons emitted varies, but lies between one and three. This is a fact of the greatest importance, for it opens up the possibility that the same process of fission can be propagated in neighboring atoms of uranium. Another important respect in which fission differs from transmutation is that the energy released in the process is many times greater.

The entry of a neutron into the nucleus of the uranium atom is the trigger which sets off the fission process. Since neutrons are also emitted in fission, they are available to act as the triggers for the fission of still other uranium atoms, and thus, under favorable conditions, whole chains of fissions can be produced, each fission being caused by a neutron released in a previous fission. In this way the process can be made self-propagating and self-increasing so that what starts as an action affecting only one or two atoms may, in a short time, affect a large proportion of the atoms in a block of material. In other words, a "chain reaction" is set up. These are the conditions which must be realized if the energy released in these nuclear processes is to be made available on a large scale. If the chain reaction builds up very quickly the energy will be released in a violent explosion as in a bomb; when the chain reaction is controlled the energy may be set free at a steady rate.

MANY DIFFICULTIES OVERCOME

The large-scale release of atomic energy depends entirely on the conservation of the neutrons produced, in order that they can cause still further fissions. If the supply of neutrons is dissipated by losses, the combustion of uranium atoms will die out like a fire that lacks air. Losses of neutrons can occur in many ways. Some of them merely escape from the uranium to the outside; others may be absorbed in the uranium itself or in foreign substances. All materials absorb neutrons. Any substance which is present with the uranium competes with it for the available supply of these particles.

Even in uranium itself not all the neutrons absorbed produce fission. In ordinary uranium, as it occurs in nature, there are three kinds of uranium atom which are distinguished by the names U-238, U-235 and U-234 atoms. They have been so named because they are respectively 238, 235 and 234 times as heavy as the lightest kind of atom hydrogen. Almost all of the fission occurs in the U-235 atoms but these are only $\frac{7}{10}$ per cent of the mixture. The number of U-234 atoms is negligibly small. The U-238 atoms absorb neutrons freely without producing fission (except to a slight extent when they are struck by neutrons of very high velocity), and unfortunately U-238 atoms greatly predominate in natural uranium. In order, therefore, that the reaction shall multiply itself at the greatest possible rate it is necessary to use U-235 alone or at least fairly free from admixture with 238.

In a mass of U-235, neutrons will be lost mainly by escape into the outer air. The importance of this effect can be reduced by increasing the size of the mass, since the production of neutrons, which is a volume effect, will increase more rapidly with size than the loss by escape, which is a surface effect. It follows that if the explosion is possible it will require at least a minimum mass of material, which is called the critical size. Thus the explosion is very different in its mechanism from the ordinary chemical explosion for it can occur only if the quantity of material is greater than this critical amount. Quantities of the material less than the critical amount are stable and perfectly safe. On the other hand, if the amount of material exceeds the critical value, it is unstable and a reaction will develop and multiply itself with enormous rapidity resulting in an explosion of unprecedented violence. Thus all that is necessary to detonate the bomb is to bring together two pieces of the active material, each less than the critical size, but which when in contact form a mass exceeding it.

The separation of the U-235 atoms, which are most useful for fission, from the comparatively inert U-238 atoms is extremely difficult. Both kinds are uranium atoms. They have identical chemical properties and therefore no chemical procedure can distinguish between them. Physical methods which depend on the very slight difference in weight must be used for their separation, and very great technical difficulties had to be overcome to develop a method which was satisfactory even on a laboratory scale. To do this on the scale required for production of the amounts of material necessary for an atomic bomb was a most formidable task and demanded a great industrial effort. The separation of the U-235 has however been accomplished in the United States.

PLUTONIUM NEW SUBSTANCE

Uranium is not the only substance that is capable of fission. Another fissile material is plutonium. This substance does not occur naturally, but must be prepared by exposing uranium to neutrons. The U-238 atoms, which contribute very little to the fission of ordinary uranium, are the ones that are transmuted to become eventually atoms of plutonium. Plutonium, like U-235, is very fissile, and it has the important advantage that it is chemically different from uranium and is therefore easily separated from it by chemical methods.

New Plant Produces Plutonium

The plant which is being built near Petawawa to produce materials for release of atomic energy, will contain uranium and heavy water. When those materials are brought together in certain proportions and in sufficient quantity chains of fissions are set up and large quantities of energy are released from the uranium in a controlled and non-explosive way.

The basic process in the Petawawa plant is the production of fission in uranium 235 by a *slow* neutron. The fission of a U-235 atom releases high speed neutrons; these collide with the heavy water molecules without being absorbed and so they lose speed until they in turn produce fission. In this way a slow neutron "chain reaction" is set up. This results in very large number of neutrons being set free. Some of these neutrons are absorbed in the U-238 atoms to produce plutonium. Later the uranium can be removed from the plant and the plutonium extracted chemically.

Aid in Research and Medicine

Other neutrons can be absorbed in materials placed round the reacting uranium. By this means interesting new radioactive materials can be produced in large quantities. The plant will therefore be a source of supply of such materials for the study of chemical and biological processes and for application in medicine.

Some of the energy of fission is released in the form of fast neutrons and energetic gamma radiation. The reacting uranium must therefore be surrounded with a great thickness of material to absorb the neutrons in order to protect the working personnel from injurious effects. The intensity of the fast neutron radiations is much greater than any previously available to physicists and presents great possibilities for scientific research.

INDUSTRIAL POWER SOURCE

The greater part of the energy of fission appears in the form of heat generated in the uranium metal. This heat has to be removed by rapidly flowing water or gas. The metal surface temperatures are too low at present for this heat to be used effectively for the generation of power, but there is a possibility that this limitation may be removed by further work.

RESEARCH COUNCIL DESIGNS PLANT

The design of uranium fission plants presents technical problems entirely different from anything previously encountered in industrial and engineering experience. It requires the combined knowledge and training of experimental and mathematical physicists, chemists and engineers and exports in other sciences. Every important feature of design has been based on difficult calculation, measurement and experiment.

This work has been carried out for the Canadian plant by the Montreal Laboratory, aided by such experience and information from the U.S. project as was authorized by agreement. The laboratory presented the basic data to Defence Industries Limited who have prepared detailed designs for the construction by the Fraser Brace Company.

The largest and most distinguished group of scientists ever assembled for a single investigation in any British country has worked in Canada on the experimental and development work on atomic energy. Canadian scientists and those from abroad who have been engaged in this scientific work have included: Dr. C. J. Mackenzie, president of the National Research Council; Dr. J. D. Cockcroft, Cambridge University, England, director of the National Research Council Laboratory in Montreal; Dr. E. W. R. Steacie, National Research Council, Ottawa, deputy director of National Research Council Laboratory, Montreal; Professor P. Auger, Ecole Normale Supérieure, Paris; Dr. H. H. Halban, Collège de France; Dr. G. C. Laurence, National Research Council; Dr. J. S. Mitchell, Cambridge University, England, and

Addenbrooke's Hospital, England; Mr. R. E. Newell, Imperial Chemical Industries, England; Professor F. A. Paneth, Vienna University, Austria, and Durham University, England; Dr. C. B. Pierce, Royal Victoria Hospital, Montreal; Dr. G. Placzek, Vienna University, Austria, and Cornell University, U.S.A.; Professor B. W. Sargent, Queen's University, Kingston, Ontario; Professor G. M. Volkoff, University of British Columbia, Vancouver.

[The Canadian statement concludes with the names and academic connections of approximately 350 Canadian and foreign scientists associated with the work of the Montreal Laboratory.]

INDEX

INDEX OF PERSONS

INDEX OF CHIEF SUBJECTS

Manchester University, p. 279

Manhattan District, 5:23, 5:29, 5:30, 5:32, 6:18, 7:4, 10:23, 11:11, 11:39, 12:2, 12:7, 13:1

Mass, conservation of, 1:2, A-1

Mass-Energy equivalence, 1:4, 1:6, 1:8, 1:38ff., p. 262

Mass number, 1:13, 1:15, 1:35; spectrograph, 1:35, 9:28ff., p. 258

Metal Hydrides Co., 4:41, 6:10, 6:15, A-4

Metallization Ltd., p. 281

Metallurgical Laboratory, 6:1ff., 7:1, 7:9, 7:10, 7:40, 7:46, 7:50, 8:2, 8:22, 8:34, 8:56, 11:2, 11:19, 12:2, 12:32. See also Chicago, University of

Metropolitan-Vickers Electrical Company, pp. 274, 280, 283

Military Policy Committee, 5:25, 7:1

Ministry of Aircraft Production, p. 272

Minnesota, University of, 3:12, 6:38

Moderator, 2:8ff., 2:11, 2:13, 2:14, 2:19, 2:20, 2:28ff., 4:1, 4:8, 8:8, 12:40, p. 270. See also Beryllium, Graphite, Heavy water

Mond Nickel Co., p. 281

Montreal Laboratory, p. 295

Multiplication factor, 4:13, 4:15, 4:16, 6:10, 6:11, 6:22, 7:19, 8:12, 8:15, A-4

M. W. Kellogg Co., 10:2, 10:11, 10:23, 10:32. See also Kellex Corp.

National Academy Committee, see Reviewing Committee

National Bureau of Standards, 3:8, 3:12, 4:36, 4:41, 4:44, 6:11, 6:16, 6:20, 6:38, 9:31

National Carbon Co., Inc., 6:20, 10:23, A-4

National Defense Research Committee (NDRC), 2:37, 3:4, 3:9, 3:10, p. 277; Section S-1, 3:14, 4:14, 4:31, 5:2. See also Advisory Committee of Uranium

National Physical Laboratory (Br.), p. 281

National Research Council (Canada), pp. 285, 288, 289

Naval Research Laboratory, 4:36, 11:38, 11:39, 11:47

Navy Department, 2:1, 3:4, 3:6, 3:11, 3:12, 4:36, 10:2, 11:39, 11:47

Neptunium, 1:58, 2:19, 6:34, 8:18, p. 267

Neutron, 1:18ff., 1:23ff., 1:33, 1:49, 2:3, 2:6, 2:19, 2:32, 12:16, pp. 263, 264, 290; absorption of, 1:47, 1:57, 2:3, 2:8ff., 2:12, 2:13, 2:19, 4:8, 4:19, 6:20ff., 8:4, 8:6, 12:8, A-5; delayed, 6:23ff., A-3, A-4; fast, 1:57, 2:1, 2:10, 2:12, 2:14, 2:21, 4:25, 6:37, 8:9; fission induced by, 1:52, 1:57, 2:21, 3:6, 4:6, 4:24, 4:25, 10:1; resonance, 2:12, 4:6, 4:8, p. 267; sources of, 1:40, 4:10, 4:14, 8:31, 8:32, 12:38, A-5, p. 263; thermal, 1:57, 2:1, 2:9, 2:14, 2:21, 3:6, 4:6, 4:25, 8:31, 8:39, 10:1, 12:40, A-1, p. 294. See also Detection of nuclear particles

Nitrogen, 1:17, 1:51

Norsk Hydro Company, p. 276

Nucleus, 1:11, 1:12; binding energy of, 1:31ff., 1:54; disintegration of, 1:15, 1:17, 1:20, 1:38, 1:49, p. 260; reactions involving, 1:38ff., 1:43, 6:37ff.; structure of, 1:23ff. See also Cross section, Fission and nuclei involved